RAVENNA DIAGRAM

*

Звезда с звездой - могучий стык,
Кремнистый путь из старой песни

A powerful junction, star with star,
A flinty path from the old song

HENRY GOULD

DOS MADRES
2018

DOS MADRES PRESS INC.
P.O.Box 294, Loveland, Ohio 45140
www.dosmadres.com editor@dosmadres.com

Dos Madres is dedicated to the belief that the small press is essential to the vitality of contemporary literature as a carrier of the new voice, as well as the older, sometimes forgotten voices of the past. And in an ever more virtual world, to the creation of fine books pleasing to the eye and hand.

Dos Madres is named in honor of Vera Murphy and Libbie Hughes, the "Dos Madres" whose contributions have made this press possible.

Dos Madres Press, Inc. is an Ohio Not For Profit Corporation and a 501 (c) (3) qualified public charity. Contributions are tax deductible.

Executive Editor: Robert J. Murphy

Illustration & Book Design: Elizabeth H. Murphy
www.illusionstudios.net

Typeset in Iowan Old Style & Charlemagne
ISBN 978-1-939929-92-1
Library of Congress Control Number: 2017960400

First Edition

Published by Dos Madres Press, Inc.

ACKNOWLEDGEMENTS

The author is grateful to the editors of the following publications, in which some of these poems appeared : *Battersea Review, Blackbox Manifold, Journal of Poetics Research, Notre Dame Review, Poetry, Truck, West Branch,* and also *Curator Aquarum,* a memorial anthology in honor of poet Regina Derieva.

Cover design by Elizabeth Murphy and Henry Gould in collaboration.

The ceramic starfish plate [p.427] by Mary R. Gould.

INTRODUCTION

Ravenna Diagram is a long poem which follows in the vein of *Leaves of Grass, The Bridge, Paterson, The Cantos, "A"*, and *The Maximus Poems*. It is an attempt to come to new terms with old epic and visionary traditions, epitomized by Dante and Milton, and carried on by Hart Crane, H.D., Louis Zukofsky, Jay Wright and others. The poet aims to take up the primordial challenge of bridging heaven and earth, the spiritual and temporal, in a new voice. There is a special affinity with the Acmeist movement of Russian poetry and Osip Mandelstam - tracing to Dante, toward the end of his life, in Ravenna, completing his *Divina Commedia* under the clear shadows of Eastern Orthodox mosaics. But this is an American poem, and a work-in-progress - juxtaposing Dante's spiritual "vertical" with the vast "horizontal" of colloquial, pilgrim American time and space.

in memory of John D. Gould

TABLE OF CONTENTS

BOOK

I

POTTER'S WHIRL

for MRG

You put away the potter's wheel
and sold the kiln, awhile
ago. You've grown too frail
to pit your clay against that steel

piled high with mud, to run your feet
in ovals round that pivot
anymore. And yet
these chipped and cheery plates complete

the still-life still – greet daylight's
glow through kitchen window
with a wave-embellished row
of sandpink starfish. Minnesota flight-

of-fancy's galaxy – so far
from any sea, but near
the Milky Way, dear
Mom (curved handmade pitcher-

cosmos, all domesticated
now). You don't eat much
yourself, it seems – a touch
of Irish oatmeal implicated

with raisins gets you through the day,
you say. You want to sail
bright clay, I think – like a whale,
maybe – trailing a turquoise ray

across a world-line I can't see.
Some dolphin sky-way,
starfish joy... some stray
and florid key, far-off there... free.

11.18.12

NATURE MORTE

The leaves turn gold before they fall.
Old alchemical autumn
traces an off-rhyme
parallelogram, a manger-stall

to shepherd the aging magus-sage
toward second childhood.
These rubicund leaves would
trope into entropy : each page

off-spun from the universal volume
a part of the fleet, an octavo,
set sail for Earth's verso
(sub-equatorial). On this loom

of time and fate, all parallels meet;
each tiny colored square
flashes in mosaic there
where Dante muttered, *È finit'*.

The season sings its elegy
upon an old man's bones;
an oak-tree carcass groans
and curses at the cagey sky.

Time slows to a halt. *Nature*
morte. A dry Bordeaux,
a frozen river-flow
of fever leaves. *Each creature*

changes here, he thinks; *I too.*
A stately turn, slow trans-
mutation... *take my hands*
in yours. Dance, Prospero.

11.19.12

SHADY BANQUET

A low sun, heavy-lidded, stands
still for a spell – hooked
in the beak of crooked
dogwood limbs (rough clock-hands).

That Raven-lord of NW Coast
– R.I.'s *Cautantowwit* –
caught the bright sheep-pelt
just so. Shade-bird. Banquet-host

of rooky wood, of Banquo's cold
last supper (in the spook-
chateau). *Look you, sly* Duke
of Caw-cawdor – *your tale's a-told,*

thin wingblade crows. *Death-mold*
clings like chilly moonlight
to your forehead. Take flight
with me! Wind sighs through old

piñatas, where a star slips now.
Day ebbs; a gone year
dwindles. *So listen; hear.*
Plummet into yon undertow

of marshland tombs (overwrit'n
ravine of shades... blind kings).
Maybe you'll catch the swing's
facetious *pas-de-deux* : a swan-

thorn, Degas eglantine, skipping
across her melancholy
diamond (feline-*folie*). Not
hop-scotch, now. Lambs (tripleting).

12.28.12

LUNAR CORONA

Brown leaf, miniature tree.
Little synecdoche
in microcosm (hardly
there) from my neck of the sea.

Picture a forlorn cathedral,
a shambles. In the salt-
marches of neglect,
for centuries... extra-sepulchral.

Your personal Rothko Chapel
full of stones and hues
where (blind) you will confuse
gray memory with colors (supple

ripple in a wheel of silence).
Unwritten ravine. Osip's
selva os... the Consul's
barranca (sea-haunted house).

My one and only love, murmurs
the speechless trumpeter.
Remote, interred, entire
saint's brow (sans crown). Whose?

What martyr from Paris or Mars
lurks here? Unshod, footloose?
Over the forest floor flies
who? Who? Some surveyor's

iris, lunar Beatrice (yours).
From rime of this tomb
of tombs (our common
doom) a shady rainbow soars.

1.9.13

UP NORTH

A fleet of ragged little cedars
harbored on a rugged
point of land (fog-
bound, sometimes – til it clears).

Wind skims burning through their
microscopic needle-
calipers. Draws cheerful
tears – ski-trails thatching frozen air.

Mnemosyne Point, on Lake
Vermilion (up north).
Time's wooden (4th
grade) ruler. *Not to break.*

The placeness of quiet places.
Watercolor (frail, subdued).
No wide-lens tin-pan mood
music. Glinting silver traces

plowlines, old broken ground.
Maybe a shimmer of poplar
at the road's end... where
sea-muck molds copper marshland.

One saturnine pedestrian paces out
the strand. His word
mutters a round solitude –
heartbroken yoke. Ultimate weight.

Lifted; torn from the soil toward
his own snowbound wedding band
(galactic, Galilean). Sand
underfoot. The stream's bright ford.

1.10.13

COLD SPRING

A raven follows its own swift crow
across a frozen lake.
Echo the black wings make
slips into tamaracks – *row, row...*

The harsh cold heretic bell
of winter. Scrawny schemer,
plot against the sun. Signature
of Cain-torn soil... doomscrawl.

Nevertheless something resolute
sets its face against you
(jeering mercenary). Blue
contrail of a smoke-dispute...

dissipating ghost-limb, drifting
wake... light morse code
for remorse – weird node
of child's play (*ping... ping*).

This chancy chancery of choices
is your own, young'un (O
Chosen One). *So*
choose, whisper the raven's

voices (many). *The only way*
is up, replies the smoke.
The chessgame in the folk-
tale is for keeps – a scary

story (winners and losers
disappear) – this the source
of raven-laughter (hoarse
sneers). Players, pick your colors.

1.15.13

GRAVE GARDEN

The shady word, the moonlit word.
The silver messenger
from Camelot, your
Lady of the Lake (shy bird).

Grey eyelash, curving round
the blue of Ireland. A sea-
gull's wing; a memory.
A song, gone underground.

Laughter of harvest dance,
wedding ring (under
the shelter of oak, sere
cottonwood). Shaky balance,

8-pt. symmetry – near the
cemetery, by the river,
(where it carves past her
garden grave). *Ephphatha.*

I follow you over the ridge,
through tombstones, tending
toward the sea. One mended
rune... one blinded footbridge...

one *saya-y-manta* in the mind.
Flung like an eye – bearing
bloodfruit (soaring, shearing
souls). Eternity's acid rind...

brave's game (a furnace dance).
Where we go beneath your shade,
Raven... your sunset, grassblade.
Tracks in the snow (redcap, lance).

1.21.13

BLACK PEAK

Crows pepper the oak trees
under gray skies (gray on
gray) at Woods-Gerry, one
dusky sundown. Persephone's

bee-day. *Proserpine,* in Roman
prose (pining for home).
Italianate *grand dame,*
civil, munificent. Domain

of archivo-kisses, soldered there
amid burnt umber brick
discards (flute-magic
tricks). Driftwood, now. Air

through pine-swords (hussar sap).
Marshland (near the sea).
Crosshatched poplars, buried
beneath your shattered satrapy

of granite, marble, mud (vacated
Porta Aurea). Twin black
brows, drawn toward a peak... ill
occhio terzo (saturnine... freighted

with guilt). Sliver-*orecchio* (mine).
Black omelet, glinting with
constitutional blinkers. Width
of irrational winch (yours, mine)...

– only ghost of a memory
(memory's host). Who lifts
twin wings (six, eight)... swift
swallow fan-tan (murk highway).

1.30.13

TOPSFIELD

A springish breeze, bright air, clean sun.
Winter's Shaker plate
of light. A simple template,
solitary hearth... sod keyed to union.

One pair of crosshairs, to survey
the plain – one steady statute
of a dauntless ghost. You
know him, too... our W. *O say*

can you see / By the Topsfield
town line / Where Endicott
ripped / The king's cross out
barehanded... Foot the unheeled

gap now, Friend. Twain'll meet
Nought, around the bend,
sometime... world *sans* end.
Amen. *Wauontam*. Let's eat.

Tempestuous word... stirs up
self-evident endowments,
wrangles regal instruments
to chartered Concorde. Hip-hop's

Charlie horse, swell's oceanic
hobby – rocking, racking
the crystalloid, tyrannic
stalactites, Putin's generic

icing on a cake of Peking
take-out orders (all
them clandestine, curial
burials). Aerial checkmate thing.

1.31.13

HOLE IN THE DAY

So much snow – we're buried today.
Salted with the occasional crow
or raven, overhead. O
raven, raven, rowing away

into the sky, where will you go
now you've left the ark?
From town to town, from dark
to dark. Furnace for scorched hero

(anti-matter X-factor) etched
against azure. Oil-power
soldered in one eye. Sower
of birdseed... fodder for wretched

prophet sent to burbling earth
to burst a boil (beloved
landscape's goat). Hovers
outside (mighty magnetic north).

Night's black, bent tenderly
to one sphere's damaged
grey. One Rahab-hair (aged,
rusted). In the theater. We

two, apart together (shadowing
you). Steep Irish profile –
Geraldine Fitzgerald's (primal
in *Wilson*). Watching the Viking

film, about the Arabian boy
and the orphan tree. *The hour*
draws nigh, when Earth will flower
like an almond (tout-monde Joie).

2.9.13

CLOUD-GIRDLE

El Anatsui, like Anansi the spider
weaves diaphanous
Byzantium veils
from bottle caps and baling wire –

cloud-gowns for a Queen of South
Ghana. *Something greater*
than fin-de-siècle *Vienna*
is here, shouts sinuous, sooth-

siring Solomon. *Makossa,*
Ebeano, Dark Sailor,
Top Squad – tesserae, beer-
bubbles – forlorn cells of Africa

welded by amiable fellowship
to spring with airy, earthy
splendor – coruscant smithy
of diamond cobra (edgy as whip).

Solomon in all his glory...
field lilies, Flanders
epitaphs. Grandfather's
brass shell, after St. Mihiel (he

saved it from the *War to End*
All Wars). Copper wire,
steel helmets... fire. There
is a greater mettle here, men –

forged in the crucible of human
union (*world with out end,*
amen). It's coming, friend –
Cosmopolis (Einstein's Gödel-heaven).

2.10.13

CLOUDY THRONE

Fog shrouds a sheepish Providence,
mild air and steam over
her carapace of snow,
my misty speech-impediments.

Far off in Rome, soft-spoken latin
girds a retiring shepherd;
punctilious and learned
grandfather, his rocky throne

stands empty now. Who will wear
the crown? *The Son of Man,*
always, I hear an unknown
Pontifex intone. *Meek dove, on fire.*

My muttering in murky circles
wheels through cloud. You hear
the sound... But will this air
grow clear – so pillars, pinnacles

appear? Stepping-stones of Chartres
unfold a forgotten, cruciform
flower – lotus, golden worm...
an iridescent almond, shattered

into sparks... a milky constellation.
A breeze moves in the center
of your eye's dark sheep-door –
the giant breathing of creation.

And down parched lanes of every
dustbowl Providence, the life-
blood of the future – strife-
worn wonder – sings : *Venite, veni...*

2.11.13

A HAND

In west window of library vault
(the Rock) afternoon sun
is veiled by oils. A Sistine
frost belt – cold, cobalt (ice-salt).

Up on the ridge (his edgy terrace)
Roger (RW) emerges
from orthogonal womb
(hers). A granite precipice

bent over Providence. His blind
man's hand held out, to seek
and bless (*padre,* meek
pioneer) – one motion (mind

swimming to the star-horizon).
Now, only stone. Memory
skims back to Prairie
Avenue, on raven wing (*my son,*

my son). Pyramidical crypt-
apartment, on River Road...
Washington and Lafayette (old
print, aloft over dinner table) tip-

toe sarabande, or minuet...
So in this time-cavern
each boy and girl will learn,
unlearn (*again, again*). Still...

novus ordo seclorum wheels (at last
reverberating through
panes of Coatlicue)
to green ink-moss (a lamb-repast).

2.22.13

ULTRAVIOLET

A father half-hidden in the pines
at Lake Vermilion.
A little like a bear... someone
half-known (curled snapshot pinned

to the fridge, half a continent
off). His get-away,
the forest primeval (shy
Hiawatha-reciter). Current

of spring silence, underground.
Earthward, anonymous
now... incognito (famous,
once). Camouflaged (homebound).

A sort of green eye on Green
Island (bordered by sand
and ocean). Unmanned
bee, beneath ziggurat (unseen,

see) – this mound (sounding beyond
Ursa Minor). *By Jiminy*!
(cracked the barrelly,
garrulous wheedler) – *yer mind*?

–*'s gone*! (as he rolled round
the smoking joint). Half-
life a year and a half
(Cathay decay) – yet wounded

Yeti may heal yet. Magellanic
clouds emerge near
Gemini... orange
Pollux casting Major Q (*Titanic*).

2.23.13

SNAKESKIN

In the old home movie (Super-8)
now surely curled in
decay (a shed snakeskin)
you hop off the see-saw, Juliet

sans warning – take me by surprise.
I land on my little ass
making a Laurel face...
crab-walk past laughing eyes

(*America's Funniest*, I guess)
beyond the lens. Then
for 44 seasons, sly cousin,
you lie in wait, to mess

with my timing one more time.
Your father's birthday –
Pearl Harbor Day – away
you fly. Wintry off-rhyme...

slight sigh... so long ago
almost forgotten now.
A Golden Gate minnow,
contrail of dive-bomb crow

inking an arc (a question
mark) across my brow.
Time slopes to earth, so
in parallel strokes, Persephone;

autumnal shades of a universe
cascade from orange prow
to one centripetal zero
beside you (spiral Beatrice-Circe).

2.25.13

MYSTERIOSO

My mute-stubborn little donkey
picks his path among
boulder-words, unsung
Pedro – all the way to Frisco, he.

Across wide heartland prairie-
memory... past West
Branch, its Belgian bequest –
statue of *mysterioso* Isis, she

who veils the numbers with her smile.
Only another broken
nation now (Belgian
or Flemish?) – her iron trial

in Flanders fields, in fresher feuds
forgot. How in this age
shall innocence prevail, O
sage, mule mine? He broods,

noses sparse Badlands clover,
four hoofs planted there
in Hoover-dust. *Somewhere...*
over the rainbow... windhover,

whirlwind. Quietly, a violet
light rays from an aster
lens (its red is blurred);
this weightless photon, set

in a deaf mule's eye, exfolds
(in atomic spirals) one
standing whirl – and her crown,
Rodinian, revolves (Pacific gold).

2.25.13

UNION-DOME

i.m. Van Cliburn

With a sigh, a rustle of rainbow fans
the audience awaits your entrance,
Fort Worth boy. *Eminence*
grise of pianissimo *détente* – musicians'

strike (a union-dome). Clash
of clayborne cymbals tears
the intellectual perma-
frost... man-forged mind-mash,

spray-thrown *vermhurl* (fear).
A dissonance of distance
between you and me haunts
this whorl (Adam's ear-trumpet) –

light triangle of iron gone gold
(*lontana*). Through jumble
of disaster, hope (humble
servant). Two doves (fire-

folded wings). So I remember
Mendelssohn, the neighborhood;
young symphonics sowed
oats there, on a farmers'

prairie (*Twin Cities*). And
Mrs. Elledge, my piano
lessons (miniature
busts of all *Three Bees*, lined

atop the piano top). Heidi
skipping across the street
(a motley scale)... sweet
whorl amid this world. *To be.*

2.28.13

CRUCIFORM

A stern St. Augustine (*Piero*
della Francesca) smolders
with sweltering bronze
gaze – massive leather quarto

(*Bible*, or *Confessions*) in
one hand – his big feet
firmly on the ground (wheat
sprouting underneath). Someone

to reckon with. His patchwork coat
of many Gospel scenes
(shaven sheepskin, shriven
palimpsest of pain) will float

us all into a new dimension
of dark *matière* (Higgs
bison, or withered fig
rinds). Raven shade-mansion.

One cruciform lifetime, splayed
into landscape. Muscle
shoals of a Michelangelo-
face, flayed by Apollo's made

man (Aretino). Untimely death
interrupting all vainglory...
passio, passio, scree
three ravens on lame limb. Beneath

this rhodomontade unreels, decamps
the bishop's crozier...
labyrinth in amber,
honeycomb spire (sheep's lamp).

3.5.13

TWIN PILLARS

The night sky, salted with stars.
Remote geometries...
an exiled *Raven* seizes
River-Serpent by a branch – spars

churn downstream, toward *Whirlpool.*
Old Narragansett god
of afterlife, uncanny bird
who summons spirits through a smokehole –

dark-twined knot of All Souls'
Eve – our shadow-self,
Your Hollowness... a sybil's
flute-servant (the *Wind* controls).

Meanwhile, on a planet of opulent day,
twin bridges (Saint Frisco's
Mary, Martha) rose –
shimmering illuminated mass (array

of *25,000 undulating...*) – waterfall
from catenary smile
of twin pillars (1.8-mile
face-to-face). *Leo Villareal*

controls each light individually
from his laptop. So
thrice-hermetic star-glow
(God of Traffic) beams (perpetually)

across cold waters of Chrysopylae;
when Raven folds his wings
to plummet, frozen things
glint in his wake. Little Bear will sigh.

3.7.13

SOLO (ARABESQUE)

The little bay at India Point
was awash in fish-scale
half-light, silvery
veils today – adrift from Mount

Athos, Zion... weightless
sails. The sun was hid
like a stone in a cloud –
its own sunspot, an S

in blinding shade of itself;
when one black bird dove
plummeting on pivot-curve
through the continental shelf

of your immaculate cosmos
(sub-rosa treasure-house
of soul – mysterious
sunstone)... O igneous *Logos*!

Centripetal, black-winged, whole.
The universal mass
you bear in a demitasse
of compact agony (one minuscule

sand grain, one drop of salt
sea... red diamond, pane
on pane). Your reign
is childhood, you are both vault

and safety net, a trampoline
swing-set – there in the park
above conclave, smoke-
hole... *dovè Cristo è* Byzantine.

3.11.13

PREGNANT AIR

Evening mist drifts into Providence,
gently (no cyclone
today). So many gone
in Oklahoma. Air grown dense,

pregnant with suspense, strung
with a perimeter
of lightning. Curls under
whiplash sun – a taut-sprung

serpent. *You haunt us, every*
little spool of wind. Dust-
fiend, circling the mast...
Elmo's cigar... *poco al poco,* see –

little mumbling flame-tips
none can control.
Through a smoke-hole
in the eye of the mouth – Egypt's

Isis, secreted in Iowa cypress
garden of Cyrus. Where
Neguses, Ravlins share
tornado shelters – low b-flatness

to the horizon. Here comes a line
of twisters... stately monsters,
slowly hoovering steers
your way, my darling Clementine.

The ground is traced with dust-signals.
Thin spider-leys, almost
not there, weightless...
light safety-knots, tied over wells.

5.22.13

OPENING NIGHT

Eyes rest on the iron skein
of the black chain-link
fence. & sight will sink
into some palimpsest of green

through the simple diamond pattern
of cross-woven wire. A
quincunx-fence for Cyrus, or
Venn diagram (for double vision).

Apollinaire on opening night
wore evening dress, & kissed
the hands of mistresses,
dowagers (*beau monde, en fête*);

the primordial rite that would
make a pall-bearing *poilu*
of him (& you, & me)
was drawing nigh. Neighborhood

St. Vitus' dance contest. Parade
of local pride. Something
for Memorial Day – wrung
tears, bells... *longueurs* wide-

open spaces enclose. Perimeter
of global civil wars (too
civil for words). Fortunes
to be told, untold – a sulfur-

cloud of unknown sailors, stung
by unbreakable ropes of fire.
Century to end here,
men. Garden the encrypted thing.

6.4.13

GRAPESKIN, EMERALD

A great change is at hand, and our task, our obligation, is to make that revolution, that change, peaceful and constructive for all. – John F. Kennedy, 6.11.1963

Strange violet light suffuses Providence
at dusk, just after
thundering rain. Your
grapeskin lens, emerald inheritance –

Venetian blinds, green-rusted
bands. *Medgar, John.*
Silver trumpet, iron
bond. Yet water flows (through busted

sluice of schoolhouse doors – Boston's
wilting, molting parishes).
Lift the sign, St. Gaudens,
Lowells – Beacon Hill to someone's

Ozark Oz. Spring vale for leprechaun,
show horse, Jackie's
jockey... where ox
& antelope lie down (both Shaun

and Shem) 'neath milky
& old-timey Alps.
Appalachian apples
rim your Eden-dream, Silky –

when the spectrum in the rain
arcs through its reign
of savory pain
(tears, nightmares... plain

full of wheat & sorrow, near &
far). Infinite fine
grain of green pine-
needle grove... King's Merlin Everland.

6.11.13

HERO'S GAME

When you're coming up from the subway,
the greatest way-finding aid is natural light.
– Craig Covil, *NY Times* 6.14.13

Evening evening light through Providence,
the ponderous turtle-
dove brain of sheepish myrtle-
browed Woe-Man slips into trance.

Unknown, they step through no-man's land
into machine-gun fire.
Spun round the perimeter
of a cemetery century (tin-can

blind alley – harmony of Red Cross
sirens). I remember
the dawnlight watercolor :
scarred Monet steeple... loose

privates sauntering toward hollow
gap, gaunt windows. Where
a Y.M.C.A. sign (fire-
truck red trident) signals *Hello,*

fellows... good morning... come on in.
Primitive Sky Reflector-Net.
Is this FOURTEENTH? *Nyet* –
Fulton Street. Half-past someone –

shivved seaman – snarls on darned annals...
a demonstration. Tilted
12 degrees, 74 feet
in diameter, 952 aluminum panels

dapple sunlight onto subway
trench fairway. A perforated
fish-scale ensign – orchestrated
12-ton El. Chamber. Dead stop. OK.

6.14.13

C'EST LA GUERRE

The old photo of the A.E.F.
in the autumn rain.
Grandpa, in mud-brown
macintosh, at the edge of the frame

somewhere in Belgium, resting horses.
After the Armistice.
Wilson will insist
on world peace – the others

a little more, and less. Sanguine.
So begin the beguine, again.
Wind up the Victrola, Marianne –
la Gloire! *C'est la guerre,* old hen.

The world rolls over on its painted
poles – a craft of spry paints
merrily caw-hawing (faint
chords unwind). No complaint

from unknown soldier. *Mistah Bones –*
he dead. Raven with an inkling
wavers over your darkling
stage – crater-caps, N.O. trombones.

Weaves latter-day lattice,
spider shade mandala –
chalked-out, phosphoric air
(*la, la*). Earth-precipice,

cave-whisper. *That's all,* sez Tommy
mule-soldier – *go figure.*
All for one, one for
all... veil between your lips & me.

6.17.13

QUIET NIGHT

Moist smell, backyard, after rain.
Quiet night, a corner
of Providence. More
darkness, earth; make it plain

why you lure us to this labyrinth.
The grave's only a black
hole, crows Raven – *back*
of Shakespeare's Head. Plinth

for *path P,* Miantonomi (Henry's
mumbling again).
Where *meet & join* mend
your charcoal diamond, Julie –

your morris dance along a golden
strand, a raven strand
(faintly to understand).
Failing, falling, flying... alone

between plinth & aegis, under shade
of owl's wing (raving).
A gate for shepherding –
lamp in your hand, far overhead.

So springs your season, Persephone;
full of rain & memory.
The Great Lakes & the sea
rhyme with air, your emissary –

down through clay rings of years
you'll take us in hand –
your humming command
a supple crane dance, spun by tears.

6.18.13

FIELD, SKY

Like these bumblebees on Fisher St.
– rapt, plastered with
mauve pearls of wayside
milkweed steeples... all's replete,

complete, somewhere, nearby.
Through ironic fence
distance casts immense
pointless topology... (field, sky);

I hand a daisy, in diapers,
through diagonal white
slats, to Heidi (58
years ago). Brittle pictures,

wry albumen, merge – one pearly
swirl, continuous photo-
synthesis (long-ago
prowl). Time is Mendelssohn (early

morn). The almond in the mind,
a half-moon salience.
Rimmed by Jacquard fence
of infinitesimal thread... *find*

yer auk, Dave, in the weaving grass.
Dance the perimeter
of grief, Doomster –
iron ring of infant innocence

gone silver, gold (earth, ash).
The century, ending, ends.
Drear Noah-flush portends
another rain. Quiet; hush.

6.19.13

LATE WREATH

Ropes on a Maltese halcyon
twirl like a windmill,
signifying betrayal.
The long day's rusted sun

lingers over Ravenna (spiny
matron of swamps, dumps).
Shade racked on stumps
soon fades into nonentity,

indifference, *accidia...*
A stern crew braids these
barbed-wire nets – Henry's
offspring, ancestors – & *mea*

culpa flutes, *coulombe*-in-hand
(your fingers, aye). My king
threw down wife, mother,
everything (laved in river-sand)

like force of nature, *force majeur* –
he conned those funerals
that echo prior burials
back to the end of time, señor.

Here, take my hand. Let's lift
the rim of your enormous
fricasseed earth-mother's
monster-memorial (fright-

mère) – see what's underneath
her sub-subway. The only soul
to come back from that halo-
hole belongs to you, lean wraith.

6.21.13

22 + 1

Facesti come quel che va di notte
che porta il lume dietro e se no giova,
ma dopo se fa persone dotte.

In cryptic silence, carrying crowns,
virgin martyrs of Sant'Apollinare
glide toward shared *peripeteia*
in Ravenna. While stony Antonioni's

lost ship, Giuliana, runs erratic
errands through wastelands
of fishing tackle – garnets &
nets for gar (automatic,

predatory pike). In an overcoat
of moss lambswool... emerald
put in a posh pocket (old
trick – bad form; *poshlost*).

& this node of sadness curls around
fickle auto-Henry :
Monica's little boy
feigning *Guillain-Barré* (old wound

unhealed, Julie). Playing with
his father's gyroscope –
bright yellow (shaped
like the sun). Henri le Width

put in his nonsense two. Yet the king
looks out from a nest of inky,
oaken script... thinking...
was it for nought, red Rhody-kins,

I plucked you? Met the Governor
today. Small city-state
of mind... chartered light
of perilous charity (stout heart, Roger). *6.22.13*

SYDNEY OBSERVATORY

We are bound one to another by
limpid, infinitesimal,
quincunctial threads – all
woven by this tiny, incredibly

brilliant golden spider, lounging
in the center of a silver net
in the backyard, Juliet.
If only (before you went plunging

off the Golden Gate) we could have
watched her leaf her veil
together. *Hear, O Israel : the*
Daughter of Man *goes into the wave*

as it is determined – but woe unto him
by whom temptation comes.
On St. John's Eve, Mom's
paper boats set sail for Utnapishtim –

little lanterns puffed by the wind
on Lake Vermilion. She
(folding out a scrappy day)
shaped extraordinary gaiety – bound

foals to cherishing, always. Inventive
muse... Mare of memories.
O Woman of the North – guileless
white-haired child – prospective

Providence glimpses a *merci-monde*.
Gilded, like this singular
gemstone in the grass... your
Southern Cross (Observatory diamond).

6.25.13

SONGLENS

If, say, like Frisbee the elf
I dance round the rim
with Irish cherubim
of Mom's pink & azure (shelf-

same) ceramic starfish plates,
with the big smiling star
& 13 sea-glimmer
points (moonlit birthdate – fate

swirling liferope fingerprints
in clay, mud-florid keys)...
If I sail like Ulysses
(blindfold) to the navel (saint's

hovel) of timespace... I'll find
you there, turning the wheel.
In trenches of surreal
violence (scars of Cain's mind-

less envy, Absalom-pride)
you are slave's servant,
martyr's martyr... a burnt
solder-casket (none can hide).

Yet these blurred bifocals mist
toward some unscent, *grisaille-*
spry osprey *fiumewerk – Île-*
de-France... Spirit of St. Louis...

rouge trawler-jenny, in the Seine
of signs (star-burst
Van Gogh). First things
first. Love's mast (cedar) o' Lebanon.

6.27.13

OUT OF EGYPT

The gold dome of Temple Emanu-El
curves over Morris Avenue
like the sun (*Typekenyoo*)
on a rainy day. Baby nutshell,

maybe, out of Egypt... *out*
of Egypt have I called
my sign. *Munde*-walled
hexagon of absolute

joie. Extremely exultant ex-
halation of exalted
gratitude. Salted
transparency of complex-

multitudinous human
cloverleaf... pirouetting
onion-dome (swing,
belle; bloom). One...

one morning. In June.
The 28th. 99
eons ago, a fine
lion (Austro-Serbian)

chalked up (along the gutter).
Trenched envies merge;
worries on. An urge
toward skill – crushbones. Utter

servitude (to death). *Freedom*
builds within. Someone
accompanies me (un-
known princelimp)... *Mandelabarum.*

6.28.13

SOUTHERN CROSSING

Up from below, like a ghost ship
over the horizon. Under
the Southern Cross. Where
from black holes, men rip & grip

diamonds. On Observatory Hill
gargantuan sentinels,
ancient figs, spread wells
of shade, above a treasury (of Milky

Way). Stars are fiery gemstones
in a crown for Lady
Liberty. *The 29th of May*
we surged across the Gate – into zones

of providence, of Promised Land.
Thin shade of soft guru
filters through *Uhuru* –
father & son, in mosaic sarabande

(a music of what happens). Paired
palm-lines whorl 10 fingertips
of grace... parched lips
murmur *freedom*. It is a flared

fishnet of durable *coraggio* –
toughing out the pressure
of the *last full measure.*
Not to shirk this dusty sorrow

to another's woe (that ever-
so-convenient victim) :
but calmly swirl to the brim
one cup of memory (to share).

7.1.13

CIPHER-ZEPHYR

Our centre held that place of graves
– Herman Melville, "Gettysburg"

Lofty dusk taps the brow of the hill
& the face of each fallen kid
beside martial stone. Crashed lid
of sightless retina. Love's torn cable

rests on the seabed (with the rest
of the wrecks). A wind lifts
their letters home. Swift
turtle-dove stronghold, out west...

strange knot of cipher-zephyr
(Iowa Isis, hieroglyph
membrane). Reflective
treble wave (*love casts out fear*)

pronged in the earth, a dragon-sign –
brave front meets firewall
(fast minie-slaughter) & *we all*
fall down. Ewe-brow, Euclidean

cognizance (steeled, stolen).
Madre-martyr's molten
wheel. Scarred Roman
thumbprint (twisted, brazen).

O thou omnipotent & deathless
providence, Who sheds
light waves through lettuce beds
of aboriginal tenderness! To bless

with hopeful kiss one *ecce*-curve,
one handshakers' arc –
ample prow of tree-bark,
elder vow (*to give, to serve*). *7.2.13*

STILL LIFE

after John F. Peto

The stillness of afterthought. Twilight
glow of reminiscence.
Old cupboard door, silence.
An absinthe green, of copper rust

or phosphorescence, lined with worn
brown seams of slats. Ticket-
scraps, a coin. Scratched
dates – photo of the Chosen One

(Abraham, as his forsaken son)
in tacked-up, black-&-white
mandorla. Paper knight
of kingdom come, & gone

now – gone (into brown centuries).
Yet the momentous dream
congeals, here... as a trireme
homes toward Knossos, from antipodes.

Is this the FOURTH? *Nope – First*
Minnesota. Cemetery Ridge.
Hope circles to the edge
of Sheol – falls (beneath a burst

of gala Jubilee) into red-white
corpuscles, flogged lines
of serried compost. Pins
each peppered skull & bone tight

to the apex of our doom. Foundering
brothers, fighting brothers...
singing : *the one who brings us*
peace is king. A starry rendering.

7.3.13

MEET & JOIN

Collect under the big tent
pegged in a postage-stamp
backyard – baby lamps of
verdant Solomon's-seal bent

on flying buttress overhead.
Your microcosmic jewel-
eye, leprechaun – *fool* !
Borne anew on dew-bred

garden-ark. *Meet & join*
within this drowsy lattice-
bed : the *bleu & grise,*
le Jean, la Marie – one stein

église-cum-synagogue (a cup
of gilded moon-foam).
An actual ransom
was paid in Palestine – game's up

there, now. Where the cross-ties
on the summer battlefield
matrix vectors sealed
in red – congeal the flutterbys'

milkweed seed-pods into one
monarch-galleon. I speak
(in geometric squeaks)
of something impossible to spin :

a mighty railroad junction, star
with star : the doom-trench
drenched with breathing (inch
by inch) swells to sail… a ship! A far

deep cri-de-coeur, fused
diamond of global
clay. Pythagorean free-
for-all – triangular junk-sail – used

chair, nailed to a tree-stump
for fun, on Morris Ave.
in Providence. You
know where Emanu-El, the Temple,

is? Right there. A throne for elves,
maybe – some little people
out of Braintree? Possible.
Sliver of blue-gray mist… moon-

salvage… Ravenna slough conjunction
(green Madonna, Monica).
Your almond salience… *ahh,*
now I see! The net of branching sun-

rays, gathered by dawn into your whiz-
dome! Light morning-after
mourning dove, on a rafter
of bender-waves… parallax fizz…

what we cannot enunciate – well,
not much. The grounded
prong of time resounded
hisstory into a lullaby – fell

swoop of singed-wing carrier pigeon's
mettle of scout's honor
badge. Wheel *o' la gloire,*
Ezekiel – *her* song (& Solomon's).

7.5.13

SCARABESQUE

Backyard evening, noticed by
mosquitoes – little winged
lancers (rusty, tinged
with ragged tears). St. Henry's

Day, *ex domicile* (Jardin
des Mousquetiers). *Boom,*
boom. Little room
on high (full of eaglets' din).

Level with me – let us speak plainly
now. Fluked in a net
among flags, words – let
this servant-surf unroll. Mary,

your wide fling-sponge... cathedral
hecatomb of feral
air (on fire). *All*
shall be welcome here (the moral

of the tale) – even the big-eared
rabbits of San Francisco.
This is America, you know.
A 51st state-of-mind's geared

toward Port-au-Prince : *tres*
riche tresses are hers,
her sails soft whirrs
(hummingbirdings)... *Say,*

Juan Fernando... those stars...
ringed round a beam
en face... trireme?
Isis barge? Rainbarrel, house?

7.15.13

MAI AUS-RIA

Blind man, uneasy seer (tear-
torn) peering at a well
of light, muttering spells
in Light Warlpiri (aboriginal ear

to her glint) – walking the maze
of my own fingerprint.
To find you at the center,
hovery hummingbird : a haze

of wings, ineffable, nonchalant...
& though my sins be scarlet
as yon bee-balm (your lancet-
lip hath pierced) you will relent

if only I stand breathing, yet –
to watch you tack between
twin flower-towers – then
careen into your tree-turret!

Awhile blind, I touch the warp-
speed shade of your path
past the high birch at *Hatch-
a-Man* – one 28-light-yarn harp

alchemical recreation, sounding
baptismal waters of Ocean-
River-Barge. O masted plan
of vertical Providence! Wounding

the even(t) horizon of these states
with doublet, upright, bruised
Empyrean... – & excused
so, hop-skip lass – to circulate!

7.16.13

INFANT ALEPH

The great oak gone this evening,
that cast its barren shipmast
shadow always southwest
toward the house. Riven, driven

away in sungold loggers' hearse,
trunk chopped into round-
table stumps; only a mound
of river litter, an empty space

where mastodon bones whispered once
green orisons. Infant Aleph,
the ruby-throated seraph-
lancer, yet flits through net-veins

of my potter-patter; the sunset
inks indelible engravings
(oakleaf shavings).
Papa calls from Minnesota

to inquire about the air-conditioning
(constant Samaritan).
What's happening : a plan
from memory (a sprinkler, sprinkling).

The signs traced in the dust remain.
Bent gesture of one hosted
arm... warm, all-enfolding
guest. An *S*, a *W*, an *M*. Amen.

Last *will be done*. Only an acorn
swims at liberty (wee
coracle-cap on cider sea) –
from broken bole a crown is borne.

7.17.13

TRINIDADIAN

The walls of my house are azure gold
& green... Trinidadian,
sly Caliban. New England
affluence (*not of this world,* O

Son of Man). & the night wind
shoves Mosquito, Raven (out
of Hartford, New Haven)
eastward, toward Block Island.

Cicadas measure treetops
with handsaws. Lone
hummingbird (Parisian)
skims heirloom zone (stop –

sip – stop – zip). All bugs
are equal in this Republic,
but God loves every tick,
hurled worm & grubby slug

with hilarious agape (ineffable
dew beyond our ken).
I am home too – like Hen in
her coop, like the King in the fable –

the one hidden in the tree
on Restoration Day,
whom they couldn't slay
for trying – *not of this world,* he

is. King in his father's eye,
his mother's arms – infant
lancer, doom-resistant
hover-over-her (here by-&-by).

7.19.13

PROMISSORY NOTE

Already the crickets serenade
bent saws in melancholy
timbre. *Every tree*
will fall, sighs the scything blade.

Beyond the last ridge, Providence
purples toward sundown.
The sky's incarnadine. A crown
with black-orange wings floats hence,

southwest... solemn everlasting
monarch (Raven, raisin from
the grave). Late autumn
corn will be your sentinel, shedding

thin gold (her silky milkweed
hair). Light lines of sun-
set time-dimension
corral us all into one knotty seed

(*diamant almondiale*). Hard
nut to fathom, arched
in gold over flare
of orange panes – my pearly pard,

my shade; out of one warp-speed
sketch-cosmos, you float
somehow, unfailing mote –
checkmate, orthogonal (decreed

on high in swaddling-thread). Once
into glissando plunged,
from natal, *étoile*-hinged
promissory notes... your dolphin-dance.

7.25.13

SERPENTINE

Another cricket evening. Sun
sets in the west : this much
I know, Juliet. Such
raven locks you spring. & the one

inimitable reedy voice –
nubile marsh-bird, your
Louisville inflection (Mary
Morrow's Hepburn-on-ice)...

This roadside shrine I collect
shore stones for... more
for me than you. Your
silhouette I resurrect

from rusted DNA of old
home movies (crumbled
ladders of a mummer's
brazen maze) is meant to hold

my soul, not yours (ineffable,
beyond me now). Limping
Hephaestus wove a lucid
skein, to save a laughable

Venus & Mars, from something worse –
divine irreconcilability;
the human capability
to shutter union in divorce

would be your parents' fate, not
theirs. Your fall (a sideshow)
turned to ash & woe
one father's light. *Unreel the net.*

7.29.13

METALLIC SHADOW

Lone cricket, stalwart Montenegrin
scraping his 1-string *gusle*
by the looming span... *hey-*
yo... a patch of Ojibwa shaman

Shakespearing pike by torchlight
(near Blue Lake). Old man
in the negative, golden
on the dometop of the sky. White

nights (birchbark, Finland). Summer
evening equals memory...
nation submerged on prairie
as massive mass, a mummer's

gimp toward Orient (that
Gate, that raven-pont).
Where you slow light, haunt
every *coot d'azure*... decelerate;

allow the effulgent diamond of
the Southern Cross to lift
above this leaky raft
of coal, iron Ur (your bargain-trove,

Lazarus). O metallic shadow-
fellow, Hephaestus at
your forge – your lariat
a silken shroud (of spidery hollow

antimatter). For rendering
one flighty refugee –
magnetic exile, she
pirouettes... in Chartres (pioneering).

7.30.13

TIPTOE

So I follow the husky-dusky cricket
chorus into brokenness.
Whisper gallery's
S.O.S. (beneath Mt. Olivet

rotunda-net). The saws break down
the tree of Poe, his raven
tottering SW – o'er Atheneum-
pen (her birdcrumb, bloody crown).

Hummingbird floats by bee-balm.
Scarlet fading into
night (winged tiptoe).
I'm by Pacific shores now. Vietnam,

Babylon. We hung upon the tree
of sighs there, Absalom...
treading the sprung moss of
our lyres (composted history

of Super-8). The decades passed...
mute *passio* of unknowns,
grave. Our bones,
translated back to truth. Mast

witnesses. Her men. *Sophia*
hovers o'er our *Western*
Sea of foolishness, our
Westernnesse... Maria's

supernatch'l sistah (*Io-Sip-Broth-Er*
too). That *Evening Star,*
that *Delta Stella* : fair
token for a Frisco ferry (*there, there*).

7.31.13

HOUSE OF AIR

The backyard rose, that bloomed
only today, is like
all other roses : unlike
in its own way. We assumed

what everyone assumed (the burden
of song) only to find
it was just for us : an Indian
mound, full of private's relics, hidden

passages (unmapped, unwritten).
This is your house of air,
your tepee on a ladder,
under cottonwood, beyond

your kin (just around the bend
of Stream River) – fair
Psyche's haunts... far
regions, which... are *Holy-Land.*

To taste your own life-crust, that Raven
plops alongside – plucked
from your grave. Ewe, tucked
in a dirigible, an air-pocket (*descend,*

ascend). This *honey of Elijah*
(secret nectar only
meant for *you,* O Henry
W. Veryman). *Selah.*

Unicorn, sealed in wild honey, mint....
whoever you are... reckon
who you are : hike on
through your galactic fingerprint

*

into the marshland of another's mark.
The ink dried long ago,
yet a raven-shadow
wavers, still (dark mirror-arc)

pivoting like negative sun
in the family album
of the human sum
under the sign of broken signs

(*open sesame*). We could
talk about it...
but the tomb is right
next to the bus-stop. Neighborhood

of former stables. Dormitory
for St. Apollinaire's
nightmares. Monica's
cul-de-sac (a cloister-clerestory).

So I rehearse the familiar hearse
here, the inside story :
pillared with hoary
martyrs, stiletto-characters,

profligate with poppies, a popular
veteran's cemetery
celebrates the memory
des hommes perdus (the ones we are).

Poplar canoe, polar *voyageur*
carry us back to her –
down *path P* (geometry's
lambarhomboid – square's circlature)

– 'til Hummingbird shows up, just
in time (silent, swift,
exact). A gift (*panis*
angelicus) in search of bee-balm (*dust-*

manna). & gone, now. *Banisht.*
My garden, full of weedy
ligatures, pushy-seedy...
yet you deign drop, fly-by. *Parish*

be visited today by Papal
poppy-feeder! *Francis-*
mite! O minuscule bliss –
O buzz-patrol! An eagle (regal,

real) dives from Empyrean,
hovers like dove
over spooky alcove –
Love! The flighty seminarian,

laughter's archivist – her
photographic memory
solves every seal – she
swims athwart spear of Africa

(Queen Candace, or Victoria)
& falls with every Falls
into delight (the walls
fall too). Dante's *theoria-*

Contessa (Beatrice-*professore*)
filters into marrow
of tomorrows... Mary
Merry's water-sparrow (sore, sole

*

star). Across the *Anansi*-weft (one
molten monarch-womb
annunciation) – *boom,*
boom, rings loom. Unicorn

emerges from thick-hammered pine,
the mountain laurel brake.
Beside silent lake
of sighing, mist... Ravenna

mast. Ravine. Immaculate.
In stony vault, bare
feet trip, slightly... bear
tin crucible, from head to foot :

a whisper round the raillery
goes hummin' (*Bluejay*
surfer? Bard of Pleiades?)
– bent reverb (*Lips Monastery*).

Stones lean over simple shepherd.
Arms lifted to horizon
of the visible – mute *orison*
unheard. Murk gesture (understood).

He stand in you pasture. The sheep
wanders, twos by four...
the star encircl'em... *O*
centurion, here be your sleepy

Lord. Hebesheeps hurtself.
Lost inner landscape
(just licked you). Tape
up her mantle. Nail up him shelf. *8.3.13*

THE SIGN

Chiropractor Doc Brocolli, across
the street, grows giant tomatoes
in his sunny side plot.
Smokes his cigar; gathers no moss.

I speak of one you do not know
very well, nor I –
just a neighborhood guy
in Providence. I lift his sign here,

now – hid in summer mutter-pool
off Hope St., near
my backyard rose – dear
little Rhody-song (of one song-fool);

on Monday, garbage-day, as the trucks
roll through (with a rumble-
crash); as we stumble
off to work. *C'est la vie deluxe.*

Look deep in the still sunny well of the word,
whoever you are; it belongs
to you. Where the sea tongues
toward the dome of the sky, a sword

of moonlight answers azure with silver :
everything is moved
by love. This is proved
on my lips, in Provence, & here

with a surge toward Sant' Apollinaris
like a wave of mosaic...
curve-matrix of heartache,
paume de promess'... Beatrice-kiss.

8.5.13

CORN MAID

One light yellow-black butterfly
leaps & pirouettes
over black-eyed Susans,
solo – in camouflage, off-rhyme;

demure, playing hard-to-get;
elusive soul! – *when*
Velje Lug comes down
to Nezuke – she skipped the net.

Yet the brittle, desiccated bronze
of history's home
movie's chaos-boredom
is somehow welded in a dome

near Trebizond – of *Holy Wisdom*;
her salience, an almond
breastwork, serried round
with complicate relief (an aerial

Rome). I'll whisper this forever
in the whisper gallery
right here, you see –
across the Mississippi River

of my lips. I'll watch the monarchs
traipsing off southwest
& taste the trace, the zest
of bee-balm trails – beneath great arcs

& flying buttresses, behold
a Venus transit through
revolving rose window... that
Beatrice-vale (gold-thread sheepfold).

8.5.13

THE HUMAN DOME

Now daughter Phoebe's salient belly
measures the girth of future
earth... *Hiya, Sophia*!
She shall be dark, but comely,

I prophesy. & coming soon,
I reckon. So the sweep
of Time's straw broom
swings reaping into sunny bloom

again, again. Let there be light
& joy, after the pain
that day – O reign,
Sophie, that day – with gentle might!

As when the heir looks out, calmly
from oaken hideaway
like Noah, into hay-
stacks of a cleanswept sea

of waving grain... *I pledge allegiance*
to the flag of the United
States of a merry, delighted,
omnibenevolent Pacific... O glance

encompassing – your quietude, your
equanimity! Your rain
that slakes the level plain
of just, unjust... onion & all!

I hear the drone of universal union
peal from bells in Petersburg
& Panama... in Denver, Darling,
& Dhaka... my child... my *matryoshka*-lion!

8.5.13

WHIRLIGIG

The *geomatrie* of *meet & join*...
let us look once more
at this. Nabokov-memoir,
translated to Lake Vermilion?

Mnemosyne – center of starfish
sea of clay? A whirligig
or maple seedling (– swig,
now, leprechaun!) – archaic Swedish-

Chinese vase, *au fond du Lac*
Victoire? C'est possible,
Phoebus, *mon chère* Ephebe.
We're riding in the way, way back,

to that primordial sketchbook cave
where Byzantium was found
near Kiev, in a mound
of horses' graves. Not Raven,

now. Some sole Arabian bard
who wings it on Hephaestus-
tongs, out of the furnace,
into the pyre – & doesn't burn! Hard

to comprehend. I understand.
But you must listen, plate-
spinner – the hand of fate
lies in your palm. A light command

set things in motion, pivoting on
one grain of bran, one
mote of wheat... & then
all Paradise broke loose (*5.29*).

8.5.13

QUATREFOIL

August, month of Caesars, smiled on me

In exitu Israel de Aegypto...
under the sign of Jubilee
the ancient thing re-
surfaces – shines through mistletoe

to live-oak tree. A tiny 4-
leaf clover, micro-*quatrefoil*
halts that August drum-roll
History, one old saint's day (your

own). The cavalcade pauses;
horses look down (near
Calvary). *Green beer*
for everyone : an Irish lass is

humming birdsong by a golden tree,
mooning through *ooblekest*
night – some nightingaelic
test, some Geraldine egged into poetry

out of Fitzgerald brood (a *matryoshka*
full of bran). Her *joie-*
mandorbelled salience, day-
limned : some scent from sepulchre

(Cheerios, sprinkled with angel-
food? Mold rust?) emanates
Emanu-el, alive... *V-gates*!
Vienna shouts – Venice, Ravenna swell

gold-tipped black wings of Neva R...
Venite, midnight sun of Man!
An ancient apple-root begin
to glow, in Providence (where all we are).

8.6.13

MILKY NUB

August. Already foretaste of autumn
in the air, although the sun's
a gold doubloon of genial dominion
in a void square (left by tall oak's doom).

Twilight comes early. With it, my
hummingbird prince (in moss-
bronze coat, silver cuirass,
black-white tails) sabers burgundy

bee-balm crowns, astride his own
moon-steed (strange
tidal pull toward grange
on high). Now cricket-violins

begin to drone, shades fade (*fado*)
toward night... evening
the globe (ravening
grown calm). A mute moon speaks so.

Beyond the chiropractor's office
over the road, meek
practitioners of *chi-rho*
break a crumblevine in peace

(ensconced in Westerly granite).
Their *poverello* Emperor is
King of Kindness, only... sire
Oasis, on a blood-orange planet

planted fast in black-gold dust.
His agate gate is lantern-
jawed, his light banter turns
molten – burns prison bars to rust.

Speaking of Alcatraz... squats in Bay
like icon of Assyrian
lion, wreaking havoc on
Turkish delight (hanging, say,

from Gelded Age). Upon twin
banks, a scream of crime
envelopes human time
in mystery. *O Romiet, O Julio*! Sins

familiar (plus your pride)
ravel surfer-nets
in twisty trees – let's
count them! *Knowledge... crucified*

... *for life*. Mummified apple-
corn, lodged at Prospect Park

*

begin to glow in the dark
like lamb, lamprey... supple

bronze emblem (threadbare sunlight).
As if pale slivers of my
hoary hair merged with dry
wheat, coarse trains of white-gold

horses' mane (*Corn Maiden*'s wavy-
raveled crown). Who tiptoes
on that span... a wild rose
widow (*Pin to Launch Pacific Navy*) –

child in her ravine-basilica,
playing with agate-eyed
serpents (unafraid). A
diamond in the surf – sail (*Ariadne-*

warp) – square, where oaken mast
once drooped (regal, abject).
Somebody nobody knew (reject-
recruit). Whose punishment would last

a lifetime. Ballast for ship,
I guess. Knot in eye
of cat-o'nine. *Him die.*
Lie-low o' Judah. Cheetah slip

net... leap off tree
at you. Sponger of *man-*
animal... Understan,
is what I secrete (*mopletry*).

Airmeal, stamped for delivery
(via milkweed pad). Fly,
lightweight buntagold (my
povera Francescan) – *you am free*!

For so the long wars led me (*One,*
Two, buckle my helmet) to
th'bole in the tree. You
know... th'eye in th'knot (sun-

glow, *quipu*). Where bread rose
in the vat, like spiderweb
of gold... milky nub
of gravity. But Raven knows

(bird hums like Bluejay, laughs
like ghost) – he be y'ownly
host, yo (holy boast). *Say,*
Juan Fernando… (happy epitaphs).

8.7.13

BOOK

II

CRICKET REALM

A surf of starry clematis
foaming once again
over the Roman iron
lozenges of chain-link fence.

The crickets of late summer
fiddling their plaintive
airs... intuitive
premonition, seasonal *no more.*

The wild sway of Jerusalem
artichokes, abandoned
citadels of rotund
bumblebees (careless flotsam)

while an enfeebled sun tends
toward foundering – sinks
into galactic night-talk
(millennial egg mintings, bends).

I whisper this out of nowhere;
only a declining garden
buried in provincial town.
The blind touch of a wheeling Bear

signals North Star somewhere.
It is near : as thought
of Guinevere for Lancelot,
as Galla Augusta's anxious care

for her boy's soft crown of hair
in the decadence of Empire.
It is nigh... near as the fire
that welds my rusty eye to golden air.

9.9.13

CHIPPEWA FALLS

Friday night. *Rosh Hashanah.*
New Year's eve. A milky moon,
gibbous (bulbous doubloon)
beams down... bright guest (selah).

Bimetallism, in itself
cannot save the Republic;
silver & gold won't stick
to the stomach (pelf

a dead issue). Hamiltonian
guile, sleek Mississippian
packing crate... insinuation
of the serpentine (Mammon,

rooted in cotton). In the beginning
gleamed the Dhaka kingdom
of a coin (whose home's
nowhere) : spectacular ringing

of strong selfish bells (bells
from Hell). Feed on this
slick commodity : it's
an ideal-collapsible waterfall.

Chippewa Falls. Where they laid
the railroad line, Grandpa.
So you pursued your hero (*baa-*
baa black sheep) in Rimini (a blade,

of course). The Renaissance, man.
America in your shoulders
like yoke, or hearse... World
mauled by haughty greed, fraud. Mine.

9.12.13

AUTUMN RITE

Crickets nibble summer's leavings,
their squeaky elegies
buried in dogwood debris.
A herd not seen (pale daylight sievings).

Time's growing old. Apollinaire
head swathed like a mummy
fluting his pipe (*fumant*
sa feuilles d'automne). Debonair

veteran (*soldat anonyme*).
Time numbers her days.
Old Tiamat, torn, crazed,
nailed above Nineveh... beam

of salt-light through bullet-holes
in the ice. Sun-bubble
in the balance – Hubble-
shot, right through that oak-bole's

honey-gal (apple of his eye).
Some telling overture
soon over, William, sir.
29th, maybe (Champs Élysées?).

The vacant chair, the lost ship...
the broken bow-strings
of the bowsprit (Noman sings
in the rigging, having fallen asleep)

...evening's quiet ark. Only *all hands*
might lift this mate from sea
of tears, moon's tendency
to swell-time (swaddling bands).

9.18.13

CHINESE LANTERN

October burnishes the oaks'
unburied treasure; Asian
maples, dogwood veins
bleed Roman gold; Sir Edw. Coke's

uncommon ghost of commonweal
lingers by Providence.
That *logos*-diamond (sun-
spangled *claritas*) will steal

way back to local color (coal-
dust gray). November's
reign... spruce embers
glimmering. Time sobers up (well-

seasoned now). We go ghostly
toward All Hallows, Eve –
all folded 'neath one eave's
projected *Shades 'r Us,* are we.

The nets of *pauvre* fishermen
(Edessa, Glasgow, Galilee)
seined with autumn bounty
strain, slacken; one gilder thread

angles from perihelion
to wheel in a high room
spoked with tongues aflame
(rare pentecostal raven)

& my chinese lantern (in buried
furze-fest) gleams, octa-
hedral : orange *docta,*
Apollinaire-berry (international bird).

10.29.13

NOVEMBERISH

The soft Bruegelish colors here
at India Point, at the end
of October. Moist diamond
apex of the bay, calm mirror

of gray sky... jade, orange.
Moss, oak leaves... quiet
water. Still boats, nets.
Strange silver vortex... plunge

past canvas now, toward
the matrix of its unknown
origin : when Time is born
from wild Eternity of limpid

rest – *Pax* lounging on the couch
of wise *Justitia*
above sunlit Siena's
supple spine (Apollonian church).

This labyrinth of All Souls' Eve
is lacèd so, interlaced
into a knot of displaced
faces – facets now, a weave

of riveted & ravelled souls
(*millions of strange shadows*).
Suddenly a voice endows
an octave's infinitely joyful

pulse with special resonance –
a *Someone,* calling you
by name. & this is how
it all begins (autumn leaf-dance).

10.30.13

IN CHAPEL

An in-between season, this –
after Halloween, before
Thanksgiving. October's
shimmering bronze carapace

scatters into ginko leavings.
Golden little Nile-
fans, pungent piles...
squashed berry-burials (stinking).

Sun sinks behind shade-landscapes,
seeks to bury its own
light (blend fire & bone).
Old fathers now turn wrinkled grapes,

frail purple... veins of melancholy,
lingering. We were in Chapel
when our shaking principal
croaked out – *President Kennedy...*

I was eleven. Unspooled young
American, ignorant
of history's unspent
venom. O *liferain*, unstrung

yet by animosity (parochial
malice) – when fresh air
waterfalls (*dawnstar*)
the arc-rim of a universal

crown – Jerusalem the hidden
hive, from raven-milky tree
lifted down... suddenly
light-riddled sepulchre of heaven.

11.18.13

ANOTHER KING

Strong end-of-November wind
sweeps clean the empty
grass, at India Point;
at Henry's Diner, Swede will find

her golden harp & silky green
gone brittle, moribund,
cadaverous. Rhode Island
keens for Danny Boy again –

morris-mazers filigree
a *J*... another *J*...
a seagull, feathered gray
(tide's salty crest). History

turns on a dim Ford Theater
in Texas (tragic pathos).
Camelot & Arthur's ghost
meander stonefields of Otranto,

Ursiana's silent forest (56
pillars, leafless now).
Ripples on her father's
brow (peering out of Styx).

Orpheus pipes a mercurial ray.
Apollo prescribes, commands.
Mary (face in her hands)
senses sunrise, Easter Day –

not the death of another king
but life of a loved one,
lifted from dungeon
of blind men (the end of burying).

11.25.13

IN RAVENNA

The season slants toward sundown now.
Short days on drowsy, lambent
streets (old Providence).
My stringy coat. A pivoting crow

pins up a forlorn battlefield
in mind – Maldon or Hastings,
Kosovo... for tempering
swords, *coraggio* (& *not to yield*).

Colors of absolute devotion.
Idols of the heart,
for whom we tear apart
body & soul (a local commotion,

team sport). Old song...
while dusk-light fades
on trumpets & parades
(lullabies of holy wrong).

Yet love itself is not to blame.
Mute adoration, innocence...
there is a recompense
diagonal (bisecting frost of fame

& morbid time). This labyrinth
or planetary waltz
of geothermal fault-
lines (feral jaguar-squint

of *quipu*-knotted, Janus-face
inkblot) is as a Venn
sketch in Ravenna : men
& women interwoven (lambs' embrace).

12.3.13

ALMOND TREE

Winter fog like cold sea-spray
filters through Providence.
Mystifying substance
of an ember hope (Isaiah... *hey*

ey yo). Long northern nights tilting
toward Pearl Harbor,
India Point (spare
rose gyroscope). Melting

through ice barricades, at last
(27 years, gone
into light). Some yarn
entangles history – a mast

for Admiral Nelson (constellation
of a heaven-yard). *The ship*!
Bound for that whisper-
signet... Southern *Chris-Craft*, spun

yonder (with Gandhi, MLK –
whorl, Milky Way). Blessed
be they who finally kissed
the sky (tall Eureka-tree

nursing Po's *Eridanus*, and
the other three). There is
a gemstone, set beneath this
coffin (folded in a flag)... grand

father of fathers, king of kings,
your little almond tree
of ripe humility
is peace-weaver tonight. Blessings.

12.5.13

SANS NET

Providence through library windows
like a snow-globe, from inside.
Out there, nowhere to hide,
sans avocat (nobody knows

the trouble) shiver-racked shades
flaked from sleek sound
systems... fine-ground,
filtered grit-roles (nice blades).

The stone man on the hill
stands for our good Will,
we ghosts – here, still
until yon Cain-&-Abel tale's

fulfilled. & by the New Year's
bubbly lens (our frothy
yea all ears attend) we
spy, at last, Apollinaire's

yew bend, *en camouflage* – a pine
amid the armèd greens,
a thorn among has-beens –
aiming toward you : like a sign

in the sky... like a snowflake
stand-in for Solomon,
dancing (all-human,
now). She be your wordless music,

harmless bairn – your New Year's
resolution, justified... your
mangy, invisible bride –
bright Pegasus, short Wain (snow tears).

1.2.14

DOUBLE NEGATIVE

i.m. Elena Shvarts & J.H. Ravlin

Just a day past Epiphany,
Elena – bright here
between me & bird-
feeder. Persephone's uncanny

winter pane... I'm interrupted
now amid wheezy insights
by light knocking – what's
going on? A pudgy robin erupts

from the dark-brilliant holly
into its window-doubled,
waxy-shiny, baubled
eidolon. Your shade, my folly?

Lambent panes of Christmas pine
lights woven with toy
sleighs, reindeer... joy
rides in kaleidoscopic acorn-

crystal latticework, Grandpa!
Your yesterday's Yule-log
pivots Demeter through fog
of Black Sea galaxies... *Brava,*

Elvira-ear! Out of scout-nymph
by pool there, *where water*
jets from the rock (shutter-
click of *camera oscura*) – triumph

of infinite depth (waltz, sarabande).
Earth your hearth, old
white-haired eagle – fold
on green fold, blue agate-in-hand.

1.7.14

STOLEN AIR

to Yevgeny Vitishko

Il y a beaucoup d'Athènes who'd rather not hear you
speak, Olympian.
Plato, perhaps. And Putin.
Judges in Sochi (policemen, too).

Go back to your Sunday tea, they pray.
Give it a rest. Poetry
in polite society
is not taken seriously – & *hurray*

for that! expound the *hoi-polloi*.
Punctiliousness is *de rigueur*
whatever that means. Sure,
it's about stuff that matters... oh boy.

Show me the riot. What's your game?
Causeries des chimps.
Gambling works – hence the
full Monty (my life, *sorry*). Shame

on innocence, or chumps. Sex
is Pharaoh's mask, Yahweh's unisex,
anyone who genuflects
otherwise... *go figure*! What next?

A naked lancer skims toward Thermopylae.
Naiads flank across frozen
lake. Siberian ozone...
Pyrrhic destination, puppy. *Hey,*

my soul's on fire. Let's put 'em there,
where they won't cause no trouble.
All's Romany rust or ruble,
Homs, *seriozhne*. Griots vein stolen air.

2.10.14

CROCUSCOPE

The longest winter in memory
waves goodbye at last.
April now will cast
chaste spells (bare Earth-mummery).

A Troy-town labyrinth. Here
every crocus, purple or
white, within its tender
crocus temblor-field, coheres –

a tiny integral crocus-cosmos,
with molten tailpipe of pure
gold (seedy *sol-miroir*)
a-blister through its petals.

The round-dance of the hills is swaddled
close. Bareness traces
sketches, improvises –
black sod dreams *goldfinch* (addled

Euro icon, scattered skeat)...
soiled sail toward Meganon.
History repeats, anon,
mayhap. The Pole wheels, replete

with hungry Bears (little or big);
the Lion roars; the Empire
spikes, way offa there
at the edge of the shelf. Echoes rig

the wistful *fado* (wars, rumors).
A yellow gyroscope
rides hopefully
on earth. Sunset bleeds headlines (ours).

4.2.14

SLOW REPEAL

I walk down Hope Street, early evening.
April's meek defenseless
light – hopelessness
just held at bay. Someone humming

through a window. Orpheus
a scattering mosaic
He died for our sake
Sheep's Clothing (by shepherdess).

Sleepy reason is a breeding
ground. Grim Viking wing
of bats, assembling
over a barn... spring seeding

under shrouds of rain. Old Hobo
lingering, trackless
by the track... his guess
as good as mine (where did she go?).

Evening light smiles in the rust
– conundrum, mystery.
Round the periphery
of ancient sound (*kerygma*-trust).

Amalgam; Alfred's anglo-lingo,
maybe. *Teach the words.*
The flimsy king herds
hailstones into church. Sorrow

is shared (*love bears it all*).
Under a millstone wheel
grain's slow repeal
melts iron hearts. Bells, toll.

4.3.14

A LINE OF CRANES

The elegiac film unreels,
familiar to me –
brownfields near the sea,
somebody's bookland (sunken keels).

Antic, doe-eyed Giuliana
swerves from San Vitale
(wild rabbit, seagull). Fey
smile for Corrado (*si lontana*).

Lost ships loom through pine barrens.
Like *Juliett 484,*
submerged long before
in my derelict harbor. No man's

land. A line of spindly cranes,
rust-orange giraffes, lift
microphones to sift
remote star-cordage – brains

over hearts tune into memory
of light. Giuliana listens
to a sandstone shoreline's
hymn. Her ghost-ship tacks away.

And who's the gloomy *vecchio,*
tout gris, cornered by
gray pots (piled high
atop gray cart) on Via Alighieri?

Grey, jasper, bronze... regrets.
Grey lightens the raven-
black of Persephone's own
crown. Doves flit behind the sets.

4.4.14

TINY SPEARS

And my last stroke, and I'm heading into the grave, I wonder what color it will be? – George W. Bush

Tread lightly through the documents
of autumn, left behind.
Oaks' fallen rind,
cemented to the ground, relents

in April. Here and there, in the pine-
swamp, tiny spears
of green lance into air
(Mary Negus would lean down

and pick them out, with rapt blue eye).
A maid of Lorraine might arc
over Memphis mud – spark
harsh skyhawk shrieks (*epithalamia*

or peals of doom). An ancient heart
is turtle-grey in spring –
in the bare clearing, droning
out of range. Flanders artillery

is ochre, rust. One Ravenna dame
swirls violet on blackboard
(touched with black and gold).
Her boy demands a tale (same

as before). A little icon
of the sea is born;
of innocence. *Mourn*
what is left, what is never gone.

Cypripedium regina (white
wing moccasin). Slow
bloomer. Slim, slight, showy,
she. Step softly toward her, light. *4.5.14*

GOOD SATURDAY

A sound like April showers of arrows
forces a ruddy eyebrow-
bridge over the flow
of customary concord. So.

The fearsome gate looms up ahead.
Westward the course of Empire
sails Berkeley to Newport harbor.
Galleys to Bermuda... *wine & bread.*

Am I in the dream, or is the dream
in me? Shades of spring
pas-de-deux, thrusting
pink magnolias, northward... a trireme

in a crossfire, diamond *Sinjun*-glare.
Burning in the front yard.
Walk on through, Hardy
boy – the tale's a jest. A dare.

She'll be watching from the garden
since the days of John.
Only tears, from now on –
like an extra eye (the size of Ocean)

as you reach for those handlebars
at the height of Mount Zion.
Cycling through the aeon
only to heft your heart (& ours)

back to her... a sailor's gift.
Our own eyes clear, so.
Humanize the sorrow,
son – lift your bracing welcome. Lift.

4.19.14

TAR, THREAD, KEEL

Flowering white cherries, dogwoods
flank pock-marked by-ways
of Summit neighborhood. Maze
for decrepit spars, tackle. Gould's

Island, a mirage of peeling shades.
Keeled over on the sidewalk,
somebody said. *Just a block*
from here. Cataracts cascade

from flimsy eyesores – Providence
is where you are, blind king.
A shroud from *Sheep's Clothing*
rivets Ariadne in RI. Nonsense-

crock, or Monarch sepulcher?
Mutual web, or recipe
for ferocity? *Quipu,*
mayhap. Counting-house, your

Gothic hoard... your Sutton Hoo,
owl-bard. Whose buried ark
is here, in Theseus Park?
Timbered differentials, fluted blue,

blister to red, white, gray...
a black sail nears the shore.
Golden forsythia, for fair
Pen's breaker-circlet – like an eye

through the thicket of a rusted coin.
A moss-beard face peers out
from angled whorls – green coot
in green coat (sunlit through rain).

4.28.14

AROUND MENDELSSOHN

Most historians and archaeologists do not consider Mount Zion to be the actual resting place of King David, but that has not deterred the faithful. – NY Times, 5.27.14

Desiccated lilacs, already shriveled
and gone. But the purple iris
still reminds me of those
root-beer rivers, vermilion-channeled

around Mendelssohn (Superior).
The music of what happens
for a shamrock tike (green
spin atop Frisbee-harbor). We're

climbing Mount Zion. Every handhold
counts – like a poem found in
college, or a found poem
in a collage. Light shoaled

in splintering dogwood, branch
scraping like a fiddle... *May*
I have this dance? OK,
Al. *Mon Dieu*! An avalanche

of joy, just held in check... Galilee
rabbi, skipping like a pinnace
with a spinnaker (slantwise,
L-ward). *We Were There* (whee,

sheesh!). Is the Pope moving in? Nobody's
had a tenant meeting in
a thousand years... spat upon
daily outside the Slumber Room. Geez.

What do they want with King David?
Let him sleep in his casket
of diamond pizza-parties. A little
bird (warp-speed drone) zips overhead.

5.27.14

SEE-SAW

> *"We do not fully understand the power of this stone yet," said Arfan Najar, an archaeologist and co-manager of the Magdala dig...* – NY Times, 5.14.14

The Mirror Lakes, in Mendelssohn.
Where we skated for happiness
in an infant innocence
guarded by ripe compassion

(*Almond Joy*) unseen, unrecognized.
The dome of acorn wisdom –
a tiny Frisbee freedom-
cap, tossed-off (misplaced, despised).

It is the window we were missing.
Evening glass, pregnant
with sunlight (regnant,
growing shady). Whistler, whistling...

rocking in the arc of a pie-chart
filled with spectral salmon.
Only light, as almond-
waif, hungry for solo part...

Hymn for Happy Amygdala,
brain-pink as a pillbox
hat (*Amen, Nox*
Aeternam). Departs. *Selah.*

The see-saw, Julie. The iron
croak... the swing (*chi-*
rho, chi-rho). You, me...
mixed-berry pie Grandma Ravlin

baked, for the 4th of July. Warped
cosmonaut in Bayeux spoon –
blind home run, fall moon.
Étrange orange (grass-harped).

5.29.14

ORIOLE WING

The double-arc of an oriole wing
caught my eye the other
morning – a pair (bird-mother
& father) skim the gutter, gabbling...

streaks of orange-black chevron
the windowsill. Only
a half-note so far (*C*
7th, dim). Patched perihelion.

A private plane mows the blue
lawn overhead. Slumber
mumbles awake yon bumble-
dream... *to be*. Solely. *For youse*.

Green shoots toward the 4th.
& tomorrow... only
a promise (of misery).
The principle of the Prince is mirth

& ruthlessness. Seamless doors,
vengeance, *ressentiment...*
an undertow. A precedent
of caustic ecstasy (sweet *Mors*).

The semaphore spools threads of blood
& melted wax. In the wings,
red, blue... rebel halo-rings... six
distempered hemispheres (*vindviper*-brood).

Dit-dah... dut-dah... Navajo chit-chat.
Nobody knows de trouble
eye bean. Only Mendelssohn-
bubble (Mirror Lake Hubble). *Fiat*.

6.27.14

DRAGON-CRASH

To exodus the snarling incoherence
of the world, my poem.
Wisdom inheres in her hem
& haw, her woolly-crowned affluence,

somehow – the almondine one,
who leapt before the whirl-
beguine (benign girl).
Before all blistered shells... the undone

Humpties, over-too-easy (melted yolk
in Sarajevo sun).
Too much no-compassion
in the guile of arsonists – those kitsch folk

heroes, harsh orange flickerings;
her mock-orange canopy
over the camel panoply
must fling flame at fire (lightning's

silver cross-stitchings). Between ISIS
& Sisi – Caesar, Assisi –
the twirling travesty
knots up your torch-catharsis

now, Antigone – loyalty of banners
& clans unties the weft
of peace-weaving (*left,*
right...). Tar-bangled spanners

on cat-walks of lambent blood-vessels
project a shadow, Sophie,
toward your candle. & it will be
a dragon-crash – thunder to deeper hells.

6.29.14

TURRET-EYE

We sleepwalk toward lost concords of the sea.
Flecked fins of turf wave
after wave... an architrave
of anglers, acute, drowsy (*see... she*).

Ocean revery (salty,
oblique). Hummingbird,
homing every word – above
that hornet's scarlet turret-eye.

Fabled shade. Sol *oeuil.* Trepanned
antique fuming the barricade –
Niagara in Texas (*Maid*
of Aureole). Your head wound,

Moises (rushes to trenches).
Unknown *solitaire*
(Bartleby *père*) –
poète maudit (chills park benches).

Diagonal trajectory.
Fireworks (*northwest,*
northwest) – some Almagest
Espiritu Santo (Mississippi

alembic). Light-pail of Milky Way.
Myrrh for the king, likely.
Turn left at Luxury
Pyramid for Mini-Ball in RI

(Rhymney Junction). Welsh the crown
from herald cranium –
Shakespook tympanum, or
Goulde, on Sybil Ha-Loon (Rouen).

6.29.14

THE LONG GRASS

The trench was like a twisted river
of manure and rust. Bent-
over Al & Bertie, faint
now in memory. That ravin' conniver

H.G., with the bloodshot eye –
souvenir de Louie? "A touch
of the royal" – not much.
Slaughtered under a Ruskin sky.

All three. South of Ypres-jeepers,
beside the sleepy Somme.
This somnolent hum
of toothy cogs must end, the weepers

say. Someday. When rabid dogs
cease racketing around by
Snuffy's Drive-in (west end
of Mendelssohn – past the Log

Cabin – in the long grass, by the lake).
Remember the Limping Lady?
Cartwheels no more, sadly.
Tears well. & for God's sake.

There is only one kingdom, only
one king. We'll see her through.
That aureole around a blue
moon, Jeanne... born before we.

She cycles through ruin, absolutely.
Up from the crooked well,
like a gleam in a lake. Sea-shell.
To bear it all, *enfant*. Anew. *Étoile-épée.*

7.1.14

COPPER STREAM

The whole summer, a river-serpent,
glides toward old St. Henry's
Day. The mole-holey geez
himself zigzags hith-yon – spent

rat between pyramids, *Ursus-Ruhr*
of the Chaldees. A Flanders
moonscape his meander's
Nile (knot nailed to trench floor).

Sigh on, ancient ear of earth.
Her truth a bunched flower
on your stone detour,
soldier. Hiding the grave's mirth,

euphony's service-symphony
(good-bye to all that).
Bad feet. *Sous le pont,*
Kipling-stripling – farewell to thee

& May. *Not good enough* (whispers
the river, creaks the stream).
Sad half-measures from
sleepy-steppes, out of wan moonlight (Ur's,

ours)... who can bear it? Raven
One-Wing, Eagle Two-Wing,
oriole in the tree (sing
low, sweet now). Bruised harvest moon.

The stump hides acorns in its rings.
Saturnine grump, abiding
another go-round – guiding
lump, firefly (hamlet-cupola, U-turning).

7.11.14

EVERY KING

In the end, every king is Humpty-
Dumpty – a pullet embryo-
omeletto, abandonato
by his own flighty mousketry.

Every king is everything,
in fact – an earthen jar
of last year's *wanderjahr* –
the war, the other war... zing,

bang, bong. The men of violence –
you know their names, O king –
would Joab your Gordian (string
you clean up) with rapier impatience

– Pamplona *virtù* in its use
(Toledo steel). *Paths of Glory.*
Tell us another story,
cher grandpère. *The Golden Goose*

is good. Steersman's an alderman
of sorts (for bloody boorish
bulls, rudderless Ishmaels,
orphan oarsmen). *Tauromachia* (Cretan).

The horn shall pierce your own soul too,
Geraldo C. This fiery worm,
Beowulf, in the doom-
scythed maize – my paw-paw, Captain, you

must face it down (weird masquerade).
Grandpa kept a brass shell
in the living room (dud
keepsake). Bells. *Le Roi est mort.*

7.11.14

LAND & SEA

FOR THE FLIGHT-VICTIMS
one if by land, two if by sea

The labyrinth of your fingerprint,
Sophie. The human touch,
impregnable (not much).
Love's murmur in sleep – rue, mint...

only rumors, next morning.
Kuala Lumpur, *O*
KL! Five years ago now.
Humid trance-kayak, flush with beaming

taxi-drivers (& one friendly Parsi
from Indie-archipelago).
Quiet storefront *Tao-*
templa. Shrines, mosques...

all side-by-side (recumbent lakes
amid brass moped squalls).
Phoebe & Khaled's
tropical apartment (your namesakes'

Polynesia to come). Long flight
Boston Los Angeles Seoul
(Malaysia Air). All
to knit my future son, in law (bright

Baba-to-be, Sophie). *They fall*
into the sea, these planes.
Or to the earth. Cranes
drift to Missouri... elegant, sprawl

(regal, awkward) in the naked stream.
All the birds of the air
shall make nests... where?
OK, acorn (steep cowpoke dream). *7.22.14*

FIGURE 8

The glittering sea-serpent
scratched a recumbent figure
8 across Ahab's poor
good eye. Poor Ahab (angry, spent).

Then out of the Pacific swam
one Captain Crozier –
his cabin cozier,
his ship ship-shape. *I am, I am*

sang the twisted rigging. Kenya
scull... stone kayak eye-
in hand... quipu sty-
wound... sunburnt amnesia...

The early bird catches the worm.
One-stringèd wreath (*trompette*
marine). Your alpha Bette
mute-pedaling (footnotes, sans harm).

That prehistoric eye, above
the pyramid. Forty
thousand years – *to be,*
from not to be... pigeon in granite alcove

cooing (*you, me*). My stout boat
braving shudders of the sea
with wispy fishline –
see, she. Will be your one whole note,

bronze herald-buoy. Milk pours
from the sky-cow, threads
cosmetic sun-shades of
green glass... yew rainforest hearse, Crozier.

7.25.14

AFTER APOLLINAIRE

That pudgy Parisian poet-vet
tattooed all over with scars –
a Queequeg of the *War*
to End All Wars (but not just yet) –

he of the blundered parentage (the
Pope was perhaps his father?)
– all that Roman bother –
a fenced-in pyramidical sage

gypsoid tumbleweed, fuming
over his Dallas *Lorelei*
across the Rhine (*goodbye,*
good luck)… O trench-spit spuming

rural rose! & the grapevine murmurs
Marne, Loire… the soil
of France – the ceaseless toil
of dew, *pour l'amour de Dieu* (showers

of tipsy fireflies in the wind-blown
hair of remote by-ways, so
gently *merveilleuse*)…
Adroit the boatman, who hath sewn

these sails – hath bent these anchored ribs
into prow, & figure-
head (one pierced *oreille*);
subtle the fisherman (Gennesareth

swab) who scanned these Galilean farms
with an ear to the waves.
Après l'Armistice, he saves
a little pipesmoke… (ashen charms).

7.28.14

SAND CASTLES

August, goldenrod of the Caesars...
& the *paisan* smile (inscrutable
& sad). Drawn to the water table
of lakes & seashore, the sea's recess.

Fold-on-fold cascades (irretrievable
decades). In the crazy-quilt
of recursive fields... your guilty
maize, & mine (South-Sea Bubble

of the mind). The Omaha train
pulls out at 7. Osage
family. On the last stage of
mourning (in the land, under the rain).

Traveling without their kids (Honduran,
Guatemalan) – refugees
from the stupidities.
Natural harbor (salty, hardpan).

Paralloid Congress troops into recess.
Up to the lake somewhere.
Collective crowd-esteem, hot air
fog spectacles with greediness –

navigators led by speech-balloons
exhale (from stingy lungs)
each bartered hearts' unsung
remorse. So an unseen moon's

ray numbers our undoing. Unkind
theoreticals & partisan
we mold a house from sand
that cannot stand. Yet, *love is blind...*

8.2.14

AIDE-MÉMOIRE

Tranquil August in the postage-stamp.
Navajo crickets already
smoking their Morse-Cody
peace pipelines. *Août,* old tramp,

old coot. Your IOU's expired.
SOS. Pronto,
posthaste. *Agosto*
cannot last. Chariot's hotwired;

roaming packs of wolves ruble
your sheep, sleepyhead.
This quipu thread's
a knot of woolly. Memory-bubble,

drifting up like Pacific
jellyfish (from Ocean
State). *Dear Someone,*
this battle is for you. Ick!

– slimed all over with holy goo.
He's in there – a She-
spidey – octo-puffy
orange squid – big eyes, too!

Octopus milk tastes like honey,
somebody said. Rumors
of warpath plant scars
in your palm, O painstaking donkey-

hoss. *Eeyore,* ASAP. Thin lifeline...
like old George's plow
on godforsaken prairie-brow.
Mute lips tread mock-marquee (a sign).

8.5.14

LITTLE HAWK EYE

Galilee, in RI, a fishing village
hidden in the green
infinity (unseen), or
summa of summers. Turn the page

of figures, unlimited bills, debts...
between heaven & earth
a broken binocular's worth
a heap (to Salvation Army). Set's

the enemy of Horus, that new hawk
droning over the backyard
pine. *Love is blind,* &
Hope's the motto (not just talk,

hopefully). Beneath the crazy-tilt
spars in sheep's own arbor –
behind the physical door,
to the mind's eye. Realm of guilt

& repentance – grief, forgiveness...
Everbiddy-plowmend's
field (Georgie's Farmstand).
Yokel-folks' unsurveyed Inverness,

so gently generous. Perhaps like a bee's
compound eye? Or Hagia
Sophia, in *peripeteia*
yonder (amid pyres of hypocrisies) –

whose heaven's not only 50 states,
or 57, but maybe
99? – in a maypole –
Whee! (*Elohim*, even!) over clover gates...

8.6.14

UNIVERSAL HUE

You can't say everything at once.
Only a little light,
a rustle, a rivulet
under a trestle, in Providence;

only as good as her next steep
command, your pilgrim is.
I commend you to this
mazy meandro-charter. Deep

grain bins of Golden Flour, tall
beside the Missus... sip
& see! Or take a dip –
your sentence will end within a small

period of time. Hence, & so forth.
The universal hue,
man. Some call it blue.
I read somewhere that violet's

the state blurred. – *Flower,* child.
There are several different
tribes in the Milky Way,
Kent. Some (Irish? Wild?)

might even be little green men &
women. Like to gab too,
I reckon – find out who
we are. Plan it? Plan it who,

then? A Providence so small,
so loco-minuscule,
so dear *me* (silly fool!)
you feel, not see. & that's not all.

8.6.14

ONLY PEACE

In the limpid silver salience
what you feel is already
a memory, already.
Be still, floaty Medusa! Immense

fog over cornfields. Ravens
having a field day. Virtual
dance of bare limbs (all
quiet in front). Some sick Ada's

X-Corps chessgame. Slick cylinder
to *Rus*. "From Russ, with
love." Cutlery, backpacks
scattered on the rim. "Don't wander

off, Alexander!" – *Don't Panic...*
Apollon in the rotten air.
Sheaves of miniature
orange trumpets vine the back

of a garage. Very muted today
(not for the last time).
Don't bother me with your crime...
everything but the bottom of the sea.

Only peace, cries the Pope. Paul,
too. The temple's gold dome
(*Emanu-El*) echoed in an emblem
on the wall – torch? Serpent? Bald,

bronze, shaky crozier-pate. *Seek
ye the Lord & live*, scrolled
overhead. In yon mossy old
Avon-cup, mayhap – cornered, meek.

8.7.14

LEBANON YEW

When that airy son of Apollo
was lifted down from Paris
aerie, on Armistice Day,
hypnotic bronze was sounding *Oh*

& *Oh* – bellowing above,
below. All that jazz
in Babylon, Ohio (sez
who?) was as an Orleans dove

a-trumpeting (encaustic *5th*
of J) – so sweet, so low...
(Lebanon ribs of yew
to barrow thee, O *Gitane*-thief).

Into the deep gills of the well
of prance-time, Capitan.
Aboard yon *caballito*
de totora, pegged to the whirlpool

pupil – magnetic anchor-weight
(a tie-dyed *quipu*-thread).
Your pointy prow heads
for Pacific meadows, those great

Medusae of the Blackfoot fleet –
enormous flowers Orpheus
smokes through torus-pipes
en voyage to obtain the *Complete*

Works of Humbaba the Wow-Mom
(Moses, Isis & Osiris
penned on Sirius). Sunblind
marine *d'amour*... your L-ship'd home.

8.8.14

TWINE-DIMENSIONAL

At noon, the bells hummed 88
harmonic tones – at St.
Sebastian's (off President
Ave.). Feisty tongs of a late

great brazen serpent, super-welded
into one still drone. 12
houris, I would have
thought – yet there were 3 threes, held

between pauses, to make a 9...
& then all 9 again,
carefully wrought round
as one. Like a *Savarin* can

by Johns – *again, again*... remembering
someone (by that name).
Beatrice is the same,
Kitty (9 times). Spirals to bring

Alighieri through the cataclysmic
chrism, to the dome
of Rhodes – *continuum-*
profundum, sounding now (abysmic

shepherdess). Soft omnipresence
of expiring conscience –
the clement constellations'
twilight, twine-dimensional... O sense

her subtle heft, who draws the peacock's
eyes into one crown
of knotted horns! Sebastian
screams. Waves fleck the rocks.

8.8.14

MACAU MACAW

Another eleventh (August this time)
on brick-silly wasteland of
one shady summer patio. Well
of hurry-up peas... bee-balm...

Joe-Pye weed... & yet this elfin
flower-team backyard
is not exempt. The hard
news (frenzied shrunken headlines)

bearbaits me too. From River Alph
to Yezidi desert, innocent
Peacock Angels get bent
down again. The gibbering gulf

twixt glib libel & Guelf remains kiln-set
in demosthenic night. Rainbows
of violets against violence? – how
coin bowl for Guinea-worm alphabet?

Sketches of Spain... Spanish Castle
Magic. Convivial Jorge
the Gardenia been draggin'
me, all over. Plays chess, too.

Iris, sez I, is a yurt-mother.
King's taken baby steps
between crooks, bishops...
Q's unreadable. & here's another

pawn to put in (yawning spacesuit).
A pair of carpenter asps
of the caduceus, Jasper –
dove from the deep. *Shalom* (checkmate).

8.11.14

SAILOR-SKETCH

O big zebra-striped cicada
with the Air Force wings
found adrift this morning
in Sophie's baby-purple wading

pool – can I identify with you?
Or maybe only your husk
was left behind. Ask
Jonah in his whale, or Zarathustra

in his Cyrus-shade (serene
weatherman). Inquire
of the Yezidi-martyrs
on their mountain. Savage scene

of human inhumanity
today. The mimic-men
love Mickey Mouse – then
spool to hate such levity;

they kill what they deny (themselves)
persecuting poor Me
in the name of purity –
pure folly (petty peevish dwarves).

I'll circulate the prose *Popeye*
instead. A sailor-sketch
of Pappy in his ketch
(the Pope, perhaps?). Only the sigh

of Peacock Angel – delicate thread,
goldfinch *trompette marine*...
yet you sense what I mean :
bright Joan – ah! – surfing from the dead.

8.12.14

HORSEGRASS SEED

The irony of this copper crown
I ring around your hair –
this semi-thick fiber for
yon russet-gold & windsown

filament of horsegrass seed (cold
dark axion out of chiral
superfield). Dear radio-loud
fermionic superpartner... my old

cartoon of your invisibility
is buried nearby (in the
cosmic attic, maybe).
As if I could draw your ability

to be wherever I be, *Yam-Wham* –
O bright magmonic tennis
gamin! (Please scan the scrim
for WIMP- or MACHO-errors, Clem.)

My silver tuning-fork, only an echo
of sea-bells (rose island
adages, Miranda).
Caustic firemasterings still flow

to the stony ceiling, where his face
beams (Galilean gallery night).
Ladders, long-neck sprites,
sword planted for a crosspiece

in that sink-point copper prow...
the oldest crown of all.
A 7x7" buttermilk burial
will cradle your cranium (for now).

8.12.14

MIRE PEBBLE

O king of kings, of kings... ping, ping...
mere pebble in the fountain's
fascinatin' facets, Hen.
Trade you my turtle for that willow thing,

pal. Love's always on the fair side
of the sketchpad – always
2 or 3 guys,
gals (sad Millicent Pip says

so). O SYNDIA MY SYNDIA BANE
THER IN MY HART REMAINS
A PANE *Madonna with Munchkin*
Surrounded by Penned B-B Gun

Pullets, or *Satan's Greatest Hits*
(kapustulation at Munich).
Uneasy lime the sick
& squirrmink soul... see, he vomits

worms, that Prince o'Poococks.
Nobody lubber him no mare.
He th'umptiest man-hare
in the stream – block-rovin' avis-ox...

Your stone weigh more'n this M-
&-M, aimin' for shore.
– Chocolish be pure
rococo-novo PIE in MY tank's giveye, Hem.

Let us contangle this convocation
on the Plain of Explanation,
Thesis. – Mizn't shum
the tautrope, needle, Addie Marion.

8.14.14

PEBBLE-HUBBUB

The mild idea of August, when the season
shifts down slowly
like a Susan (dark-eyed
teetering sun). & how then

untie this Cornish nut? Old man
of concrete sorrows, clay-
foot minnow-tar, so thickly
barnacled, gillied o'er wi' tin-can

regalia... highland loading-docks
for lotos-haggles. Knot
for Gordon or McNutt
indeed! *Go & tell that phlox*

something greener than Macbee
be here! In humble Hubble
pebble-hubbub, stubble
of autumnal sensibility... you'll see.

Rook through the crooked mirror,
maven. Some Thanksgiving
nods in the riddling
rhizome's kid-scrawled wisdom (barely

there). Somebody's paw, leafing
from the aqua liner
like a buoy – slim silver
bone-whistle (*Asclepios*-thief).

A wheel of emerald palms (Phoebus
folk-art). Very unique
linen, spun with coral eye-
drops reefed to each lifeline (*outré* rebus).

8.15.14

STRUM SOFTLY

If I extend a handle on
this raven-winged
diagram – & spring
an abstract of some gamelan-

hieratic chessbud's ovoid willow-
drawings – some Abyssinian
synthesis (elephant-clown
in boxer-trainers)... Grace might go

with you, Cindy, to the well.
Fallacious, maybe, but
archaic, too. Something attic-
mitten Hittite's southern belle's

Ptolemy about him. *Might be*
the beginning of some word
or name Edwardian
Antiquaries overlooky-lookied –

crucigerous *Ensigne*-navvy, or
chiasmo-rhomboid
chippy's waterboard...
Aye-aye, Chaplain. Too heavy

& too knotty by half, Bogey-
man. O this victorious
waterfowl of senseless
adoration – peacock's *Jubilee-*

midéwe dalliance! Only memory
of your hermetic lips'
vermilion... while ships
strum softly on up to Itasca (for thee).

8.15.14

COPPER PROFILE

In gaol, a bookish Boethius
will set his house in order
with quiet cricket-whisper
of raven feather. Pocahontas

or Beatrice... quick Milaneasy muse
levitates gravity
from the grave (the pity
remains). Busy emperors use

Martian pylons to cement their rule;
a double accident
(habit & precedent)
steers Beat to barber stool.

In the 9th dimension (philosophic
ladybug-land) some shady
Eeyore irradiates me
with graceful simplicity of means : full-

phantom-five strange spiracle
of copperhead small
change (one wheeling hail's
sea-serpentine green double-

spun encircled peon-eye).
& a whole glob of noodling
nations starts caboodling
their common-aspirin opinion-pie

until Providence intervenes
(eddying Pole's tree-
sliver in ocean – see?)
Crowns Galaxy with Dairy Queens.

8.18.14

SAFETY NET

August crickets are singing to someone
far off, or not so.
Thread dangling below
tangerine peaks, out in San Fran –

a catenary smile. Eureka,
Eeyore-Eurydice!
They plan to (finally)
ravel a safety net. OK,

Ophie – all right, Juliet.
The ocean has a mind
of its own. So find
the sliver in my coral circlet,

Señor. The vertigo's a mere
(*blnk*) mirror (covert
parish) – tense-converter's
home yurt hug-generator – sheer

Miranda-linen, for the chess-
mate brine-fest (welding-
day). A raincoat's pedaling
across the drops, from Inverness

to Octahebron... only a black dot
in your pupil, eye
of your own summabody. &
the tighter she whorls this river-knot

the quieter the whisper moistens
my lips. *Aye-aye.*
Ding-dong. We only die
once in a dream, dear pastel cousin.

8.19.14

PERSIAN CARPET

Often, some undulant Vermilion
afternoon, I'd lean
across the canoe-beam
& gaze down, past reflection

of water-lily, through sweet well
of quiet lake... to the white
sand floor – where a clam might
linger, molding layers of gray shell,

its coral palimpsest (secret
stone ossifer, or ocean-
oval). & so someone
might spin a maze of Persian carpet

out of a welter of overlapping
memories, half-
lost... (some lamprey-staff
Menominee, maybe, from Happy

Hunting Ground). *You must be born*
anew, Henry, the ghost
flutters – out of her moist
mosaic, its inward rime of horn

(purling Itasca-masque). *But how*
might an old man... ? Iowa's
peony, her mind flows
into mine, clear agate stream (slow

octahedral chirhodendron-star).
Love's Jonah sweeps
one hand through leaps
of sheep-years... wavelets lap scar.

8.19.14

RABBIT-SCHOOL

In the decline of this most August month
some rumors surface near
White Bear Pool – y'hear?
New Rabbit-school – sunny bar none –

with talk of *Kingdom Come* (again).
No Roman umpire, see
(*all the world shall be X'd*
to a T) – but 9 full innings (for children)

& all the brine you can surf ('pon
some rainbird Gal Marie's
waist-deep pad for lilies).
O primordial world of Mendelssohn...

where we lumbered, Heidi, from the slough
with an antique rusty plow
to set up as prow
for Spanish galleon (all things made new

by way of *Harold & his Purple Crayon*)...
Time seems to linger
near summer's pioneer
(Jiminy Dave Cricket, Fiddlin' Son

of Paw-Paw Pete); by willow breaks
& cottonwood banks,
there we'll give thanks
with Milky Zed, & Abby Jakes

& all the company of kid-run things –
companions in that realm
where Jay goes roaming... &
even Evelyn Raven rests (relents & sings).

8.20.14

WOBBLY STARS

A king was once the centerpiece
of the turntable – LP
as long as he could be.
Just. Magnanimous (he's

a darn good reign maker, too).
Like your own father,
only farther along
the fat of the land. & his voodoo

ancestors applied special powers
to orchestrate the tribe's
jet stream (hit songs, jibes,
bribes in the Happy Hut). Ours

was such a kingdom, these many
tins of tousands of cheers –
life's crofters & beers
harmoni-choraled by Volant Benny

the Goodman, his sons, & yes, grandsons.
Merrily, merrily, merrily,
merrily (sometimes scarily)
the lifeboat filled with hams & yammuns

& sailed into last night's Sydney
dreamsong (full of sheep
& mermaids). & if you keep
looking down, you might (soddenly)

up periscope!... into another
hemisphere. *Big Bear,*
Wobbly Crane, North Star...
where *Milky Gal* curlicues forever.

8.21.14

ROSY CIRCE

My task – a blessed one, if you
are willing to accept –
to measure one precept
from the deep June flowers to

the flow. Shakespearean headwaters,
if you like. One coppery
tilt of yon Po' Bobby
riverbuoy, still upright (all that

matters). Nehushnow, hon (sun
of flying Nun) – the quiet
suits your Narragansett
fleet (tarry southwest now, Harry Dan).

One life, one path (a windy one).
A blinded canopy – fiery
as that hoop-swept, unweary
cardinal, whose scar-etched crown

peeks out from clematis, mock-orange.
Through a tin-can twin-
doored Mexican
mirror, sense these rays' strange

personal summons (between paired
dovebirds under trumpet-
vines). Mote-delicate net
of proto-galaxies, that snared

all worlds, before all whorls, whim-whirled...
A Someone, huggin' our skin –
Proto-Indo-Ethiopian-She-
brew PIE-Spinner? (– pumpkin, Honey-Pearl.)

8.21.14

ANOTHER NINE

O shaggy, quincunctial
September garden, when
snows of greeny-golden
clematis surmount the wall

of tangled wire, again. A year,
squaredanced. Galilee
means *a circle,* gals –
whole whorl a rollercoastering sphere

screeching on a subway, hugging
silvery Smolak the bear,
whose shoulder's a sheer
tear-drop. Metaphysical thing,

singuhilarity. Black hole
atlatl-crozier,
quartz-quartered (in your
mazified curls' timespace ear).

Surprise... the royal touch opens
a blind eye. You behold
the homely dimpled portals
of a venerable smile. *Humans*

cannot comprehend their own
good fortune, hums
yon infinitely humble,
bearable Rabbi. *These bones*

shall rise, out of the dusty plot –
origami galore unfold
from one hypnotic cold
Polaris-9. Corral-bells drone (b-flat).

9.9.14

CRICKET CIRCUS

September. Cusp of somno-autumn
yet again. But not
to sleep this time, not yet.
The cricket-circuitry's low hum,

its infinite lowliness, invisible
glee. Sad-happy blues
way back beyond Memphis,
herm-green hills. *Anything is possible*

he cricketoons, *with the power*
of soul. With the power
of *you.* Out of mellow-
bright sunset-wheat, one flowering

morning star. Time pivots thus
on beautiful pin-
prick (airborne origin).
Panopticon. Archimedes'

hand, full of trusting levity –
a cantilevered moon
of cosmic acumen...
all the kingdoms of this planetary

pollen-harvester not worth
your soul (orange oriole-
feather, pumpkin bowl).
So follow the lightfoot fiddler forth

from Julian calendar to 7th-day
Jubilee, my friend –
all the way to the end
of Frisco Bay. Let us make hay,

by George, I say! The time-vine ripens. *9.10.14*

GRAVE FICTION

Drove through the watershed (cusp
of Mississippi, Great
Lakes). To catch a late
wave function, beyond my grasp.

The first king was a dead king.
My father's wrack (nine
seamen-Liefs). Line
of Hillsboro generations, lo, I sing...

behind bronze wheel of Buick ('tween
Columbus & Ravenna,
OH). O Manna-
man of Heaven (outlier now, keel-

gone). A grassland salience.
Soft tread of mountain-
feet, dewlap fountain.
Ancient hunter-scent. *Silence!*

Hawk sweeps nordeast, above
my head (in Providence).
Continue hum, dense
dream (pinedraft). A twin-dove,

two-door Mexican tin-moon (gift
from Twin Cities). Crazy
paisan poisson-prance – he
do the Shy Entrail! Too swift

the yarrow of her Thoth (blink-murk
of Suger-queen, the maze
of scairn)... – O pinioned blaze
of Solomon – blank buffalo-spark!

9.11.14

NICKED MIRROR

62-yr-old Providence Man
Lost in Late-Summer
Sunlight. Beachcomber?
Like Big Rabbit in Rabbit Clan

or hidden Hiawatha-wannabe
he snoozes in ripe shade
(old *mini-aha* Corn Maid
fan). A tiny, gilded, bee-

like fly rides light upon his knee.
He nobody – only
this calm tranquility
of crystalline transparency.

The Day itself, he mumble, it
might be like so, someday.
Dressed in garden togs, hey.
Vacating the rites of Ugotit

& Wegrabit, of Big Cat Fear
& Hard-Heart Recipe
(brune soup). Black Sea
of caustic raven-ink, draw near –

engrave your lettuce-wave across
the sky's nicked mirror.
Something strange is here.
Beyond pre-Stonehenge Way-Back, toss

your diamond octopus right through
the cosmic gauze. One
grave, brave moon-
gaze harbors you (hail, Manitou).

9.12.14

BEYOND TREBIZOND

In gaol, Boethius beats out
a Greek-Byzantine tune
set to old Roman
type. Hand spans a lute

now, in his memory (that's all,
folks). Curtains flare
down like swan wings air.
Les jeux sont faits, Apollodorus,

mon ami. Waves (medium-
grey OK-fingertips)
remind him of those lips,
O Wisdom... salt over tedium.

Beyond Trebizond. Outa sight,
Detroit. The chariot's
invisibilità (thought's
light portion of your sweet

anti-Octavian proportion)
– prelude to the mangy
grand finale (strange
unsnarl of trench-contortion).

In a lamb's cat's-cradle (*ojo
de Dios*) the golden wool
ravels every spill,
for carrots! Stubby fir-iron boho –

him Assisi grapejay giveaway!
Such humiliated gold
still shine from sheepfold...
um daily bread. Him loco honey.

9.12.14

JONAH-LAND

Your presence, in the drift of a day;
one sheep-cloud overhead
shades the vermilion thread-
medallion (a hobo child's play).

While clay labors in wide circles
& iron rings, to finish
the furrow-mosaic. The fish
of Justinian exceed his net – sparkles

brim in the aquamarine. Leviathan
or Spinosaurus, a gatemouthed
Mammon squeezes north-
south-east-west... & out pops Gill-man

(with Martian friend) – cuts corners
for Pluto, speeds templates
to placate (for a while at least)
implacable Moloch (corn-mill for shirkers)...

Your presence, a voice in the leaves;
capstone of the whisper-poem,
persistent victim-lamb,
at sea (Ravenna's gloom-lit eaves).

Who keeps climbing from the cave
until we understand
at last – good Will's demand
was kept before we knew. Only save

this token of a broken safety net;
my memoir of unraveling
starts hobo-traveling
toward Jonah-land... will be there yet.

9.15.14

WRINKLED HEIGHTS

Summer's last gold, in these weeds
burnished by constant crickets.
Jasper, rose, the violets.
Drowsy Apollinaire proceeds

through thunder-blooms (repetitions
of a dated jealousy)
toward his Texas Annie-
Ariadne (*chanteuse* convolutions,

Cherson harbor-sound). The rites
of autumn's Oklahoma
oak. Dusky Jonah
twinkles over wrinkled heights

out west. Margarita in Mexico,
Procurator & Monarch-
mast – one syrinx-irenic arc
for sleepy sun. *Monsieur, les jeux*

sont faits. A Petersburg, hélàs.
Bees hover, dive into
late clematis... you bowline
one poor wreath for your Francesca

under Frisco sun. From Mendelssohn
to Providence, from shanty-
town to Olneyville, from Anti-
Christ to Chosen One, the molten

haze gets fluted into unison. Low song
welds tungsten hammers
into infant stammers...
calumet marine (peace-prong).

9.15.14

LIGHTWEIGHT PENDENTIVE

The raven in a land of shades
is caustic ink. Remains.
Inca child in mountain
sacrifice – there's gold in spades.

This raincloud looms in purple-grey.
For everyone. & then
one hunted black-orange sign
skips over fence – *hey-yo, ey-hey.*

Sole monarch is a butterfly.
En route to Mexico
Kedron (ground zero) –
grey-green needles, blue bull's-eye.

Soul monarch. Psyche-melody,
tangential, tentative.
Lightweight pendentive
shepherd in mosaic (friendly

rabbi-lamb, in ferrous wheel
of morpho blue). Not far
from Ursiana cedar –
Route 56 (exit for Israel).

This king bears all. *Ursus is us* :
service stations, Rus
to U.S. The humble ass
shoulders each blow, does not resist,

does not concede. Smolak or Bruno,
eye on the sky, burning –
dove-star, yearning, turning
soil. Barefoot basilica (fresco).

9.16.14

BOOK

III

SHEEPSKIN INTEGUMENT

That downward eagle, calligraphed
in Calabrian parchment
(sheepskin integument
for Joachim, his flowercraft)

sheds colors of an evening
down Ravenna side-street
past sepulchre of Dante-poet
requiescat (wolf-world unravening).

So eyebrow & eye elope
together, sloping down
toward blind renown –
just when ox & ass lose hope.

Toward Jerusalem he goes,
then – riding backward
to a king's reward –
just so the Son of Man undoes

the sun (his own). Like melancholy
Berryman, burying
his dad again – beginning
from the ghostly end of Galilee.

So spread the ragged Sicilian scroll
out flat as Morning Star
upon the prairie, like a jar
in Dallas, '63. This earthen bowl

will lift her wings (past Phoenix
AZ) toward Mexico
aflame, anew – gh-ghost
lancing (to lofty tense apex).

9.16.14

SOLE CARILLON

An earth-flute, omnipresent,
infiltrates lyre's jangle,
wrangles over laurel.
Suddenly the veil is rent,

sounding. Smokes from mouth to mouth
across flat latitudes,
prosy interludes –
a whirring praying-mantis oath,

Veracruz-craft. A matrix
in Ravenna (oval casket
rimmed in stream-quartet)
harbors marzipan & brick-

red dust for such mercurial
Venusian transfusions,
whose lute-foam effusions
swell spinnaker, gild sun-dial...

Only a local bread-boat in the Ocean-
loafer's milk-train fleet.
The pattern of *petit*
feet, maze-dancing – corny motion

or complete rapture-redemption?
You decide, pilgrim.
After all, her kalimba-
hymn is your sole carillon,

or none. Like the tendril elegance
of the balancing tread
between twin towers... sped
by kismet-calumet toward Providence.

9.17.14

POMMEL-TWIN

Beneath the 5 and 29
bright gears of Alighieri
old Lady Memory
(Ceres? Maid of Orleans?)

spins yarns (midway *midéwewe*
maybe)... – over the river
from St. Louee – under
some clobbered almond-shards of clay.

& say a Dauphin or Merman emerged
from her serpentine skein –
some magic pommel-twin
Guillem d'Orange, or synergetic

Demiurge – he'd be a jolly *enfant*
lifted from the bath,
just born (transflouting wrath).
There be no ghostlier intent,

say we (according to a gloss
of all the poetry
from shaken spoketree's bee-
enlivened, lightning-riven moss).

This autumn rite springs from an earthen
tree-rung dancing-floor
much older & more
permafrost (storm-resistant too) than

triste-pleurant poppyfields of France
or *heils* of Germany –
her only country's many
crane-bone flutes (in one sneak glance).

9.19.14

CORNCOB SPAN

A praying mantis on the autumn
laundry rope. A remnant
of green thread, his Martian
ant-head like a musty seed (one

hypocrite lecteur indeed, my
Hannibal Caliban!) – his
shriveled corncob span
clutches the line like a castaway

Jonah. Who will save him now?
His fathers lied & killed
like he, with pious guile (though
he'd critique them at the Insect Show).

Below the wire, a shuffling friar
packs weeds into a willow
basket... remedies for now
(until the Halloween bonfire).

A caw-caw Kali decorates
Verona's tombs with purple
violence. White-steepled
Providence (Cautantowwit's)

is not exempt. My antic heart
twirls in its labyrinth.
Wormwood & absinthe
halve dove, slice lark – unless this art

of Raven-nut unravel in the light
of day. For these we pray
in Mantua, mantis – *hey-*
yo, ey-hey... (brief Romeo, slight Juliet).

9.23.14

MOLTEN BRACE

The chronicles of history-play
scroll into a double-whorl.
Theaters of war,
shifty hunters' perjury

– old Uncle Bear, it was not we
that slew thee, but those
wily Russian Jews, or
maybe Georgian Romany –

plot death-marked love into recursive
déjà-vu : the tomb
a piquant little room
where flakes of Romeo's elusive

raven-mask (with white bone-streaks)
form lambent constellations
in the ceiling's tessellation.
Satirical asides, poison-pen leaks,

bladders, packthread, straw-men, fish-
shaped manatee... the whole
Leviathanic rigmarole
of nightly sea-snakes (onto-gulpish)...

Yet note how mere soft light (reflected
by lily-pard) lances
cataracting circumstance,
until twin ferris wheels of salt

grind to a halt. Patched in dry ice,
Baby & Mama Bear
revolve in state, up there –
one molten brace, one Paradise.

9.24.14

BLACK MAGNET

The ferris wheel of seasons creaks
toward rust now. Starlings,
magnetized by molting
dogwood, cackle through stiletto-beaks

& whistle from their spiral summit
(orange, rose, maroon).
Every raven soon
will flit, exit stage left, evaporate

(– an oblong glance, a Frisbee-skim
between slant flakes of twilight
cold). So hum the bright
Finn finish-song, old Smolak-hymn –

his haunter's tune draws nigh the stars
to circle round the heaven-
heart... his iron pen
rings Pegasus, Orion, Kiril's Cart...

– & all the rest. Winter's a black
bear cave, a hibernation-
hole. Celebration
of the hunter's cap – of bone (way back

behind your figurehead of stream-
bred gold). But Honeypaw
will growl no more, Grandma.
Your heart's a broken kettledrum

that smolders something darker even
than my song. *Drone,*
black magnet of the crone –
light bends, somehow (a crown for Stephen).

9.25.14

MUTTERING HALO

The Crown of Stephen, a legal person
& a double one
(*couronne grecque-latine*).
Rimmed with 12 pearls, icons 19 –

Pantokrator, & Emperors,
Sts. George & Damian,
Cosmas, Demetrius...
kept in gold-vault at Fort Knox

until Epiphany (back in '78).
Grandpa's birthday (1.6).
St. Stephen's Day (12.26)
is Mom's. Today's September light

moist honey & rust through dogwood leaves
is food for wheeling starlings &
fat robins, yodely-nibbling
ruby berries. So... who sieves

our personal potions? How?
Some snake-den matrix
gamma-guest pinpricks
pawprints of dogwood blood, O

Stephen (stiffening *fer-de-lance*).
Some humble Berryman-
DuBerry, daughter of her son
(a vein of Rabbit-heir's long-distance

almandine). Lone polar bear
who bears all things,
madre of one messy king –
muttering *Halo, freedom-friar...*

9.26.14

BEAST-MOLD

Under an overcast gray sea
of sheep, October shades
turn radiant. Parades
of moss-green tendrils... prickly

batons of some domesticated
thistle, in their mantle
purple borne aslant
across a limestone cricket-

moat. The season loops toward
Martian anniversary.
Apollinaire (jolly
ubiquitous *Tuba-Roi*) lowered

by casket from his garret
À bas, Guillaume! (*11*
11) unto his best *paisan-*
royaume (*la paix*, more great

than *tous les guerres*). & Ezra
Pound, *à Paris appartement* –
tight-coiled, truculent
comet-slingshot (Goliath-kithara).

Old autumn kings of Indian summer
bear all our sins. Mad George
& his red-coated bowling-
pins... Hernando Bloody-Flummer

nipped by Crazy Horse. One glass
agate-eye lies beneath
them all (blind rabid wraith
no more, but frigid hut) – Time's last

beast-mold. *10.2.14*

DR. SOMEONE

The whole earth sketches itself
into a corona
of some sort, Mona,
around the moon. A little elf

told me. Honest. Small green man
from Mars, or Skerryland –
canna but not understand
a wee bit, only. This great nation

that wum nursed wim fingerpainting
– *"Dang George's fault – that bad,*
mad King – we all been had!" –
squished into gouache, wid fingerpointing.

Like a rain-map by John the Daubist
of Ethiopia,
the cornucopia's
lost tramp-vein – 50 states list

overboard, almost (into Atlan,
Hell, or bust). *The bath*
of wax & caustic wrath
is either the beginning of the end

of the nigredo, *or alchemical*
nadir (Dr. Someone
moaned). Perihelion.
Prospero's booked, Ariel –

y'on y'own, my piñon sprite.
Cussed black-orange wing
skims (westering,
impoverished) toward Golden Gate.

10.6.14

JAYBIRD VOODOO

Your climbing spiral – tier-
on-tier of spiny
terraces – maybe
the Tiny People's hair-

line pathway to the sun (blue-
green, translucent).
Absorbs me too, volant
Ariel. Via jaybird voodoo

I'm the last monarch in Mexico –
oaring, mesmerized, my
melange-bateau (capsized,
stranded in the trees' tress-glow).

So into the anonymous pattern
of Everyman is folded
one longhand *John Doldrum*
Hancock-Colchis anagram (stern

wake for Black Sea golden ham).
Under the starlings' pole
of the telepathic yodel-
scroll, where 3 Bears swim

& one bold peacock eyes the eagle's
beak – that raptor-hawk,
who silences their talk
with airy stalk (gyro-elliptical)...

Ariel, ho, Ariel!
Come back – your pining
monarch in retirement
zigzags off... farewell, farewell!

10.6.14

BURCHFIELD SCENE

The lusty guest of a mid-October
breeze bisects my rusty
dogwood's forked *V*
de la Victoire – while the composer

of this Compostela wayfares through
nostalgias of imagination
(near the compost bin).
Visions of Paris cleaved by dew

compel one heart's Ohio-land –
wind-bent Burchfield scene
with odors of old barn,
latrine. Some seedy hand

on a vagrant tangent, muttering
his chert-chat, cross-eyed
double-vision – plied
over flimsy plaid, worn, stuttering...

some rheumy Rimini parallax –
Pound in the round, pounded
into the ground (of mind
unsound). Yet past *cinq* sunken acts,

maybe, the duplex of twin lips'
ellipse melds into one
crepuscular *saison-*
chateau. Full fathom. Fleet, ships...

So set your caw-caw calipers
for spinnaker, Hobo –
wide as can go.
One gale encircles all the reapers.

10.7.14

ELKHART

Elkhart. Planed (horizontal)
onto flat plate of the fields.
Winnebago windshields
flock to leeward (behind motel).

I mosey through October park.
Light amid oaks, the old
Masonic bandstand. Lake-bound
rivers intermingle through dark

Indiana valves. Small-town museum
could be Russian (one
spare Burchfield windblown
farm, out of Depression). Hum

the highways, south of the lake (U.S.
80). Truck route, grain-
belt shuttle. Hymnal (plain-
song). Bible radio. Esso, S.O.S....

Black Elk might have passed through here
(on the train). The Buick
shuttles east-west, slick
with amaranth, milkweed... sheer

sunset loom-dust (grain elevators).
My father in rehab,
voice faint (grabs
phone with one good hand's

bone grip) at the end of the line.
The left-side vision's
gone. Yet mind's precision
lifts hoarse laughter (like a highway sign).

11.20.14

BLUE PRONG

This evergreen's a blue prong
mizzen, steady as
she goes. Under the sky's
G-minor (melancholy song) –

the empty feeling of concave
November (full of wind
& rain). Gold ginko-rind
spearheads (fantails of Isis-navy)

pasted with brown oak leaves
onto moist pavement
(brittle syllables). Bent
Demeter hugs the dry sheaves

to spent breast. *If we scourge the corn*
for the sake of oil, we will find
no grapes to trundle... signed
a poor mason (Thanksgiving morn).

If we spoil the wheat for glint of gold...
if hunter tramp over maiden-
slope (sulfurous Milton-
masque)... if the trail gone cold...

Into the hollow of the year
spins the spruce ghost
who mirrors most.
Into the still life of the ear

sounds coiling spring (seedy
acorn grave). Moist earth
remembers us (Arthur's
maze – Theseus, Ariadne).

11.24.14

MIRROR LAKES

The drizzle of sleet, monotonous
snare drum. New England gloom
(Nor'easter coming). To whom
shall we give thanks, U.S.?

Fields furl their cornucopia
to pumpkin horns. Blow,
milkweed, for Fergus now –
so low on oil of gladness. Yeah.

Can you loop some snarly comet
with your lariat? Invite
that hobo down the street?
Unleash the joy in Joyce – the might

in Lincoln's painful mite? Mosey
on up with Moses, Jordan
way – beach Promised Land
in Plymouth sand? Say yes in Yeshuee?

Wampum rests with Wampanoags.
Holidays rewind
red Vinland soil – to bind
the serpent to Kid George's

fleecy cradle-calumet. Your eyes
are Mirror Lakes, child;
Mendelssohn's a neighborhood
for Minnesota symphonies;

the deep stars comprehend our schemes.
The bears all harmonize
& tumble through the skies
their growling round (hearth-beams).

11.26.14

COLDFRAME

Green arugula in the coldframe,
my little Garden of Adonis
beneath dove-grey mist
of December sky. Low blue flame

(Apollonian, lukewarm) steams
the last orange leaves
on the horizon. Grieving
Aphrodite (black-haired now) dreams

round the corner (Morris Ave.
& Sessions) – purple plum
gone brown. The gilded dome
of *Emanu-el,* its perfect curve

a grave measure of your acute
sorrow – one small hamlet's
sins in microcosm (gimlet
eye of narcissism) writ

in hen-scratches around the eyes
(hers, mine). O Time
& folly (off-rhyme
butterfly)... only a child's disguise.

I hear the wind blow through the slats
in the manger, catch a star
in the corner of a tear –
wells in your eye, a tiny frigate's

mast. Ember of sail... some ghost-
ship trails across prairie
toward San Francisco, see –
some Ariadne's *farfalla-nostos.*

12.3.14

MEDUSA THREADS

In Ferrara they're working out a formula
for iron, using minus 38+1
plank-beams through a bunion-
universe. Grandma Ravlin's Gamma-

Ray Space Teleharp hovers
right over Hooverville,
Iowa – droning still-
lives using Watchbird cameras.

Dark mutters meet dark energy
there – O feel her still
small microwave, Ophelia! –
Medusa threads North Sea

with covenants of broken vows
in her evil eye. *IN RI.*
A microcosmic sigh
sets timewoof cresting (infant nows)

full of disturbances for Peeping Toms,
exponential Tomahawks –
tom-tom powerhummocks
powdering interstellar pom-poms

(twice, thrice). Finger your blind
eye-in-hand, señor –
genetic memoir
primed for persecution's double-bind.

Only low murmur will save
her appearances. Wind
through blue-green pines.
Mute hazel eye (convex, concave).

12.3.14

TARNISHED OVAL

Your hazel eye, the color of clay,
light amber shade. Witch-
hazel – gnarled saddle-stitch
of jagged bones, so frail. Someday

(late March) blinking to life again
as baby stars, mustered
sun-yellow to the tree...
one lumbering local Orion

in your glance. Maritime charts
map undercurrents in the Ocean
State – mind's murky projection,
tarnished oval mandorla. Horus

for your Isis-bark, aquiline raptor's
white crosshairs. A bald
abstraction (Hamlet, stalled
on high). Iris will report

back to the King, immured in oak-bole
like a Roundhead's womb.
Frescos lap the room
of your servant, incarnadine scroll

of congealed thunder. An almond shell
rolls under the table
of the Emperor – feeble
now, on life-support (spooned from the Grail).

Meanwhile young Roger on the ridge-crest,
old Blackstone by his *Catholic*
Oak, play hide & seek
(brown turtleshell, mud Phoenix-nest).

12.5.14

GREEN CRYPT

Yesterday the memorial.
The Navy man's entombed
there, under the gloom
of salt water. Ariel,

ho, Ariel! I need you now.
Miranda's lost at sea,
by *Porta Aurea* –
it's a mystery. Right off the prow.

Them frosty pearls... like a snow-globe
swirling salt sea air.
Let's not go there.
Literature's for creeps, Hobo

sez – forcing a smile a mile
over that mariner's
cimetière (Jonah
C. Joiner). Stay awhile,

smoke a cigarette. *Love
is strong as Death* (crafted
into the Carrie Tower) –
tripped over that sepulcher-alcove

just getting here (*where are your
eyes?*). In the corroded
mirror (Venice, *Hérodiade*)
the magnet springs to life... surges

in waves. Ocean sounds in its well.
Where four streams run
back whence they began –
to a green crypt (your amygdala).

12.8.14

CORONA BOREALIS

The young blue spruce in the backyard
mantled in silver frost
spirals its vertical mast
past haze of gray December cold.

A pillar of forest, here in town.
A pilgrim form (*climb*
higher, seraphim
chorale). Earth, put on your gown

of snow – swathe winter hills
with infant innocence.
Sky, sprinkle the adamant's
bark with fiery spearpoints, spilled

from Corona Borealis (muttered
from cave of Papa Bear).
I am my mother's potter's
clay, whispers the starfish shard

from the shaman's hoard. The feminine soul
is naturally Christian;
she delights in moonshine,
baubles, Rin-Tin-Tin, the ocean's roll...

a box of almonds under the tree.
If only we measured the labor
that hauls pomodori *to harbor;*
if only we knew how to set them free.

A twine frame shines through Gotham mist
where Ariadne's thread
cat's-cradles round a head
of Colchis gold (pine-mesmerist).

12.10.14

IN THE RIVER

Listen to the waterfall.
Late-autumn rain.
Shadow of a raven
passing. Mirror on the wall.

Through this hollowness of things
reflected... way-off echo
of a chord. Blow,
Memphis trump. The milk-train sings

at dawn. I see a pine-swamp
in the background. Gaunt
figure, shoulders bent
into the wash. Her upright tramp.

The long fields, where trashmen sang,
collecting time, scars.
Equal among stars
is your little lamp, my lambchild. Strong.

Underwater, in the river, borne
downstream... your friend.
In my beginning... end.
Blackboard scrape of railroad horn.

We seek a broad place, a place
to land. Slave quarters,
the servants' house (yours).
Squire's antic foal is full of grace,

Jessie. The minister of joy
praises with baritone,
bearing the tune (bone-
dry). So we give thanks, Dante.

12.10.14

ANTIC GLIDE

Focus the lens, Antonioni.
Emerald blur of winter
moss, wool, off-center...
streak of dark rust on gray

slab of shipyard. Raggedy string
like an arc of Johns
winds through a maze
of *melancholia* – to the King

of Gray, pinned in a corner
like a fisherman of salt.
Time comes to a halt
in your eye, or hers (Giuliana).

The bronze vise of human longing
grins among smokestacks;
the pressure builds, racks
bolt into buttresses, rigging –

like Stravinsky thundering toward a sacrifice
of Morning Star – the blithe
child teetering to death
in the hunters' myth (not very nice).

A tear wells on the underside
of the retina. Still
life. Giuliana will
testify, after her antic glide

into San Vitale : one green almond eye.
In the distance, the sanguine
pigeon-man, crooning again –
what's his name? *She will not die.*

12.12.14

LOCAL KINGDOM

Solidarity of persons manifest in stone.
Sky-curve of quiet dome,
breastwork of tranquil freedom
after mortification (flesh to bone).

Fire in the marrow purifies,
a cryptic syzygy
transmuting infamy
to fellowship (as the crow flies,

scribbling glee with mourning dove).
Walk to the green recess
cleft in wilderness
by spring water (Jonah's cove) –

let the waterfall open your eyes.
The leper walked there, shunned
by fear – scapegoated, stoned
against your wall. Maze of Chartres,

gleaming throne of Christendom,
bow down before this blood-
thread gauntlet, neighborhood
ghetto – your painful local kingdom

come. A raven zigzags silently
over the sepulcher;
just before Easter
ground is adamant, empty.

Mary whispers to her bridegroom
gone. Her swollen eye
looks inward. Sky
clouds (grey). Lips curve our doom.

12.14.14

HILARIOUS BIRD

The little leaf-plastered shoebox
of a playground in December
gloom. No kids clamber
over grimy plastic, nobody rocks

the swing – only shades giggle
on the jungle gym, crowing,
piloting their string-and-
cardboard (balding) golden eagle.

Little ghosts under hazel thickets,
making the best of things.
Rated higher than kings,
more breakable than cigarettes

by almond eyes (with reason, too).
Like elves in crevices
of one vast northern spruce
in Embla, or Vermilion, or Sutton Hoo –

a scene unseen, a herd unheard –
where the body lies, and the mind
is true. Where the eagle (blind)
zeroes on Everest (hilarious bird).

Such a microcosm you are, child –
a little wonder-world
in whom all flags are furled.
A mule carries your father (mild

& wild) back to Bethlehem,
where a spangled bangle
hovers, lambent (angle
of crown) over Mendelssohn limb.

12.16.14

GRAY MATTER

Bluejay poised on a blue chair
out the backyard window.
December light so
delicate (threadbare vernacular).

I douse your watercolors – jasper,
bronze. A gooey gouache,
imperial mish-mash –
metropolis of birdman whisper.

There's the outline of a sheep
tangled in mainmast shroud;
a shepherd, roped toward
urban crowd across purple deep.

Beneath frescoes of gray matter
foisted into festive stone
one pearl aches – lone
Ishmael, or Nazarene (scatter-

brained Ebionite recluse,
mayhap). In Baptistry
of lightbulb history,
Johnny draws a circle (obtuse

angel) onto a palm. Hopes
his telescape's smoke-
signal might just work
(if Smolak film develops) as

in Ravenna – where Dante, Boethius
linger with Chaadev, Williams
over the crypt of freedom's
chosen (wintry moonlit space).

12.18.14

GRAPHENE WALL

This local sunshine, elevating
slightly toward orthodox
Epiphany (Grandpa's
own *God Jul,* with Yule-log tree).

Anthropos is microcosm
in spacetime bird's-eye.
Ancient Kiev, Ravenna
not so far away – hum

straight through this graphene wall
(my personal mossy vale
of Maia). So sing wassail
for Maximus, late-blooming viol

of Chalcedon! His mute chalice
at Wisdom's altitude
waits for swells to subside
in salty scrolls (transmuting malice).

All the byzantine wars of belief
somehow missed the Man
himself. Blues, Greens,
blur of red-blue states... reef

of fatal battlements – the world's
Black Wednesdays folded
into bone-hold (barnacles
of scrimshaw, ribbed, pearled).

The sun sinks behind Providence
pine branches. In a rustic
Newport yard, historic
tendrils ravel up strange opulence.

12.29.14

CAT'S EYE

My little pony-mule's a fancy-
dancer, she pulls the grass
of graves between her jaws.
Over there, in the old *cimetière*

by early Newport synagogue.
Near the brown-gray church
where Jack & Jackie search,
still, for one sea-rose – *Rogue*

Island Mermaid, Miramar...
(pink petals tossed by wind).
Who knows what they might find
beyond the graphene raven-mirror!

Winter earth holds autumn choirs
in brazen ice-tongs.
My longest longing longs
from coast to coast, until desires

expire – their expiration date
stamped on a milk carton
from *Land o'Lakes* (maiden
made in maiden-land – infinite

Gal of Galaxies). She dances there,
in deerskin, in a mule's
bull's-eye – one hobo-fool's
wise guy-rope, dangling *catenaire*

(9-lived). Where Solomon's cat's eye
pings against an almond
yew, & me, in Mendelssohn –
in Cana, or in Galilee (Rhode I.).

12.30.14

SIMPLE PRELUDE

Quietness in Providence,
for them that can afford.
Calm streets (no Ford
Blunders). Sabbath silence.

Another year is gathered in
to history. Beautiful
vast former battlefields
blend into distance now (someone

booms a bell across a plain).
Only earth remains.
Infinity stains
each rusted blade, unreckoned pain.

Have you not felt, have you not seen
the lovely icon of
her face, beamed from above
on limpid threads – buried in the grass

so green? Trepanned Apollinaire
smokes by her bedside,
spies stars in tears that slide
across her wide land's cheek. There,

there. *Everywoman wears*
Night's 99 candles now,
he mumbles. On your brow
anonymous rain rinses the lairs

of lost crusaders, broken kings.
Your rustic diorama's
humble panorama
magnifies in miniature – brings

crèche-gifts from the galaxy
to crushed *paisan*, bent
slave, dishonored filament
of glory. A raven's orthodoxy,

player's rule – world-overturning
in one mild eye's glance.
Epiphany or trance
transfigured into bird-learning –

the earth seen through a blade of grass,
a child's infinity –
cosmic society
of spooky charity – forgiveness

born of magnanimity (*O just*
justice) & gratitude
(*just being*). Simple prelude...
groaning Shostakovich, glittering dust

of Bach & Mendelssohn – a swirl
of sound now shapes your
ghostly figure (hour-
glass, bright everlasting Pearl) –

*

Two strands crossed, hidden in a field.
Of night & day, of earth
& sky, of raven-black
& light-brown, blonde. A low tone sealed

their bond, a hum, a servant-song –
& then a lens caught fire
magnifying everywhere
Love's equanimity (calm tuning-prong).

12.31.14

YELLOW RIVER

One bitter blast (Alberta Clipper)
curls your mild December
dream into ice-comber
horn (arctic Big Dipper).

& you must ravel up thread-crossed
prayer-stick Mnemosyne
within Kickapoo tent's
evening apex – *Ariadne's Crown*

(embossèd round with shields vermilion).
To the *House of 4 Pines*
where a spiral winds
through Itasca springs (in winter sun).

Raven & Phoenix meet there on
Turtle's back – Guillain-
Barré, Guillem d'Orange home
into one *ange d'or* (*cher* throne).

Gold was Henry's first color.
A Yellow River through
Brahmaniac slough –
Blackstone's original stream, before

the mill-wheel broke. Martyrs crown
each Wounded Knee – time
bleeds each limb (*hymn,*
you & me) – the earth's our own,

in limping speech (of fishermen
& governors). My cracked
mosaic leaps into cataract –
Espiritu Santo floods the lion's den.

1.5.15

ROYAL OAK

i.m. J.H. Ravlin

Strings of tiny Christmas lights
buried in prickly green
spine-fans, almost unseen.
Grandpa's *Tannenbaum,* his birthday

night. Where trillions of miniature
Lincoln logs emerge
(Railsplitter's urge
to mend all men, amen). Within your

triple rainbow, Alighieri.
Omnipresent OMO,
eagle's starry memo...
Beatrice glowing in your eye.

Starlight, moonlight, chill, ghostly
behind those tamaracks.
Swamplands (weathered shacks,
old rowboats). Adriatic Sea.

You trace the ineluctable distinctions
of your fork-tongue land –
Chief Broken Hand
or Florence Ainsworth – widows, orphans –

Juliet, my lost Ophelia-
Ravlin – granddaughter –
twig-bent ever after
from that bridge – *ey yo...*

Wrath simmers in the stolen earth
many buffalo years.
Pathos echoes, whispers
from your ghost-dance birth-

*

star (veinous branchings from
on high thread winglets
for an infant Jonah's
prow). & each squaw-mummer

bears the whole universe
bundled on her back –
houseboat, tepee or shack,
motel or *Royal Oak* – all mangers

everywhere. That gangly monk
with the blue-white beard
felt your pulse, heard
your wedding-sigh (on Black Sea bunk

in prison cell) – beheld the chaste
conjunction of a cosmos
with its heart's anonymous
warm hand, bright eye... *Make haste,*

make haste to find her here, him
there, hid in the vineyard,
my Beloved, O... (weird
Janus-coign of almond bloom,

warm elbow of imperial yardarm).
Charlie sleeps in the oak,
a slumber-king, a bloke
with head round as an apple. Charm

in a name there be, like Charmion
or Charlemagne... a rose
smiles through its rainbow's
reign, your charity incarnadine.

1.6.15

LEAP-SECONDS

Fresh snow crowns a fresh year
with infinite white
diamonds – even the summit
of that garage in back, a pyramid

of blinding hexagons, brilliant.
Don't know if I'll ever see
Mont Saint-Michel – may
have to cross that Jordan very ancient

& in secret, like Mayor Bernard,
Great Escapee
(of blessed memory).
Not Proust nor any Time Lord

in Paris can hold back the earth
entirely (though she's
ralentir, apparently)
from wheeling pear-wise (O mirth-

cunning ham) toward her favorite
star. Thus my mental
golden spider must recoil –
revert apsidal synapses, knot

quipu cloverleaf across
this bubble-octagon
(*Emanu-El*, the sun).
Apollinaire dreams toward his *Croix-*

de-Guerre; Bernard pops into PX
for a final cigarette;
Stravinsky's Juliet
leap-seconds to St. Vitus rite (*La Paix*).

1.7.15

OLD BERET

Cherish yet this goblin-goblet
buried in George's field.
Iron curve, silvered
by time & rain – thin graphene net.

Your delicate recursive thread
bears planetary load.
Her slow gait (pigeon-toed)
& long brown coat, her bowed head

musing down the street, black hair
beneath an old beret.
Agenbite of inwit,
egret; sad, by shoreline (ancient ire).

Time shunts loom's backbrace (thundering
boom). Young Charlie's oak,
febrile with Hebrew spokes
(dove-speak). *Gdspd,* my blundering

cartoon – your secret sunny man
is safe with me. I fell
from towers of Notre Belle
Dame, late of Galilee (bold Magdalen)

when the lights went out. *Hawk's eye*
& raven's wing, a shadow-
script of Jonah's prow
just now emerging from the sea,

the Southern Cross of everything.
Rose octahedron in
your heart... ponderous bronze
groaning (*pain*)... OK, Ahaz. Palm-king.

1.8.15

MAGNETIC NORTH

Snow on backyard pine, a winter
scene. With bitter words
the hunters return. Bird's-
eye view. A raven's splintered mirror

integrates the earth with cold
& calm – ravenous fire
with ice-skating, the hounds'
dire hunger with a master's hold.

Strange distance in this place of graves.
Graven with flames... a tinder
touch. So you will render
up the whole of life, in silent waves

windblown, articulate (ash-
hexagon from one
remote hearth-rune).
Only dappled light (reed-wash,

acacia screen). In the continuum
of strange dream-song, a black
milk pours into Black Elk,
Melchizedek... slips back to you, O

Somno-Man (where sparrows hum
across the mirrored ice). Your
wing-palms print once, twice
beneath aurora burial (*drum-*

roll, funereal). Snow gathers
at magnetic north. Rose
dust & wilderness
meet on your lips (coal-cinders).

1.9.15

PATH P

I thread Route 80 like a sad arachnid
retreats into her silver
shell (another winter's
tale). Pennsylvania sepia –

Bruegel bird's-eye road (through pining
hills). Dad's thin veins.
Horsehair, strokes of pain
into amygdala (each numb-lumbering

day). Threads from Twin Cities
back to Providence
& back again... suspense
knitting your mystery, old Oedipus.

S.S. Normandie – her maiden voyage
on your birthday. *Vive*
La Paix! Rise from the wave,
Hermione! Your hermitage

on wheaty heights is shedding snow –
springs open stolid gates!
Limed by nimble Fates
one sweet blind mummer's pas de deux

traipses my lips. A logorhythmic
miracle skims through
your fingertips – Bayeux
or Neva-land... Raven-abysmic

light takes flight! We'll take *Path P*
to Eridanus now,
my Paiute Pyotr – 144
hum-yawns of supervoids – Pappy's prairie!

2.20.15

CEDAR REPLICA

There were scruffy local prophets
just beyond cannon-range
in every hamlet. Door-Hinge
Guillem, say, in Lebanon, OH – gets

no respect – or Josh the Carpenter,
for example, out on a limb
in Galilee, RI. Him
they tend to snub, until winter

cracks the mast off the yacht, &
the tub starts to founder
petrified in flounder-
nets (Ocean's cold reprimand).

Time gets old, echoes grow faint;
the statue in the park
steps into evening dark,
amnesia puts on war-paint.

Your icon, buried in the garden
sank like a thousand ships
into the grass. Those lips
still graze my ear, sheep-warden –

whispering forgotten words
out of a lichen-book.
Words of the sea. Look,
their wave-trace in the woods –

a cedar replica. Her milky kingdom
was a salt-spray splinter,
Noah's rudder-stump – her
shuddering Shaker-wheel spelled *freedom.*

2.24.15

SHADY MOUNTAIN

Little boy Jasper's snowman
(beyond the backyard sea-
drifts) smiles at me
with half-moon curve of red twine –

penetrates my white wasteland
of jealous discontent
& chants *Repent, repent*
between twin wide-flung twig-hands,

silently – only to me.
Through a green door on the rim
of Ezekiel's wheel the seraphim
erupt – a Shaker replica

cracks at the seams – Raven rows
back into Shady Mountain
(mined by Justinian
for classy gold). *The* Shadow *knows,*

my father used to say, out of
his infant comic book
of dreams. John's look
of baby pigeon-light... loon alcove

of your soul. How much invented
to clothe a Pharaoh's grandeur?
Isis in Iowa, each Hoover-
ville of holy stage-fright... tented

with frankincense & myrrh, & whizzing
meteors above Earth's camel-
back... Behold, the enamel
flakes from her scriptorium (glazing).

2.26.15

SHEAF GARDENER

In Puget Sound sounded... Davy
Jeanne's own Dauphin dove...
& wholesome Slow-Come John
hove-to, with gal aboard, full of glee.

The whole almond droned then,
from Ferrara to Ravenna,
OH... & shades of henna
plumed for the Prince (formerly known

as Art) – who merely stamped himself
Sheaf Gardener, by dream-
shires of Missus Ship-away
(*I am, I amble*). So rang the belfry

sonorous & sinuous of bronze.
You must not mistake Phinehas
for any final Finn – he has
a Viking shark upon's prow (Cain's

ivory man, gone chill beneath
the salty hill). Jealousy
suits not the wormy V
that threads vermilion cross a breath

of floe – it is hermaphrodite
Hermione that Phoebus
loves, & checkmates (rebus
put in Ukraine grain, held tight

with ISIS ice). The cargo of the Pharaoh
moseys down the stream;
Joseph, in his dream,
spells Josephine – globes rugged Clio

with a *miroir* (she). *2.26.15*

HENRY'S ADAM

This backyard dogwood blooming now
with strange maroon nail-holes
at the cruciform petals'
4 corners, keeps a chronicle too –

ringed with ragged pale-grey bark
over tombs of cicada husks.
Her inscrutable codex
marks the plots of folded peacock-

fans... slow-diminishing pulse
of a certain father's deathbed
childhood-sigh (old
John's apple, at the grave matrix).

Each local anecdote of global
Providence springs
scraggly lightning rings
in some such way. Calder mobile

or Statue of Liberty – Apollonian Sophie's
purple plastic wading
poolful of Bangladeshing
Roma genes... remnant refugees

sketching poppy fields of Paradise.
Grafted by wilderness,
the archaic ravenous
vernacular grows foreign lives –

yet still your father's face peeks out
between waves of metal sleet.
Incorruptible, complete
now (serious dog-star Scout).

5.8.15

DAY-LILY

Like a solitaire somnambulist
(or gilded mini-Jacques
in Nabokov juke-box)
I thread the maze of musty East

Side mansions, under curtained oaks
of this fey seacoast town,
to Blackstone's emerald crown –
a light-filled rectangle, with spokes

of ash-grey pillars, branching backwards
under spells of timeless
testimonies (green plateaus
of sunken continents). The words

anathema maranatha sound
no more (full fathom five) –
in hummingbird's dome-hive
revert to a bung mara pun

(like Jonah in a bird's-eye view
of seashell Paradise).
Pearls that were his eyes
are yours now; nought can keep you

(*nor height, nor depth, nor things present,*
nor things to come) love-
lorn from me, my sister-dove,
who left behind only this cerement

of melted ceiling wax. Your eyes
in the dome linger for me,
rusty Galilee day-lily –
their magenta rims make nations rise.

6.10.15

A POSTCARD

Farewell, little microcosm! Soon
I must begin to say
goodbye, my hideaway –
goodbye, good boy, my elfin garden...

O tiny postage-stamp backyard,
less than one-fiftieth
the size of Lil Lilith
(a.k.a. her Rhody OK retard-

reward for a state of island-mind).
Send me a postcard from
that future then – hum
me a bumblebee signet (blind

Pharoah, roving mare). An unseen
Gould hand (o' Jeremy's tribe)
still keeps this grave scribe
scalloping through summer rain...

to keep the mocking peers & jeering
mice from troubling
the outcoast pliers-king
(Jonah's mother's pioneering

wailer – tom-tom thumbing liar!). Where
then shall we go, my dear?
Into the interior –
not far from here. The raven's dare

lifts through that inky smokehole, Blackstone –
your mother's home (North
Star). Strange mire-eye-berth,
hearth-casket. Steady on Shoshone shone.

6.11.15

CORNISH HAZE

As I begin again to remember
you, you reconstitute
me, in the absolute
mirror of this syllable-blur

(systole,diastole...). & I pledge
allegiance to our binary
aye, ornery Alighieri –
you with your golden morris hedge

(chartreuse whorl) – I with flatland
cornish haze... I owe,
I know, an Iowa
Isis hoover-craft – whole hand

full of diamonds, Jack! – her maiden
voyage through a Butter-
milky Way is all my
muttering. In the lion's den

Dan the Welder smiles – a very
catenary *accent*
grave. Worn, lifespent
shoes left on the edge (at *Porta Aurea*)

only the molting keys to Beatrice-
track (her flight, Europa-
limpid, here to *Via*
Eterna). Nut-gold archer, Never-Miss

Everland, your ingrained hills
spread wide upon the tables
of my heart – twine cables
(gracious gate) for a hamlet's mills.

6.12.15

CANE-MARK

A cool, rainwashed mid-June day.
Summer rain in Newport
or Catawba. Playful snort
of Jack & Jackie's colt – a roundelay

or song of songs. Remote chesspieces
trace the wheel's design –
from *Philae P67*
roping comets through their paces

to cypress shade of synagogue
where Gould & Gödel meet
in Princeton tesseract
(a decussation in pine-fog).

Remains unprovable, but golden –
like Coke's annotation
of law's conjunction
with natural rights of Englishmen,

extrapolated by Blackstone
(Wm.) & Williams
(Rog.) – *what I am*
will be soul liberty, O Solomon.

Quakers guard my graves, the whisper
refrained. The little tree
from primitive Galilee
bent from far over that sepulchre;

as distant as an old man's walk
with *primavera* filly
round the sun. See his
faint cane-mark in the children's chalk!

6.15.15

RUSTY COP

Stars lift beneath Edith
in Ethiopia,
align the *camera*
oscura to one blinking zenith.

Katherine & Humphrey too
zigzag the permanent
jungle, fundamental
river-flow (bog-burnt canoe).

Overhead, mild Cassiopeia
writes her W (im-
mense memo to you)
across the mirror of Medusa,

where Pegeen has stamped another
U (green tread of rusty
cop) Hephaestus
used (to wrap his Martian bro

in sleep). Tell another story,
Francesca – the one
about your mule (*Zion*
or Bust). The power & the glory –

copperhead theocracy
vs. one clumpy donkey
lambent in RI –
Eeyore (crazy *yurodivy*-

odyssey). Thread the whole whorl
a-knot one almond *J* –
he's coming from the sty
like a beam from Orion (vermilion earl).

6.15.15

SHADOW-BRIDGE

White swans on Blackstone
tiptoe across the water.
Wingèd liftoff. Were
angels perched in that April midden,

or only Morpho blues? No one
will say. Of course
it might have been a Paris
rain... nitrate of mafia drone

in Dallas haze... an ordinary
human end. Design
from nature, grim, benign –
the maker's nick (encaustic jay).

This park's a quiet hideaway.
Oaks on the steep ridge
cast a shadow-bridge
for Andes orioles. Say,

Francisco, if you can – why
the proud builders missed
the mark? I would have kissed
you, cuz, who embraced the sky

too soon (*Psyche, Persephone...*
ravined by gravity).
One eucalyptus tree
(*Eeyore, Eurydice...*) must (line

by limb) restore your salty skein
of handprints, raveled
veins – *Eureka, you have*
found me! (jade Qosqo refrain).

6.17.15

PIGEON-RUMOR

The Blackstone is a gray seashell
this morning. From the ridge
facing east she'll fledge
an eaglet, fold a rose from notional

velveteen rabbit out of a hat
& float (harmonic pencil)
origami pearl-
boat parallels (oyster octet).

Was that a unicorn, playing
tuba on the river-sand?
A cloud, I understand –
wind only a breath now, straying

through shady cottonwoods.
No rain has fallen in years.
Turn, & she disappears –
smiles a tear for Ukraine moods

(Calabrian, or Cheyenne Romany) –
an iris orrery
so gyro-promissory,
ornery... her corn grows honey-

bee hexagonals all over D.C.
Mud-pilasters, almond
cherry-bombs... her fund
of Florentine well-water glee

fountains right up to 4th of July
for at least a century –
her statutes of liberty
today's pigeon-rumor (plumb from sky).

6.18.15

MINER'S GIFT

The longest summer day flits by
in a hummingbird's heartbeat.
Stay, hold me, sweet
Seekonk-time, in your rabbi's eye –

immeasurably tender *King*
of Guess, meek mule
& brother to that Yule
fell off the log (near sing-sing

Alcatraz). Earth-flutes congeal
their subway threads (cars
2-5, A, C, J, R,
Z – always on the left please

bend down back into the dark
abode of predators –
droning inheritors
of sub-men *D, N, A...*) – our shark-

tooth seal, batting Italian despair
(indefinitely suffering
Ravenn) into a freezing
stump of iron shriek-sparks... *there,*

there. There are these 88
light arcs (too tendril
for faux guile) lend
one beam-tier (gold plate

of purple peon-ear) will lift
the wayfinder into
her breathing mirror-net's
RI crochet... late miner's gift.

6.20.15

OLD GLORY

The tiny whiz-bird hums & floats,
hovering over my rose
pontoon, her paradise.
A flint blade chimes bell-notes

out of Grime's Graves (neolithic).
By the grey Blackstone
Hilario J. Robin
snake-charms knotty hillside oak –

dauntless redbreast, passionate
Guillem d'Orange. Whose cell
is gathering mass (black
wholeful o'moss) in triplicate

like an Old Glory spun of Greenville
jasper – caustic wax
to burn each switchback's
cussed fer-de-lance (eternal

jail) into a trillion spangle-tiers
of morning (milky spider-
barn). Haul it down before
nightfall. The soul in tatters

seeks a deeper, quieter call –
Jonah's Pacific hum
from whale *profundum* – bee-
balm croon for Memphis Emanuel.

Will set you free. Sweetly now
the offspring of the sun
are fielded, droning, into
one (*farfalla*-Gaspee... rain bough).

6.23.15

GREEN ALPHABET

When ruthlessness wreaks havoc in the fields
& rules by plunder, rapine
& the sword, how then
shall innocence prevail? Where are the shields?

Thus Boethius pondered, gaol-bound.
A sort of violin
of joint tradition
(Athena-Jerusalem) he found

his body living out his mind's
refrain – grey leaf-rain
spelt from ash-tree (pain).
Yet he would live again. Love signs

& underscores each scintillant
syllable, each weathered
hieroglyph – his feathered
Sophie laughs down petulant

violence, blear death – cures fear.
Because he met her implicate
cloudline, or a Hand met
his... where the Clue draws near

in Galilee, or Mendelssohn...
children leaping sprightly
to her dawn tambour (*look,*
see!) – red bird, Franciscan

berry. Into the grimpen habitat
of Mammon, Moloch, must
we go, be ground to dust...
& rise again (green alphabet).

6.23.15

ANCIENT GLASS

That mourning dove hid in maple trees
flutes dirge-like lovesong.
Da-dye doo, doo, doo... hung
up, lovelorn... croons yearning & unease.

This morning at summer's dawn
the cantor-carpenter,
enchanted, winds a copper
strand around his staff (asklepian) –

his sunswing mesmerizing still,
his rowboat frame become
a kind of Smolak world-
imperium – Rain Bear's meek will

a template of peacepipe benevolence
anoints the orb. Scapegoat
o'scapegoats, he will note
graves of serpentine intolerance,

each murder bitten in his name, or not.
Shaman-psychologist,
he ripples down each twist
of hurt mind's ideolatry, unbinds each knot –

yours, mine. But how it came to pass...
out of the grotto & the spring
elliptical circumferencing
from shepherd hills. Some ancient glass

polished to shine all-human light
crimped yet again by Roman
might, Pharaoh-dominion –
until whale-ribs reverberate

Ravenn, Apollinaire, Pastoravenn... *6.24.15*

DEFT WARP

Another time, another landscape.
Here an octaped,
invisible, threaded
through the night from cape to cape

(clothesline to purple peony).
Now an inch of neon
spectrum shuttles on
that bridge – deft warp of memory

in Morse (must be an international
engineer). Pearl Harbor Day
your figure hit the Bay
(from 8 to zero). Tears shall well

from pole to pole (sailor's memorial).
Stars blaze to ash
for one black eyelash –
scatter from galactic wheel

each infant spark, original.
Yet wingèd light that burned
through rippling Jordan
spirals, indestructible –

beginning ends, ending begins.
Around Ravenna dome's
perimeter, kingdoms
etch wave-patterns, mordant signs

beyond dust-motes, buoyant, glinting...
Sophia's everlasting
fire (serene, unmoving,
clear) forever welded in a ring.

6.25.15

TIN MIRROR

The color of those clouds, above
that soaring pine (her arms
flung wide, green Miriam
bedecked with cones) – vague echo of

El Greco, Michelangelo –
a bit marmoreal.
Disconsolate King of Coal,
Concrete... former *Numero Uno,*

about to send tears stumbling down
again... So we sketch the local
monarch. Him we all
know (*Only-Two-Well*). Then someone

in Michoacán – Rosario Ocampo,
maybe – fashions a fine
tin mirror, sealed with twin
doves on double doors (closed, now)

& mails it to a mountaintop
in Galilee (just north
of El Grotto). *The earth*
is in travail, he murmurs – *ope*

mi puerta – up periscope, Jésus!
Stormclouds part for a flint
moment (lightning) – slate,
smile! *El rey ha muerto, vivez*

le rêve! From grassland salience
(Tower Hill, or Mount
Zion) her milkweed font
purls into sylvan stream (pine-sense).

6.25.15

GRACE RAVLIN

The summer's Sky-Reflector-Net
is replicated in a gentle
eye : matrix of the spindle,
mote where lattice angles meet.

From Providence to Paradise
a simple triple-step,
sideways & back. Steep
recapitulation – say, Toulouse

to Matilda, Queensland to Provence –
by cavern candlelight;
those hallowed aliens might
be us; San Vitale's green silence

the dawn of some Franciscan renaissance.
She is the tender sphere's
orbit... her love inheres
in eggshell domes, the garden's permanence

Apollinaire after the war
ash in his peace pipe
Georgina with ripe
plum   to hand   so far

from feral death's-head   pride   spite
the nations sleep   their rage
assuaged   hate in its cage
for now   low flute   *bonsoir, bonne nuit*

Grace Ravlin sets her easel there
Overlooking George Washington's
Garden   good evening, Cyrus
greetings, Rose   *O somersault*   sweet air

6.26.15

MASON'S PIN

The gray underside of these
dogwood leaves, clustered
over my head. The blistered,
lingering pussy willow. Evening's

repose *à Providence*, which I
must exit before long.
Into the slough I'm diving...
weedy heartland (lake country).

Roger Williams' apple-root,
Blackstone's Yellow Sweeting
will remain. A meeting
at Swan Point – starry circuit,

milky wheel (Pappy's birthday
pivots on your mother's
grave). Some Vladimir's
renunciation – icon of clay

starfish, her lambswool tracery
around a baptistry –
Boethius in ecstasy
after the rack is rolled away.

Uncle Henry weaves his spiderweb
out of one gold strand
of maidenhair. Trebizond
cell for Guillem, Maximus – ebb-

tide for violence, with violins.
A child skips over granite.
Spinning, inviolate
djinn, dynamic Virgo (mason's pin).

6.29.15

CLAY LIPS

If I whisper out of this backyard garden
& word went forth from Ramah
Rachel weeps... no more
a cricket shuttles through the iron

lattice – churring *chi-rho, chi-rho*
a pigeon croons *là-bas*
là-bas... labarum... *abba...*
baa... lambs on a radius go

round, skip stones, elliptical
(up to the mountaintop).
Rough clay lips elope
for steppes, ignite pyramidical

lens – Nile *coming-forth-of-July*
in one almond canoe;
wooden frame for yew
rainbow (*adieu* beyond river-eye).

Beneath an avalanche of violence
the lattice rusts, the eye
corrodes. Still clay
will coalesce, in tinder hands;

Giuliana in her mossy coat
& frowning eye signal
another way; lips channel
shapes (mosaic, inchoate)...

Ravenna diagram, vertiginous cross-
road into Washington.
Path P, star-tangled almond
tree – here chariots bloom (manes toss).

6.30.15

ATTIC SCRAPBOOK

i.m. Sir Nicholas Winton, 1909-2015

The wonder of such strange & serpentine
inversions – the fugitive figure
of a mote-motif (Apollinaire
in pipesmoke, say) turned adamantine

ground-bass. Children of Nicholas
trained by tomb-cocoon
back to civilization –
little seedling-waifs to distant witness

stand for a hero's welcome, basketed
in attic scrapbook (almost
lost). So inside-out
(a Chaplin's chaplaincy). O helmeted

spouse of almond biosphere,
whose pergola or grape-
vine lattice lifted up
one speckled shadow, brazen spear –

sere monarch-leaf... to re-appear!
Wave-shield for life arrested –
lacquered, casketed
sybil of Sibelius, flown clear

in V-formation, still alive...
So Dante's Florence, my
grand motherland, might be
a molting rhyme, prairie beehive

as forth from Juliet or Maggie's den
Earth arcs one Saarinen
cat-grin – fireworks begin
to boom at dusk (Frisco, Ravenn).

7.2.15

AMERICAN DREAM

The flag, lacquered with encaustic
in Greenville, S.C. –
like a sand story
in Queensland, or mosaic patchwork

quilt (outside Ravenna, OH).
Her palm inscribes a circle
as she chuckles out the tale.
We Walbiri live on the ground. So

dry in California – only
the Bridge keeps orange in
her shroud, Florence (thrown
into fishnet soon, my little tree).

Love is the criterion.
Your only manly mistake
was pride – it is to take
power as entitlement, my son.

E pluribus unum – tears fall
as rain from Manitou,
Black Elk whistles. You
see the Mandan dancing – Jubilee

a joint venture, people. American
Dream. Not to be tarnished
by malice, nor the fish-
mash fables of the shellfish. Someone

turtles through the brazen image...
flutes across my tables
of thanksgiving. Seven Gables?
Stephen's Gate? Iris, in sage.

7.4.15

BOOK

IV

OCEAN STATE

Bridget flings her emerald
signal flags SE,
NW – kicks her heels
& gyroscopes along a thread

of starfish glisten (penciled
Cornish involution).
You follow her confusion
of species, her grave mongreloid

ellipse, toward the vault of your own
vertigo (*in exitu*
del mio Gypsy-o) –
the weight of this diamond casket (sun-

burnt charcoal). Mark the black rings
beneath her eyes, ringlets
of raven-hair, her fits
& stirs. How the pain sings

on the way to Mendelssohn, or
Littletree – way back
to the cricket-shack.
Venite, powerful western star...

or is it North, now (dizziness
part of the package)? I'm
packing my leaving rhyme,
my Rhody limes. I guess this is

a goodbye tootle. Ocean state.
Vast in our eye, your
jewelry gum (*Glee*-ore) –
the giving was the thing, chic mate.

7.6.15

IONA'S HAIR

The s-curved spine of attainted king
snakes up from parking lot.
Not Prospero, not quite
Macbeth. The plot's the thing

for knucklebones. Woodvilles & Nevilles
in the nether woods – phosphorus
Warwick, glowing in the dust.
Someone's gotta pay the bills

for Renaissance magnificence.
The wolfish gusto of these
alpha *bêtes*! Rimini's
laird, Ezra's ravening prince –

shades in the hollows of Sherwood,
old artifacts of violence.
How did we survive this?
How will we yet? Pappy understood,

somehow – head bowed with meekness
to a mud-stained plow.
All yang, no yin, was how
blind stick-up men went down. No sense

of the spider's tensile teetering
with dewy tread, on thread...
black widow's offspring (death's-
head remonstrance for buccaneering

sports). Be with me, Columba,
bright dove-bird padre
from cloud-slopes of Eire.
Proud kings lie hidden in Iona's hair.

7.7.15

BRADY NEGATIVE

The angry sun's a perfect mirror
of our wrath. General Mills
& Private Fleece – their wills
be done, on earth as it is down there.

Someone walks beside your car,
needing a lift. Limping
goat or skimping lamb,
cricket-bat in rookie empire...

Passage to Indiana? – O, more.
Like Brady negative
of Raven-Shaker native,
sun in her beak (one of your

Slocum cousins) – she's an Iris
with an ark on her shoulder –
Apollinaire-boulder
beneath *girasole,* in Paris...

& arose out of my treasure-chest
a great corn-mandala,
wheeling round Tower Hill
like Glastonbury Almagest;

the flatiron plate of blazing Midway
(*midéwé* amid Twin Cities)
spinning projectivities
into harmonic pencil-cones... I say

these peaks, in a bubble-bole below
Iona (north of Io-Ariel)
are buoyed by level-eye –
shine everywhere, Horatio!

7.7.15

SCARLET HUE

How to espy that singleness of porpoise
through a welter of drift?
Violet in a red shift
like graceful huntress, or Beatrice

slicing through time & oblivion –
Love is strong as death
sky-writ in clouds' breath-
chords (Lear jet?)... *L'Hermione*

afloat again (with laughing Lafayette
on board) from Normandy
to wheaty heights... O alchemy
of welded verbs! – your statuette

in salt repose (*La Paix*) revives...
I see an orange arc
through spray – Rothko's dark
palette thunder into lightning-hives

of dawn, as when great apes face east
to meet the sun – it's you,
Agape, riding scarlet hue
& cry, as Ethiopian whirring wings

feast (*hummingbird*) on David's craggy
bee-balm crown (a jester's
thorn zips round her
ladder-throne). *The poetry*

is like a buzzing in the air, he wrote;
it's everywhere. Transparent
keel of solid air... lips bent
our bows, *Ange d'Or,* into one boat.

7.8.15

WOODEN RULER

This hummingbird skims through the dusk
bee-balm to bee-balm
in the evening calm.
Each blood-red crown already crumpled

husk – Rouault's King David, gaze
fixed into paint, back
into time. *Alack,*
milord, where shalt thy lambs graze

now? The wooden ruler frames
a contrite attitude,
plucks mournful chord
in minor mode (whom earth reclaims).

The wingèd thing needles his pate.
A hum sleeps in its beak –
a scimitar-smile or streak
of luck (metaphysical template

drifting down thru feathery emerald-
azure horn). Your dome
lights up... sparks of freedom
stream into a firefly world

(back behind the Bye's old place,
in Mendelssohn). Childhood
Apollo strums into
bold oaks... only an echo of her face;

the *Wars to End All Wars* are laid
to rest, put out to pasture;
head-bound Apollinaire
sports hardy laurel now (Jeanne-made).

7.27.15

MOSAIC CITY

The wrinkled grapes left behind
on Fox Point backyard
arbor. Unseen, ignored
sweet local globules (Bruno's kind

of infinite). A multiplicity
of meek facts well
into salience (pell-
mell) – as if the air's haecceity

merged a mosaic city (lego-
integral?) east of Lincoln,
Nebraska maybe (someone
said). Time, Now... *Don't go,*

don't go, Daddy-o. We love you so.
Upon a rooftop dome
of far-off time, Smolak
snares Siloam into tuneful flow,

stones breathe with Orpheus in Galilee.
Tall stilts of gold,
emerald & sapphire hold
up deepwater wind in counterpoint – see

how your soul emerges like Osiris
from the Isis-clay
of ordinary day!
Bifocals in the grass... field glasses

teeter over trench-grave (in
contra dance con tottering
crone). She's muttering
again, old raven-heart. Bear's den.

7.28.15

HONEY, RUST

Summer just begins to wane now
by the Seekonk (or
Blackstone). Oaks are
seething with cicadas; this mosquito

getting sleepy now... so long,
little unknit needle. Old
King Richard suffered cold
& heat, endured many-pronged

reversals. Like this black butterfly
striped with orange wounds –
a kind of monarch inside-
out. His gaucheness was our *gaucherie,*

his stumbles our own stumbling –
he's *Lily-King for 1 Day*
Only, always passing away...
like summer's white rose (crumbling).

Through this file of droning oaks
I glimpse his ghost, his
goatishness. St. Stephen's
twin – always the alpha blokes'

black mark, always the mourning tread
of Mary's grey eyelash
around salt blue. A morris-
maze of autumn. Roy is Mort.

He's us, our Danny Boy. 56 years
under Sign of the Bear –
like Henry Church, or
Ursiana – hunched, compact of honey, rust.

7.28.15

FOREST ROAD

Sultry late July... the mind
creeps along like a deep-
sea worm, a Noman
Tepee. Funnel for humankind

out of our depth – faint eidolon
beyond pineland marshes.
Trees mark the arcs
of her vanishing point. Shade-zone

of upright, tremulous poplar spines...
Coraggio, cries caw-
caw Crow – *old Grandma*
says so (her forest road lines

your forehead). The sea is full of seamen
who once walked these planks –
the frightened eye draws blanks,
compass overboard – amen, amen,

Jonah. One tear swallows the sky.
Wings trace, erase overhead.
Sun rises from his bed
again, her Ocean State... (rose in RI).

Chordal, concordant, our troubled waves
of love... betrayal and
redemption too : your hand
full of liferain, from salty graves.

How your Ravenna shipmate speaks
of refuge, domicile!
Watch Roger reconcile
Crown & Ecclesia – hear the mast creak.

7.29.15

DAPPLED SNOW

Bumblebees happy in the
sweet pepper &
Joe-Pye weed.
The clematis. Invisible crickets

ululate – Augustan chorus
circling in couplets
round the summer scapegoat's
pinched perimeter (he's us).

The king was a stand-in for an almond
tree. He stalked the wild
rudraksha berry... piled
ossuaries on pelican ponds...

all for the glimmer of a veiled
cosmographer (her name
arrowed across tame
unicorn manes). *Earth for sale!*

cried her bark's barkers (they didn't know).
Her leaf was a mandorla,
a man door, *là*...
the *clé* itself was dappled snow.

We might collect some black-eyed susans
in the Hippodrome,
before summer's doom.
Galla Placidia sleeps in Ravenna's

Androscoggin. Cree gold
in your eye is *napakikinosew*
(in the rain). Slight
tilt toward autumn. Icon (sold).

8.13.15

ROLAND WAVES

She hides now, like a bit of clay
dissolved in the Pacific.
& you hear my heartsick
braying, like that sovereign Sunday

mule – foalish, stubborn, somehow
barnless in Verona
(down the trail from Dante
à Ravenna – *è finit*). How now,

Ariel? Where to, Joachim?
At the end of the third *aevum* –
crowned with the cosmic hum
of a trillion honeybees (Love's hymn)?

There's some empyreal *raisin*
soleil, raison d'état
in my four-legged squat –
stray goose-honks trying a bassoon

for the implicate symphony to come.
Maestro di colori, turtle-
dove monarch of universals...
flame-whisper, omnivagrant kingdom-

Sikh of butterflies... Vladimir's
Veracruz (shy
brown bird, swampy sigh
of cedars). Single yarn (gray hair).

Grey sea. *Matière de Bretagne.*
Whole whorl in curl
of eyelash (salty pearl) –
Roland waves (to Charlemagne).

8.14.15

VIENNA VEINS

Klimt was a kind of crooked wicket
out on a creaky limb
in Cricket City (rim
of Rimini, Parisian rivulet).

Gold. Vienna veins of Ravlin
violins (*we were there,*
Agnes). *Do not compare.*
It's only an American Robin

Redbreast, hooded, yodeling...
he's calling out your name.
Not *Stephano* (fair game
for Fame) nor *Nunzio* (clipping

the locks that flood across your face)
– though they are near. The Boot
strides on. The man is moot.
Your Crown is *Everwhirr* – mesh-lace

of spy-veil, ambling the source...
a poverty of materials
in a land of burials
& sunshine (Italy, of course).

Klimt limns the anguish in your eyes.
Through vales of Solomon
or Sheba, all the broken
kingdoms, poppy-fields (Grandpappy's

ripe Epiphany). Pain circulates
through straitened means
somehow – corny Earth-scenes
beyond our ken (Thanksgiving plates).

8.17.15

WICKER BASKET

A spry brown bird suddenly trills
out of the blue spruce
behind my head – scoots
into weary lilacs. Rhenish hills

of Carolina calling to him,
limbs the courteous artist
etched in Tuscan glass...
birchbark, shipped to Byzantium.

Unmindful of anti-theodicy
Wren frescoes the span
between word & hand.
Light was. What will be will be.

To comprehend bright anguish of JB,
or Everyman – when the sign
flags, & a jasper John
flings caustic clay into the sea...

when the onion domes rot from below
where the booty lies, & the tongue
betrays, & a scrap iron lung
pumps the gremlin mask (cash-flow)...

Brother tangling with brother
for a father's love, across
somnolent *versts* (brass,
moss). Your wicker basket, mother.

Burchfield sleeping in a field
of birches, fluent waterspider
sped downstream (a gilded
glider). Then the far bells pealed.

8.29.15

ROYAL BLUE

Among the quiet oaks, on a ridge
over the steel-gray Seekonk,
at the end of August. Think
how words glance, carom off the edge

of wherever you are. Skip into
the river, & submerge.
Three good shepherds urged
the flock along, beneath contralto

almond-shade. They leapt the fences
thatched with riven oak,
abba, baa-baa – a little joke
the lambs repleat (condolences

for Papa Bear). Old Pappy grew
a little seedy toward
the end. The family buried
him beneath an evergreen, so blue

beside Vermilion. Bread & wine
of dailiness belie
our verbal formulae...
someone must daub these tears (mine,

yourn) with coronation oil
that willna fade nor fail.
As the great Gal's sail
lifts on pendentive golden foil

into the royal blue, crimson
of Eden at the crown,
sheep gather on their own –
brushing the violet of seen, unseen.

8.31.15

WOODEN LOGS

August departure... evening crickets
elegize on wooden
logs. In Peto's brownian
study, a sad decade disintegrates

like Queen Zeno's palm-fronds, in
Palmyra. One wing-scratched hand
pleads Washington's jarred band
of masons (keening for Syrian

widows, orphan sons). *Important*
information inside.
Your gravy train can't hide
from Grace, her chaste Nubian portent –

always arriving never quite,
a Paradise for turtle-
dives. So melt the mortal
Quito coin, our double-down knight

(shy U-bird cycling her parking
lot). Concentric wheels
of Nummulitic seals...
one bears dawn for Ursus (barking

Mammon flipping tails) – the other
gyrates toward his irate
Beatrice – oceanic
ex, Czech mate (cyclonic mother

coated in cute limestone slime).
One down, one to go
up again, Horatio.
Antique Atlantis corals rime.

8.31.15

FRISKY PARD

This rangy herd of Jerusalem
artichokes, aspiring
sunward, gold-burnishing
against black lozenges of Rome

(a chain-link fence). & so I sketch
my scrappy chronicle –
home videos unreel –
& is it real? Might be a stretch.

In earliest April, crocuses unfurl –
their cruciform gold spokes
accelerate – *That's all, folks!*
– spin to counter clocks' whirl,

cock's crow. Each arm's a mast,
the vortex reels them in –
by crozier & theremin
the serpentine veins (vast,

American) glimmer under wind vanes...
paint flecks of crocus-gold
a gyro-calumet (hold
steady, gaffer). That nesting wren's

a mother hen – would gather acorns
in the moon's half-light.
Half-seen, the Green Knight
Liberty silvers her shoe-horn –

plows under sparks of minuet-mustard
that will leap again (*ange
d'or*) – right through orange
western gates... – O frisky pard!

9.1.15

LACUSTRINE CIRCLE

This delicate native wanderer
like a dusty monarch (rusty-
orange) might just be
traveling incognito somewhere –

on white-winged moccasin, from
flower to flower – her agate
glance like Grandma's (great) –
in West Branch, near the Iowa farm.

I dream of a different Isis there,
no punitive Hooverville;
another Cyrus too (there will
be no clicking Mileyhahas to prepare

with die-cut revelry your family's
despair). She will be veiled
only with cloudy knowledge
of the bright round pearl; salt seas

will anchor plumb her understanding;
Solomon will test
& be tested, & she
will best him (at the Ontario Fling

& other things). A whippoorwill
accompanies their evening;
Caroline will be singing
like a wren from the oaks, a royal

Charlie... like a gal you met once –
Cal? – along the shore...
– that lacustrine circle where,
of yore, the monarch floats, hunts...

9.1.15

STILL NOTES

In ED's garden, a brotherly ghost
would slip across Northampton
grass – a-charming Someone
with a sweet ride-broom (*...Thou lovest*

Will). His word was planted like
a blade, a thorn, beneath
white veils. Rugged wreath,
rough crown – Ophelia's fell spike

of russet hyacinth (discuss).
In burn-tarnished coeval,
meanwhile, War is all
the rage. Each shallow Salamis-

pontoon is *mustard op* – the tribes
prime bellows in unison, &
prink for each pore mold-green
mirror. *Fetch me red wedding robes!*

Man, the soul of her intelligence,
lives on the Yangtze or
the Platte – drives car or
shepherds camels into tense

oasis-shade, cloud-seedy mountain.
I'm only dreaming now.
A sower went out to sow...
someone stand waitin' by them stolen

plow. Good shepherd, shepherdess,
where is my home? The grass
is withered & the sun is brass...
Still notes on a piano. Felix? Bess?

9.2.15

WOLSEY RED

On a sultry 16th, in the month of Caesar
I was ambling down by the Blind
King, on Wickenden –
betwixt the Golden Sheaf (or Fleece) &

her Sheep's Clothing – like a raven
in wolf gear, or some Pierre
o'Cesca – like *That Man* there,
following his own tattoos into an Inchon

Dept. of the Interior.
Aboard the good ship *Keep-U*
(between *Racquel* & *Rue* –
achh...) skirting an ice curtain

somewhere... in a Wolsey red, mate.
Weaving around blind
cataracts, muzzled
shoals – paring bears in the Strait

below White Narrows (it was 1728).
I don't know why 'twas done.
The Inuit intuit none
of our designs. Split Diomede? Great.

They look you in your eye as though
you were in RI! Weird.
I only see weed (black widow's
weed). A coffin exchange came through

the aerial, Mira – maybe
amygdaloid inside?
Keep the white slide
for video, Queequeg. That's my knee.

9.2.15

PETAL-FAN

September. One late crimson backyard
rose remains. Knot
not exactly Ruby, not
Desire – but Steadfast Fire (framed

by maroon foundation of the house).
Afloat upon your thorns,
a crozier, or serpent's
copperhead – magenta compass,

planetary pole. Away beyond
all foregone Oregon
disputes – those Diomedan
straits of Fenris-Greyhound –

54°32-by-Four! *Ringing*
the International Date
Line – must I hesitate?
Princess in a shower, singing.

We clambered to the clear high room
where SF in a bay flamed
orange bloom – became
entangled like a *quipu* sum (loom,

cedars). Weight of one iron anchor
filled that octagon
with spray of azure ocean
when Evening Star fired his tangential

thread of light into shade-womb
of piers – that San Franciscan
adamant, where limestone
Rhodi petal-fan (leaf-shaken hum).

9.3.15

RIVER STREET

i.m. Edwin Honig

That Bluejay with a raven on
his shoulder, that trickster
was a local fixture –
like cornered kid on stony Roman

pavement, Maggie. Now you see him
in your mind's eye, whom you knew
from streamy childhood (blue
was the mussel surf, where the Rephilim

stamped a sweet circumference
with giant feet). & Babe
the Blue Ox, & Gabriel
w'hm seraphim, & the fish fragrance

of White Bear Lake (*miroir* today)...
all the waters in the world
seem to coalesce now, pearled
to a cedar point of windy memory.

Only the shrill *cree-crow* of the tall
iron swing on River Street
reminds you of the weight
of all that autumn. One free fall...

Weigh, anchor. To the bottom you shall go,
infant infantryman –
loaded with *diamond*
mondiale. A Seekonk conch will carry you

across her retina's black sail, into
the womb of *Imago*.
Full *fado* five... just so,
Pessoa. *La vida es sueño*. Ephphatha.

9.4.15

SHY COLOSSUS

In the events all around you
at this moment – like
that cabbage moth taking
a hike around the arugula –

there is one Event, like the breeze
cooling your sultry end-
of-summer haze. Send
to Gilead for news – release

those carrier pigeons from the rooftops!
Take a message to Garcia!
Summon our immune
militia (Firecracker Pops

& Marty King to lead the way).
None shall die in vain.
The long day wanes.
Like Max in Mexico, the monarchs play

hide-&-seek behind bronze pillars,
Lebanon cedar.
One beloved figure –
footnote painted in a corner –

shy colossus in Rhode Island
pasted with primary
color – Hurricane Mary
(Maggie to her friends) will stand

for every cyclone & dust-storm
of tears. Here's looking
at you, kid. Bring
apples, Rosie... comfort Everyworm.

9.9.15

SPARKLING EYE

Erica Tagliabue Dorf, 1918-2007

Rain falling on your birthday, Erica;
after an August drought
these gray skies float
down water lifelines, *pioggia*

povera e preziosa.
Your green & copper
wooden cabinet
like something out of old Ferrara

still stands guard quietly
in the dining room;
out of the city's boom
& boffo, to this rustic hideaway.

Memory is mother of the arts.
You were a hidden matrix
deep in that beehive-vortex
(10 W. 66th) where music starts

up from the frescoed scene –
that Lincoln Center fount
of gaiety in sound, that
plummet of gravity & Balanchine;

ferrying Fellini to his grand entrance
or steering Isaac Stern
toward the stage, you were
the dancing master's high romance –

sparkling eye of the champagne
della vita. In your wide
Gypsy glass, hide
me now, Rose – the globe's your reign.

9.10.15

BLUE SCHWINN

Out of the vernal vernacular,
low to the ground, weedy,
where the plane (on its way
to the White House) took a detour –

in the park, where the kids play
& choose up sides, & dream
of glory, & ice cream –
someone planted (in post-igneous clay)

a wedge of limestone, with an antique
bicycle saddled to
its pinnacle (blue
Schwinn, I think). Joints creak,

wheels wobble in the barnyard breeze.
My kingdom for a horse,
cried desolate hoarse
Richard, knocked to his attainted knees,

blood-drenched. Phrases mumbled
as we read along, in school –
Eli lama sabachthani... rue
the day – gave pause. We fumbled

for our lunchboxes. We floated
spitballs toward the furthest
pate. Life in the West
was always evening toward sunset –

where Thunderbird lifts hefty wing
above snow mastodons,
& Mulberry Bay runs
rosy, toward plum Everything.

9.11.15

TWO THREADS

Rite of Spring twirls out of Paris,
1913 (tight-coiled
as a Springfield
bullet-train). Apollinaire's

the latest Dionysus – tranquil
eye of Martian hurricane,
versifying inane
Europe's *Grande Guerre Nonpareil.*

He will die too (head-wound).
Le Roi Ubu est mort.
Two threads, athwart
a catenary arc (gray ground,

blue sky) form slow raincloud;
two notes, or three
make melody
like a wedding day, a shimmer-shroud

of mutuality. The King's
in Memphis for the evening;
Queen's busy restoring
an old carol (*Acorn Tree-Ring*);

Lincoln's going to the theater
of the war tonight.
Curvature of sharp flint
Choctaw cheekbones, at the center

of the storm – a smiling ridge
of tears. Pocahontas
cartwheels one meticulous
$J^2 = Mx/Mn \times 1132$ (thread-bridge).

9.12.15

AMERICA'S CUP

An *Ocean State* sky, color
of sleep or turtledove
today. *Don't move,*
let the wind speak. Late summer

mandorla of ripenings –
a little boat in your hand.
John off Rhode Island,
lounging, relaxed. Bare shins

& feet propped up against gunnel.
Good book on deck,
half-moon of wooden oarlock
framing calm harbor. Sea-knell

through the photo (Pietà).
When we go back to the sea,
whether to sail or to watch... we
are going back from whence we came.

America's Cup... can you drink it with me?
The Round Table, the Lady
in the Lake... a malady
in the Grail (of all humanity).

One raven-prong drills through the human.
Black Sea sunlight rays
from the depths. Maximus
with one hand frames the circle's rim :

one sail traces its catenary arc
along a thread of fleece.
Ariadne's peace, which
passeth fathom five... Mark.

9.13.15

LATTICE-WORK

If we can shrink down small as Frisbee
the little leprechaun
from Arthur Street (in
Mendelssohn), we might just barely

wiggle through the lattice-work
of Erica's Ferrara
cabinet (*dove sta*
memoria). Such delicate

moss-green & gold! Almost as bright
as your sea-iris – sun-
flecked, pregnant lens
of summer season (cave-light,

river-carved limestone... lakes
of glacier-deft sketches).
Time's a yarn, that catches
history in *quipu*-knots. Oak aches

for each acorn – the great light
diamondiale, that lifts
each person (infinite
è finit, unbreakable). Slight

limp, unfinished manuscript...
slow clay, Mendelssohn
relief operation –
Berryman in Resurrection crypt

or Pound à Venice (perilous seat
in dolorous gondola)...
Dante sets down Ravenna
raven-feather (*geste* complete).

9.14.15

LOW RELIEF

Air is mirror-brilliant today, even
shadows cut clean
across Touro slate.
Mid-September, slanting sun,

a New Year for an old people.
Someone plays a flute
off Morris Ave... fleet
foot sails into New World marble.

As in a low relief in Rimini –
an august Agostino
Venus, or Diana
whorled in limestone dithyramb

out of the sea. The jutting cliff
crusted with barnacles
whittles its pinnacle's
bowsprit, figurehead – her glyph

(lifted in one hand-wave) twin
scallop-shells, like
castanets (break,
crashing surf...) where time began.

Your moon along the shore, Apollinaire.
Limestone foundations
crest across seasons,
granite castles – seagull's mother,

feathering horsegrass in your hair.
1321... 1132...
Joachim voodoo;
Jeanne's grey-eyed icon (Galla's lair).

9.15.15

LITTLE STEPS

Halcyon late summer day
in the ancient yard.
Soft came the word
from kayak lips... like one stray

Chinese lantern, swinging orange
over weedy greens.
Quiet river scenes –
Yulong threading bamboo (drafty *ange*

d'or fisherman) between karst hills
& water buffalo –
bull's-eye, ground zero
for the monsoon spring. God wills

fish from such limestone streams.
The way to Promised Land runs
through your heart, O branded
Everyman. Job's hook redeems.

A living soul talks back to hieroglyphs
until they come to life.
Osiris in the loosestrife
with French polio – Ravenna stiffs

in sketchy skiffs, rafting a mossy
Giuliana to her sunny
son – sweet honey
from a shack smokehole, in Galilee.

You won't get it right away.
The flags are thick
with gold encaustic –
targets flip like livid hay

in a tornado eye – the limp
thread hangs from one
thread or another in
a Mandan sundance. Nails crimp

crumpled limbs beneath a cloud
of starlings... when one
raven, crowing, spun
through your aching pupil – proud

oculus of Solomon,
Galla's ripe acorn
crown of sylvan
horn – an evergreen

Ravenna Pinetop, skipping 88s around
your retina. The iris
in her sheaf of cornea is
larval now – pupa plummets down

octagonal, folded to ground –
Hero in milkweed,
featherweight... freed
fiddlehead wing, cedar-bound.

The mountain lurks above the trees.
Imago flies to her source.
Monarch wafts a deft Morse
code in air – needles sing *breeze*.

A message-smudge, still incomplete,
yet untranslated.
Fisher King... checkmated?
Will fly again lambchild. Beat?

Through bearskin smokehole, near
the North Pole, Glenn
plays baby Bach again –
so grand, these little steps! So dear.

9.17.15

MOSES-KAYAK

The soul's a kind of mirror, they
used to say – the old
mystical sheepfold;
you'll find it on baptism day

refracted in an oval, seen
through water. Incidental
angels rim the cave-wall
(all elongate, string-bean

apparitions, seraphim)
till harvest ripens
& a scythe descends
dividing wheat from empty flim-

flam... everlasting Judgement
Day. That Galilean
gospeller, Samoan
wrestler, flipped oval Testament

into tight spring – a seventh wave
reversed the Jordan-flow,
the eye of Moses-kayak now
recursive back to Adam's grave

(SW of Lake Victoria,
no doubt). My Mirror Lakes
were Mendelssohn out-takes,
rehearsals for a Globe-historia –

the young king, hidden in an oak tree
still, waits for his mother's
signal – climbs from a mummer's
moth-shroud – floats to the Sea...

9.18.15

ALMOND EYE

The half-moon curve of the golden dome
of Temple Emanu-El,
so calm on Morris Avenue
in Providence. Only an emblem

of transparent well-being – invisible ties
that loop us in a web
of lovingkindness... (hub
of the universe – clear Paradise).

You know – it knots your heart, whoever
you are. Like the bursting-forth
of a smiling cloud, one 4th
of July, or 19th of September –

like that lunar opalescent gleam
toward autumn equinox,
when they shepherd flocks
of lambkins, & piles of pumpkins beam

like orange suns toward Thanksgiving.
Then you will remember
the anchor in the harbor
under the safety net – the sea-bells' ding

for one lost sailor. Radius of sound,
a palm leaf of repose;
her memory a rose
pendentive (over Indian mound) –

Ferrara iron, sounding to the depths
of pain & memory.
I am your soul, Henry;
that almond eye Pacific keeps.

9.19.15

TAPROOT

Observatory Hill, atop the crest
of Sydney Harbor – guarded
by phalanx of great-aged,
magnanimous fig trees – like a nest

for visionary eagles – keeps a lens
trained on stars down
under (twinkling diamond
octahedron, Southern Cross).

Yet here, in a nearby yard, one pine
soars higher than those figs,
flings moth-wide wings –
lime branches drooping like a pinecone

honeycomb – leans into evening
at acute angle (a golden
mean). Jack's cheekbones
were so sharp – as that pining

Rail-splitter's, in the cracked-plate
portrait – like the *pyx*
flung aloft by priest
or angler's scale-scorèd blade –

the vertical taproot must plunge deep.
Against sandstorm &
flood, the blistering worm,
a maze of chains... rusted keep

of treason's *rigor mortis* – fatal
spire of *PX*'ed Magdalen.
Where buffalo pern
to droughtland hollow (fetal, natal).

9.20.15

BRUEGEL SCENE

Summer loses weight, becomes
translucent at the end.
Sunlight slants graveward
with a farewell glance, & autumn's

trumpet-call is barely audible
amid hilarious
alarums in the circuits
of the starlings (swarming, risible).

& so you wonder where you are
on earth. John Berryman's
in jasper, John's in grey;
Man's in a graveyard green (so far

from here). Splat in a corner
one cloud-turtle (from
Iona) lifts her drum-
shell from the sea – almost another

comber, very salt & watery.
I'll join the starling circus,
friends – I'll whistle us
to Minneapolis, SE of Rimini.

That raven's in the Bruegel scene.
His glance is like one
wintry *oeuil* upon
her apron – by the deep tureen,

at dawn, in the spare refectory;
feathered in soft silence
on a wall of remembrance.
What's up, Dad? Unwritten history.

9.21.15

MAZY SIMONE

Equinox : a bridge between seasons.
Nay, no *night-mare*;
articulate as horsehair
& as serviceable. *Musique de* balance,

équilibre – night & day,
reason & faith. Of summer,
d'automne... (mordant humor,
luminous grief)... *Hey-hey,*

giddy-up, Old Paint! We galumphin' to see
the Pope touch down, in D.C.!
Strait o' Columba, maybe –
where turtles kick through tough gray

curves – like a mess o' limbic pigeons
decorating limestone
from the air. Everyone
behold her, now – mazy Simone's

the River Queen. Like Ariadne
with her golden seine,
or murmurous Magdalen
of sunburnt feet, she will meander

underneath each Maximus
(from Po to Eridanus,
Neva-Neva to the rusty
Don)... O Theseus, she's mulish US!

Chart the way-way back now, Mary.
Through this labyrinth
of dinosaurs, a kitten's
coracle will bless – make merry.

9.22.15

BRIGHT GAL

> "Look instead at the canoe, I beg you, and observe
> its honesty, dignity, and moral courage..."
>
> – *The Garden of the Finzi-Continis*

The last full drop of summer sun
plays out across a falling
garden. Dogwood, shedding
scarlet berries, rattles in

cool air. Leaving Lil' Rhody soon
(for North Star State). Exile
is a state of, meanwhile.
Yom Kippur whispers *repent, atone;*

Francis in Washington lifts up
his rod of Aaron (bloom
of magnanimity &
doom). *A star from David's cap*

came forth... a cedar replica
from Lebanon – like Wanda's
wand (the State Fair Queen,
robed in golden Land o'Lakes

boxim (within more boxim)) -
aimed, centripetal,
toward glimmer-portal
of the Milky Way. *The little foxes*

all stacked up, O my beloved.
Monarch is an imago
out of the cocoon
of long ago. A turtledove,

the El of El – Francesco
out of San Francisco – ark
within an arc of light, or
Galilean galaxy (an Okie oak).

9.23.15

HOME PLATE

the game ain't over till it's over

How the figure of a man at 90
(any man or woman, see)
becomes transparently
rough diamond, somehow... Yogi?

Behind home plate, in empty lot
traced over waste land,
he crouches – hokey Panda
Bear (rye antic square root

bassist of the base, Neanderthal).
Signals from the crotch
each crypto-kingfish pitch
plumb perfect (Sasquatch cone-ball).

Yankee stars wheel over stadium
where Little Bear paints
himself into pinstripe
corner (gray silo *Te Deum*);

Big Bear, worried, waves him off
Indian mound (a brave
9 innings) – takes a dive.
Let's go explore the bottom of

the harbor, little lamb of mine.
I'm gonna let *you* shine.
Beatrice was a 9-
man game – for 28 seasons

soused us with spray of lilac
Liberty bells (for free).
Between you & me
the wave flows everywhere, Smolak.

9.24.15

CAUTANTOWWIT

The sweet old pussy willow's gone
that once o'ershadowed Pushkin's
backyard grave (great Russian
cat). Leaves not a leaf behind –

only an empty space (alas,
alack) anchors a magic
carpet o' masticated
stump. So we hung up our lyres

on the bow of that stubby caravel,
Acacia – stuffed to the gills
with incoherent motorings,
burbling Barranca Straits – with Mal

& Papa consulting the cabinet
non-stop... coat, liquor...
What have I left her,
now, here? *These were all spirits,*

veering toward Prince Eddy's Island.
Wracking my brains... hollow
ravine in the pupil, *valley*
so low... black hole of Depression

Inlet. Perdita, somewhere in
the safety net, under
the ark at *Porta Aurea* –
dear lightsome daughter! Ravlin,

unraveled so. Now rainbows flash
Medusa-shells, O
Mountainous Sad Shadowship –
to wit, to woo... (by Narragansett ash).

9.25.15

FERRARA MIRROR

If I fade into the low relief
of Minnesota limestone
hedgerow cliffs – a zone
of Ice Age gypsy moths (brief

lives of dashing hummingbirds
& wingèd Peacock Angels
fixed in river-angled
banks of sediment) – my words

would bend into the grain, grow
rude & wooden – like
that bridge or flood-dike
scored by slashing Viking prow...

you'll read about it in the paper.
World events (*Pope*
Francis Whirring Hopeful
Wings – Blood Moon a Rusty Copper

Penny – Putin Barricades
Himself in Alabama)
refract in your Ferrara
mirror (juvenescent shades

of gaiety & heartbreak, green
& bronze between twin cypress
ribs). My wilderness
a Mendelssohn continuum (scene

from the window of a Roman train).
The mast is dogwood too,
Mama – I made it for you
all by myself. The rain in Spain...

9.29.15

STEELY PRONG

Heidi, it's been many a year
since we went a-Maying together
down Arthur St., in Hopkins
(Glastonbury? Mendelssohn) –

but next door, in the autumn rain
a misty hawthorn silvers
bright chartreuse berries
for the birds (windhover, crane,

starling) who may alight someday.
Just down the ancient lane
my father's granite urn
abides, along the Minnehaha;

ravens stitch the cooling air
above the stream – a shade
those oak-leaf hands once made
over our heads (good chevalier-

Samaritan). Yon turtledove
coos from a russet square –
fieldstone embrasure, where
vaults rise on sable ribs (alcove

beyond alcove, into the light).
Bring me your thorny ring-
around-the-rose, Heidi;
I'm ready now to dance & sing

athwart the maypole-chariot.
One drop of scarlet raven-
ink, one graven letter's
steely prong... (one grail-griot).

9.30.15

HOME FREE

Set adrift down Providence streets,
blown along by chilly air,
this autumn Atlantic weather
in the Ocean State... gray cloud-fleets

follow birthday Hobo, his big-baby
muttering – a nonsense
tremolo from Jonah's
whale-gut habitat (her kingdom's *maybe*

someday). Like Apollinaire slaloming
dolphin-rime atop a marble
door in Rimini, warbling
his *trompette marine* (something

about a Frisco treasure chest
in a hurricane eye) – or
Bluejay Slocum, Shaker
salt in pauper's Dauphin-quest...

your sailor's air, so fortunate
pipes down from the future
on Ariadne lure.
Hookline for deep sinker – bright

hand who flew from the poop deck
waving from waves his
palm-leaf radius
(JJ-pendant, octahedral speck).

Wisdom's justified in all her children
plays out the line from high-
strung Miriam. Sky milk-
train sounds – all home free then.

10.1.15

TRAIN-HORNS

The raven-message in the ink gets blurred
in the dark. Signal fades
over badlands. Wade's
gone upstream, Charlie – overheard

her talking about the telephone.
One with the wheel-dial
we used to use. I'll
call you in three days, Persephone.

Grace made this little linen hanging
with palm greenery, with
red specks for eyes. So Phoebe
set to compass-pointing in a painting –

hand-prints, fingerprints, green
dolphins breaching in
a fling... theremin
flute-song – ghost dance for Iowa

maiden (midden remains). 400 years
in Utah, seems like,
they danced. A snake
coppered up in a trance – cheers

for the livid buffalo (the one
who got away)! I
don't know, Charlie –
she's pretty mad. The whole corn

crop is blown to smithereens.
Hazel threw her whistle
in the purple thistle –
thorns crown hills. Train-horns...

10.2.15

LOST PHOTO

Spotty grackles swarm the dogwood,
chatty starlings nibbling
scarlet berries, quibbling
around each drooping leaf (old

ruddy father). They traipse a happy
nonsense o'er the remnant
garden. Sir Thomas Browne,
strum softly til I end my Rhody

nap (it won't be long). Your Persian
paradise (precisely drawn)
will do for Gödel, Dante –
not so simple to sketch that Abyssinian

abyss, encircling the human plow
through history. Your soul
is touched by lost photo
whose courteous artist limns her now –

an April child glimpsed through November
shades (*All Souls,* Grandpa).
One unicorn grace, *selah.*
O woe to me, that scarred the moon (her

face still gleams from autumn grass).
A soft Franciscan Rimini
rhymes in the memory
of your basilica (*on ne passe pas*).

Dear evening Matilda, 1-3-2...
(Beethoven, fowled & quartered –
decussation – weathered
sprite). *All shall be well,* hums Manitou.

10.5.15

DOUBLE-WE

Something inherent in the stone,
the milky, the snow-seasoned
Winnebago (Indian mound).
A pregnant plot, expectant zone...

one-stringèd salt-shanty, or tent
of tentative meeting.
Limestone Mediterranean
USA, moon-galloping... unspent

Ethiopian Edith (double-we).
String's stretch-to-break
(real Rimini headache)
loops through Persephone-tragedy –

Tiresias whispering mother-wit
or pock-marked moon
keening her Dionysus-loon
(*rive-marine* beyond yon Key West

jetty). *If the Greeks could see...*
but it's not necessary.
Stout military
Perseus will refract the sea

into a trillion dolphin-heaps;
Poseidon's jealousy
toss Cassiopeia
upside to her throne (for keeps).

The circle of the sea (deep Circe)
revolves round Galilee –
Pygmalion will be
revived in thee, Pocahontas-B.

10.6.15

SNOW-CONFESSIONAL

These scarlet dogwood berries
sprinkling the patio
like drops of blood, O
thou October pale marine. Seas

mottle thy face more than they should –
scars, age-spots, drawn
across youth long gone. *Her*
billows drowned there, Robin Hood.

So the copper-pronged harpoon
dove deep, to sea-floor known
before Bronze Age – ravens
intone their learnèd funeral tune

& crows can recognize your face,
Cautantowwit. *The moon*
be pierced to russet soon;
your soul, also, cannot erase

persistent chronic blood-pain's trace
that stains each chronicle
of hero-miracle,
mutters Antigone (in Mary's place).

A coral circlet rings her hair –
aquamarine, full fathom
five; another kingdom
circumscribes (asper coin-lair).

You know it, Henry Buried-Man;
your snow-confessional
remorse codes – *Rez is all.*
Be reconciled, sez Rabbi Dan.

10.7.15

OLD HYMN

Somewhere out on the wide flatlands,
on a highway, on a prairie
where you are, lonely
Manitou (man, too – man-

woman)... beneath neon signals
through the rich gas fumes,
something threadbare looms –
a used-up catenary cradle's

rag. An old hymn, scored for coral
shell. My coffee cup
out of Byzantium – wave-top
mosaic with a dolphin's hurl

of blue-green (lofty ruby-diamond
star) – I'd set you down
upon a lake so round
like glass, in Galilee – let the almond

world, centripetal, converge,
surge into your matrix
grave. These raven-tricks
the wind plays – Ishmael's urge

to ride Q's coffin-cup, to surface
near your lifeboat, Rachel...
left me alone to tell
the tale, Jonah. This carapace

of turtleshell, this heavy salience
is near silence – closer yet
to your own ear, my pet.
Black Elk in Elkhart... life-sentence.

10.8.15

PUMPKIN MAN

in memory E.H.

This windy gray October day,
fat robin camouflaged
(hoodie?) in dogwood's
rusty green... & then the great gray

beech I passed this morning (Slater
& Lincoln). Elephantine,
primordial, in motion
still (old pre-Socratic critter)...

Edwin's tree, his 100-branching
crown – the graying *King*
of Gray, still whistling
to *Even Dove*, down never-dying

Dolphin Way (led by leaping sparks
into Ravenna). O patient
rude dream-sponge – intent
to wrestle safety shroud across stark

span! – your International Pumpkin Man
lit from within (warm
orange flame)... *No harm*
shall come to thee, my child – listen!

In a corner of a lumber yard
one sharp-eyed old saint
(framed by gray paint
cans, wagon) waves palm upward

toward the dark sheep-door, just
over his shoulder – where
one candle shivers fire.
An endless jet, he whispers. *Trust.*

10.9.15

TREASURE CHEST

A bird hums low through human sleep,
hums softly lullaby,
aubade. Ohio
bifocals their Burchfields reap.

Columbus is a Jonah still.
The outcast Genoese
casts off, a shifty breeze
of shuttered Inquisition swells

bright spinnaker for Spanish Main.
Indies glimmer in the grain;
Powhatan's skipping maid
knots scalp & *quipu* in one braid –

taps down lost gold of tumbleweed
& prairie memory
to one wide planetary
estuary (harvest mead).

The bird floats feathered in her gypsy
treasure chest. The ship
is *Holigost* – Time's keep
(unfathomed yet). Each Henry V,

grandee Philip will drop the knee
her way; each hungry soul
will stand renewed & whole
upon New Land someday (you'll see).

Thus in the globe of Jonah's word
the world comes round, & so
one wing's carefree proportion
curls each creaking mast homeward.

10.13.15

LIPS MONASTERY

This bright transparency of mid-
October Providence –
sweet-sad remembrance
of the princely sun (Caesar's eyelid,

drooping into Ides). Boethius,
last of the Romans, slips
away into *Sophia*-deeps,
drowses beneath dogwood leaves;

little feathery flesh-tone coins
of wild oats dangle, sway
on pale green stalks today.
She'll plant them with Galla's remains,

he mutters to himself. The monarch's
just a social butterfly;
none need any longer die
in her doctrine. Light-waves, arcs

of arches, radiating from
a central hearth... archaic
woodland (near Itasca)
where the springing pendulum

of springs is born. Moss-green Alph
to mauve Omega, vibrant
strings (O most ancient
of lays!) knot Ocarina Everysylph

into her vale of Inca-tiers –
a tinder Lips Monastery,
quicksilver Philosophy
lifts Rome to Mexican cedars.

10.15.15

SUNDANCE POLE

A poem might commence with this
little hawthorn tree
on Fisher St., fairly
overflowing with deep rose-red berries

like fireworks on the 4th of July
flaring & bursting in free
association – a liberty
of uncommon fiery wheels across midnight

sky – the pale stars in the background
steadfast lights, bespeaking
deep-down goodness (Hopkins,
maybe... Mendelssohn) – the silver sound

of a tender, melancholy trumpet
(memory of mourning dove,
her all-compassing love
that wanders wild, like autumn blade

of maple seed). The streamlet of speech
emerges from wilderness
of your own soul – manifest
in scar-chronicles of flesh (*we beseech*

thee, YHWH, *forgive our ingrained wrong*);
the language snakes its way
along a jagged ray
of peace pipe lightning (*atlatl*-prong

of brazen serpent) back to the source
rippling from limestone,
primordial marrow-bone –
a familiar voice, whose gentle force

you recognize from long before.
Comes with a question, like
a music teacher – *Mike,*
Jenny... will you try this score?

Do you know where you are? Bright lens
(rose-red, white, blue) surrounds
her limpid lamp – sounds
stir from the keys – the earth sends

radiance from ground-bass depths
(a b-flat flint enchantment
striking flame – tent
flaring firelight toward the Great

Bear's ring). *It is the sundance pole*
that gathers every Morning

*

Star to Thanksgiving
from every tribe & people in the whole

wide Universe. The Commonweal
of Cosmos-Wheel, the breeze
of *Manitou* through trees
in Lebanon, South Central

L.A. – a whisper through the pines
of Mississippi, Kansas,
California... Memphis
Tennessee... on any railroad lines

through space & time. Even here
on Fisher Street, in Little
Rhody, her turtleshell
murmurs statutes of liberty (*I hear*

you, there). Gray hawthorn branches
merge the black & white
of factional dispute,
pretentious politics – brace avalanches

of fanatics, stem the feuding tide;
her leaf-shades balance vision
with experience, precision
with that draft of lifeline magnitude –

fresh air of gratitude & calm
compassion (openness,
grace, charity). Less
dogma, more enthusiasm –

where blossoming cities lift from soil
of civil equity,
brave ingenuity –
American can-do, granted to all

who will. Old promise of a justice
overflowing, paid
in full – the freedom-chord,
rung with a joyful crash-caprice

of fife & drum, guitar & harp –
O let it roll down now!
That red berry you sow
in morning will be blooming bright C-sharp

by noon! Song's equilibrium
rests on her branch –
Love will enfranchise
multitudes (world freedom plumb).

10.16.15

BEE-STING

The rough sketch reaches back
so deep into beforetimes
like those caves of limestone
dolphins, walking... some refraction

in the water-filter flips Time over
into clear half-moonlight,
where *Word-is-Psyche*
typed into a graveyard clover

prints snowfeet along Minnesota
River, cemetery
ridge of Irish faery-
land (Apollinaire in Georgia).

Hard to explain. Grace Ravlin
what thou lovest well
this garden, under spell
of summer sun (your Washington

laboratory). Someone brave
magnanimous & kind
who vaults the epic rind
from orange threadspan (architrave

of salt-blue ice). An *Ocean State*
of mind, where ships sail
slowly down to Coral
Sound, abeam some forthright

rabbit lighthouse, trembling.
Forgive me, it is so.
Earth is very slow
a-borning. Here (one dead bee-sting).

10.19.15

SPIDER-PARADIGM

Emperor Yu, beside the Yellow River
noticed a painted turtle's
dome poke from the yurtling
current... crosshatched with a magic square.

Was struck with wonder – enlightenment.
The order of the world
arrayed, made clear – curled
around one salient shell. A tent

of meeting at the end of time,
a mote embedded with
encaustic gold... the myth
fleshed out by spider-paradigm –

one woof of mutuality
supernal company
dovetailing tympani
to turtle-immortality.

The character of a place reflects
the character of those
who dwell therein. Flows
of time illumine the limestone text,

the lambswool poncho, shrouded cave –
where we will meet again
old Roger Gentle-Hand,
bright Guillaume Apple-Mare... Genevieve

Little Tree... dear Juliet Bluejay...
where the matrix wheels
an April love... seals
1200 tribes with *alma-joie.*

10.21.15

BLUE MIDWAY

In the drift of autumn distances
leaves sail their own Pacific
toward a blue midway
air-matrix. Somewhere East

of Henry's passionate history
(mercurial Möbius strip
or Klein bottle – just flip
one *M* to *W*). Love's mystery

refracts – deflected by the rage
for mastery, an infant
flummoxed by ambivalent
shrugs... until the splintered stage

is suddenly quiet, spooky as old age.
& so he takes *Path P*
(which intersects roughly
at *X*) to make a mirror-image

of her wounded face – the child
she was, and is, always
(beneath time-tears, nail-
scars... Hen's self-betrayals, chilled

on wheels). Meanwhile, in soft Atlantic
Delft, deft delvers deal
a double-diamond parallel –
quick *Jackie-Joanie* seesaw flick

like *Leo flipped a Lei by*
Oahu Gal in Galilee.
Sol sighs, *it's only Me.*
Love's integral resolves in sky.

10.22.15

EARTHY TAVERN

This polished late October light.
Burnishes each diamond
of the backyard iron
fence. One survivor-cricket

churrs behind spruce (indomitable
busker). Over the rail
a wave of clematis still
surfs; the massive parasol

of luminous russet dogwood leaves
still braces (on its sturdy
mast) against a gusty
autumn breeze. Halloween in the eaves.

I'm leaving very soon. The golden
spider packs his poison-
bag, curls (frozen)
in a thread-vortex. I be beholden

to my Ariadne. In her hazel eye
the gold lambswool, yellow
Corn Maid poncho flow
into one clay design – pendentive sigh

of wild oats panicle (brown
dangling bird-feet
elegant & neat
as many-rimmed Ravenna urn).

My host is flown. Like *Stella Maris*
over the ridge, at Swan
Point – pivoting on *équinoxe*
de printemps (April 12 it was

*

this year)... like Beatrice's Florence,
born *le 4 Juillet* – or taut
Francesca, by her net
of Inca wool... *ou sont les neiges,*

maintenant? They'll ride my splintered
coracle back home.
Or (gone threadbare) roam
my prairie west – O mulish cowherd

wind-wag, tickled to Frisco Bay!
Morning Star, look homeward
kind upon yon way-weird
son. Apollinaire, with calumet...

the wars is over, anyway
– wars in my old heart.
Ravenna's where we start
again (light *brdftprnt* of Dante).

Motif of a sacrifice.
Eternity turned
ice-cold (solid,
absolute). Not nice –

unless you reckon yet again.
The dogwood mast is creaking
in the slanting afternoon;
winter will be coming soon

for Hen, who gathers everyone
into his earthy tavern
(like a Grecian urn)
across far distances... (American).

10.23.15

BOOK

V

MAMMOTH SNAKE

By the River Road, under the tall
bare cottonwoods, on the last
warm day, before the blast
of ice descends from the North Pole

I think of this Mississippi
constancy (unbending
loops & bends, winding
serpent-wise out of prehistory)

& of my frailty, my brevity
having forsook soft sand-
castle *petite* Rhode Island
for some territorial interiority –

inward cthonic Mendelssohn
where Mirror Lakes echo
down Arthur Street (so
far-off in the way-back zone).

The cottonwoods lean toward the sun.
Gravity pulls at
the Franklin Bridge (that
spider-thread my brother swan-

dived off, & lived). Flatland anguish
drags at Minneapolis –
down gridiron avenues
of gray snow, hunkered refugees...

The low sun, like a paradigm
hovers just over the mammoth
snake. The face in the cloth
shudders – furls birchbark (trireme).

11.19.15

COFFIN-CUSP

Here in the cozy habitat
of Cecil St. – Chester-
cat, snug in his nest
(or hut) near the Witch's Hat

on Tower Hill (old Clifton
Fadiman abode) – *Le Roi*
est mort, Vive le Roi
brazen carillons cry (Berryman

fleet flute-plot) – I'm remembering
Rhode Island. Ocean State.
Providence, full spate –
tight-furled concert, in a spring

of industrial silver (*Jewelry*
Capital of the World).
Hazelnut head, all pearled
with raven breakers... like the sea

my gong-struck muse (Medusa chord).
Apollinaire will bear
the burden of the air
leaning against brick wall... absurd

farewell to fiery squid (*trompette*
marine). Buried in roses,
granite Roger poses
on Tin-Top Terrace – a light

unto both Gentile & Jew (washed-up
driftwood apple tree
in prow of *paddle-me*);
balances books on his coffin-cusp.

11.20.15

INCA BIRD

Mississippi sundown. Meek
flock of cottonwoods
leans toward sand-
bank... listen to the river speak.

Noah's raven criss-crossed the ocean
weaving black on blue,
salt over salt (sez you).
My splotchy gouache representation

wings away north, south... follows
Big Muddy to her delta
denouement, *selah*.
Breathes on clay (rows, rose).

This Inca bird, like a Cuzco condor
(or Marshall St. bridge
bald eagle)... no prison-
pigeon, but flight to the rondure –

a well of black water, with stars
in a lattice (for stories).
The Ghost, says Maximus,
prehends the insolence of wars –

lift up your hearts, she cries,
lift up. Paradise
is a habit of eyes &
hands, not formulae;

lips rim a coracle (of cedar
curve & silver plow)
so that you too may know,
my child – the Earth (from a star).

11.21.15

PAPER SAILBOAT

His profile in shining lunar silver
twinkles with Dublin glee
on the half-dollar (JFK,
insouciant). Camelot forever.

I was born in '52, believe
it or not, but only
52 years ago I
lost my innocence (heave

sigh). I was 11 years old
when they shattered the crown
of the redhead king. My own.
A double birthday, dubbed. Fold

up the deck of your paper sailboat, son;
in Newport they will mourn
the people's chosen one,
killed by the backlash of the gun.

A still life, now. *Brown Decades*
(Peto). *Reminiscences*
of Lincoln. Whitman's
chrysanthemum (cresting cascades

of lilacs). Memphis underworld –
I gather the limbs of Osiris
(52-pickup, Rimini-Venice).
First king, dead king. Neighborhood

gossip has it, Solomon,
he's coming back. He
never died. Like Jonah
Houdini, he'll eat fish in Hebron

yet again. *11.22.15*

AKIMBO-LEAP

That poet in Ravenna caught
a cold in Rimini,
or Venice. Passed away
to Beatrice, Juliet.

Love's adamant majesty, a sign
strong as death, cruel
as the grave. Well
from the heartsprings, evergreen.

Out of salt pine-swamps (north, south)
a chastening, straight-
ening... hero-fate
an odd Sioux stratagem (mouth-

harp buffalo). The reediness
is all. On a cliff
near the harbor, stiff
WPA Roger-Osiris

lifts one granite hand in blessing –
& for what? The dignity
of an old pine tree.
Tell me how God made everything,

demands the little hopping child
whose dancing illustrates
the answer (pirhouettes
toward Paris now). One wild

akimbo-leap – Puerto Rican
hip, maybe? She's
learning fast. Trees
watch, cast shadows (almost human).

11.24.15

HIGH SOPHIA

My mother's golden watercolor
of a corner by the porch
door – let us approach
this summer morning autumn splendor

as it was, & will be once again.
An open door in Hopkins
Minnesota spins
its Manitou of teeming *pain*

et vin (an infinite childhood);
Alighieri in Ravenna
summons high Sophia
in the guise of Beatrice... would

she still circumference all human
knowledge in her arms?
Beyond Hell's harms
stands Boethius – *Consolation*

rhymes (decline & fall of Rome)
with Dante's *futurismo*
(*Roma onde Cristo*
è Romano) – one bright sunlit home.

Paisans, turkeys, sheep draw near.
The meal *c'est commencé*.
Massasoit & Williams here play
host – what was a funeral pyre

unfolds to cornucopia.
The crux of natural law
is liberty's *Commedia* –
all-human Earth joins Milky Way.

11.25.15

ROYAL FLUSH

Bald eagles wheel over Marshall Ave.
Bridge. The clouds drift
north. Lakota shift
west, into Dakotas. *Have*

Black Elk, will travel (Wild West
Show). In a circle.
Until the icicle
of White Bear Lake's a poltergeist

in the story (frozen Minnehaha).
Carry her over the water,
Hiawatha, Longfellow
(*this is the forest primeval*). Eh,

sighed my father, *c'est la guerre*.
He bears it all, with grace
before each meal (Minneapolis
Falcon-Ace); now I live in his eyrie-

lair. It's a strange situation (*home
to his mother's house
quiet return'd*). Oedipus
& the royal flush (a kingly game,

poker). Every Hamlet plays
the odds (instinctual
evolution, hell
to grail)... *Alla Mistakeo*, sez

Poe. But he's wrong (as usual).
The water from the creek
whispers my father... *speak*.
He's earned that urn. Mississippi, roll.

11.26.15

ANCIENT AIR

Articulate inchworm, lifting
little arches across
King Tut's chambers –
shape-shifting hero (glyphic

frogman), testing the submerged
crevasse for Nefertiti.
O Jealous Fertility
Goddess of the Wine-Splurged

Sea! Accept our offerings –
these cracked amphorae
full of ancient air
& semaphore (dusty grain bins).

Do whatever he tells you, she
directed them; the wine
from prehistoric pine-
nuts will transport us into Galilee.

But you have saved the good wine
until last. These grapes
are not Israeli types,
nor Palestinian; they shine

in the landscape; this is beautiful.
The purple embroidery
around your lips, my
Queen! The fiery eye of Yule,

the burning hearth of infantile
desire. A trim Beatrice
flickers through bound hay-
bales (kayak, limping up the Nile).

12.2.15

RAVENNA DOOR

This winter Mississippi, silver-
blue as a kingfisher,
must be my Ocean here,
now. Old Rhode Island (Roger

Williams tugging at his oar
along the Narragansett
shore) is like an inlet
glinting on Ravenna door.

This plain flatland's no nacre
objet d'art – no Rimini-
Jiminy jingle-tree
nor fizzle-pop of firecracker.

It's the tip of a massive iceberg
mound, with Ojibwa scrawls
from International Falls.
It's a raven-furled ironwork

Father of Waters (*del Espiritu*
Santo). The dark ink spills
from Andean condor hills
like shade from a single pine... you,

yew. One sinuous dove-grey thread
from woolen crown (above
almond eyes) – Love's
quipu, drawn from riverbed –

the peacock bow of freedom's O
(a circuit of Noahtic leaps
that signal seamanship).
Her line grips like a sheepfold

fence (through centuries of snow). *12.3.15*

INFANT BIRDS

In the ruffled mirror of the lake
scatter sibylline shards
of ice-light – winsome chaos
fabulating carousels a child might make.

To the attunement of a ball of clay
dissolving into Mendelssohn
spring mud – spry union-
unison of infant birds (with day).

It cannot last, cry Paul & Augustine.
Yet lasted long enough,
croons woodman Joseph's
son – *justifying all her children.*

Afternoons of used-up antique men
shift with shy Psyche –
hope to melancholy,
grief to resolve (determination).

Dusk filters into codex ink.
The dapple of the harbor
shrinks to one iron
anchor, parallactic (in the drink).

Yet teeming Earth still whispers
its new whorl – the mind
rewinds, sea-myths unbind
their clams. Heroes (Coke, Roger)

ripple in the river, over the rim
of light birch canoe;
Psyche's eyelids flicker too,
tap signals from tall Joachim.

12.4.15

LIFE-SAVERS

A warm December, Pearl Harbor Day.
Pale & luminous radiance
suffuses the primary colors
of the workmen's big machinery

in the river (below Franklin Bridge).
Dazzling maternal uncle
Jim's birthday – a Ravlin
clé to the mystery. Mrs. Elledge

added those little busts of Bach,
Mozart, & Beethoven
to my piano-lesson
collection (when I finished each book);

I loved her. Jim waltzed Agnes,
the Viennese musician's
daughter, around Lincoln
Center – while his own *jeune fille* was

in the shrouds of late-adolescent
angst, despair. O
Juliet... swallowed at last
by Frisco Bay (*agenbite*

of inwit, James). The pearl in the harbor
was a vivid soul, before
that fall; maybe somewhere
the wind still ruffles her black hair.

The soul, like a robin redbreast, wavers
high on its dogwood branch
over each day's routine
avalanche. Hunts for life-savers.

12.7.15

DARK HEART

A droning of iron chariots on
U.S. 80. Straight through
Elkhart. Winnebago
memory (in the amygdala). One

whisper groans like an oak in Mendelssohn.
Becomes a benevolence,
a shade for Sabbath silence.
Word become flesh (my father's own

right hand, gripping mine, until
he was gone). Amygdala,
a tower, a butterfly
net for memory (little

Rorschach mirror-wings); the stone
with the 12-leafed rosette,
with Abraham's whetted
blade, upheld in time... (*atone,*

atone). Little portable temple,
your body (innocent son
of mine) – odd grail-stone
now, for a trial in Jerusalem.

Where they open bronze doors for Jubilee.
Let the land rest every 50
years, in the name of mercy;
let the mind roam in humility

of Franciscan donkey (chariot
of Elijah, sparking fire
of futurity). Dear
Mary, with your high dark heart...

12.9.15

HUNTER'S GLOVE

Gray world, wind washing rain across
the enormous limestone crevasse
down River Road. Slant layers
of pre-Cambrian scrawls (wrinkles

of periwinkles, snails, seashells)
pre-date the hieroglyphs –
those Isis-&-Osiris skiffs
loaded with already-hoary piles

of Horus-eyes, gold scarab beads...
Cottonwoods like willows here –
divining rods bent to the River's
imperturbable Runnymede.

The stream's a mobile parallax.
One touch of tuning fork
will resonate through stark
tenebrous time-caverns – axe-

marks of *Raven* shadow *Dove*
into a treasure-trove
of hunter's glove (apes
channel fright to constellation-love).

I would sound that iron undertone
down through the catacomb
of trench-war years – hum
Psyche-Wisdom's *will be done,*

track Ariadne's thread, from Chartres
to Notre Dame, from Magna
Carta to the Frisco Bay –
where *Lady* knots her safety net.

12.10.15

RAVEN-VERSTS

In the film like a dream, or film-like dream,
amid inalienable pine-
swamps of yourself, a line
scratched by crow divides team

from ox, sheep from flock. Ineluctable
quiddity of ramshackle
vernacular. You will tackle
each day's unaccountable trouble,

snaking sly-inching replicas
of raven-versts across
your brow (Voronezh
barb-shears). *& those hills, alas!*

in Tuscany... & here the tang
of spoiled fish, seaweed,
salt-marsh... Hobo-reedy
outcast, you'll note the rusty clang

from vertical train-tracks – glamorous
icons of onion-dome
supremacy, driven home
by battery ram. Yet *chasteness*

still shines from Black Sea mirror
(gray pebble in a seagull's
beak). Galilean silence
rustles on lakeshore. After the furor

of a jealous djinn tears past, the sun
will peek forth without wrath –
retrace your raven-path
in filaments of violet, moss-green.

12.14.15

HOBO SPAN

Nocturnal nadir of the year.
Gray oaks along the river
nestle in a manger
of their own dry leaves. Cold here

for the wanderer, the no-count
strangeling (shiver-er).
Bring them in, Pierre.
We have room. Starlight will haunt

the here & now (parochial).
Already the axe is laid
to the waste land, cried
Granddad (civil engineer). *O*

Tannenbaum... (his favorite carol).
Would save the sacrificial
pine (last year's Noël)
for this year's fire. King Cole

in Mississippi wood (sacred) –
The Bear, a Memphis barge
in Iowa (suspect
at large). Uriah (*Scapegoat Snared*).

Bathsheba Takes a Bath (sit tight,
Hittite). In poetry
Hamlet will flip & fry –
like Salem for bluff Endicott,

Sweet William in the vacant pine
(a free perennial).
Romany iron, after all.
This hobo span beams red & green.

12.17.15

TWIG-NESTS

Who draws the wheels of the year-circle
in galactic flight, spokes
of a flame-spectrum? Oaks
brighten a little in December murk

outside my window; the anemic slant
of milky light stirs colors
in an old rug. El Alto's
orange Aymara beams make chant

more vivid than Ravenna's haunted
choirs. Freddy Sylvestre
rivals Juliano here
(Argentario) – one silver thread

(*trompette marine*) of interstellar
spiderweb (to quipu knot)
is sign of Noah Cosmonaut,
set sail for infinite hearth-fire...

The shipbuilders of Solomon
weave twig-nests in their sleep.
Fey Sheba *baa-baa* sheep
foretell each fatal monarch's tune

with cat's-cradles of quantum wool.
In crosshairs of the *here*
& now, Prince Chanticleer
crows every fox from every hole –

& only the mentor of a humble mule
looks down (wise Everyhen)
from speckled Empyrean.
Compassionate one! *Her child shall rule.*

12.18.15

SPARKLING SPOKE

after Handel's Messiah, *in concert at the Basilica of St. Mary, Minneapolis (December 18, 2015)*

If you listen to the chorus plow
like a river through tectonic
locks, sometimes an eccentric
voice will skim the crest, akimbo...

surfacing (plainly) like a Canadian
counter-tenor – wafting
on mellifluous wing
to plangent threnody (Isaiah

keening, hopefully). Under
the plush gray monotone
hulking Baroque stone
replica, weighted with plunder

from the Vatican... Handel's *Water*
Music (for a *King*
of Kings). & everything
coheres, in knots (of prophetic cheer);

unheimlich gemma-ovum *Yearned-For*
– out of an abject manger
breathing mortal danger –
Nazarene eloquence! – a scar-

etched, unquenchable, smoking
brand (the *wrrd*, made
burnt tattoo). Conceived
by a miner (chaste soprano, blasting

beneath birch-ponderosa doom)
through perfect boredom
of *logos-mysterium*
one sparkling spoke (O kindly kingdom). *12.19.15*

UMBRIAN BEAM

On the shortest day, in these northern parts
the river is quiet, the sky
is gray. *A heaving sigh*
of flesh, my body is... (the old poet's

confession). Too heavy for
this rusted lattice, locked
in Mississippi ice (rock-
frigid rictus). JB – metaphor

for Job, mayhap. Job, an icon
of hectored humanity –
who *in latter day will see*
my Redeemer stand before me, on

the earth. Sparse light, thin
calumet of raven-smoke...
parting curtains with a stroke
of ink, an Ariadne-thread (woolen

quipu). The trumpet plays tattoo
above furled Flemish loess
in Queequeg runes (*remorse*);
lambfields of returning, clumps of yew

veiling a furtive limestone chapel.
Under an alcove of
blu oltramar, Piero's dove
rays Mary's robe into mandorla

made with fingertips – Umbrian beam
piercing raven-umber
(barely). & *though they slumber*
now, soon shall they wake... in Jerusalem.

12.21.15

i.m. OM

You might visualize an image
now (your mind's eye)
of this ponderous, steady
trundle of train across iron bridge.

Brown rust & steel through clean snow.
You might think of another train
(to Vladivostok). The crane-
flight of deerskin moccasins... how

many pairs worn through, leaving pink signs
in the ice? Of a man
on the bridge, in winter,
at the end of his rope (Berryman's

remorse, nearby). Old prophets shuddered
with typhoons, unheralded –
deep vocals from childhood
(Solomon's, might be). *Henry stood*

clad in diapers, by whitewashed fence
handing daisies through
labarum-crossbar (to
Heidi, ancient puppy-flame). Immense

Mnemosyne of unsprung Spring!
Skatings of raven-wing
over Mirror Lakes, echoing
out of yesterday... some drowsy inkling

of spousal sunlight, some eagle-crown.
By all the authority
vested in poetry...
scratched into birchbark (Elijah-renown).

12.27.15

MELODIOUS EMBLEM

Dante paced the perimeter of Florence
with mumbling *gravitas*
& halting step. He was
building a grainy microcosm, dense

as diamond, light as linden leaf;
light as this Minnesota
snowfall (speechless *alpha*
blanketing state fairgrounds beef

– bandstand *omega*). Orientation
toward *North Star* becomes
entangled with kingdoms
of heaven, world – a mule's way station

to a Gold Rush claim, staked down at last
in San Francisco (keystone
of stark orange span).
A vortex (raven-blonde, vertiginous)

immurèd round painful iconic pair;
a song of *songe* (statute
of liberty) no more astute
than any lovebeat California dreamer

in midsummer. Melodious emblem
for those deeper waters
(azure heights) that course
around foundations... Jerusalem

temple under Roman beams, arch
that forms the tensile wing
of eaglet eyrie (singing
scroll)... knife-edge of Raven-church.

12.27.15

GHOST-SHIP

The long year closes on snowfall,
finally. Over the ridge
to the Witch's Hat, a ledge
over Arthur Ave. (#33 – *les*

jeux sont faits, John Berryman).
My father's flinty ashes
by the creek, that washes
through my mother's thoughts. A man,

c'est tout. Her lacquered plate
of autumn gold (Yeats'
Tower Hill, almost)
shines for the poet now, like fate.

A circle, fiery wheel of light...
Apollo's chariot,
or Noah's boat... a plot
of Plotinus, from cloudy height

of thunderherd – heart-mirth
of chuckling Apollinaire
(his swaddled head a pear
donated to interstellar 4th

or 14th (Q) Juillet). The pattern
gold, shot through by fencing
needles, under the glancing
plectrum of wind-beaten mast. Stern

heights & forthright gunnel-curves
of one gaunt ghost-ship
surging through the deep –
one orange *alba-ange* flares (swerves).

12.30.15

BLADE-POINT

You there – coiled on quiet side street
in Ravenna, your flickering
sabre-tooth tongue barely
echoing now – like that complete

grey gentleman, cornered by paint-cans
in Antonioni's stony
Red Desert (who is he?)
mutely suffering blessed senseless

Giuliana's windblown St. Vitus dance...
Maybe he beheld
her triple rainbow, welded
somehow over arctic heavens;

or this winter-silvered river, slowly
inexorably mirroring
its way to New Orleans.
An emblem of continuum (sea-

borne). *All things are moved by love;*
thus you conclude your song,
rapt raptor, eagle-prong –
wisdom Minerva signaled Jove

among hard-bitten Romans. Glancing
blow, ineffable blade-
point (that steely Maid
of Orleans would ratify) – slung

thread-thin from remotest eye
of polar bear (*Mama*
& Papa Bear... ah, now
I see!). Heart-music. Organ-sigh.

12.31.15

STRANGE TENT

Nothing will be exactly as predicted
when the poem sets out,
like this ice-hung behemoth
heading south (serpent-conflicted

Mississippi, Father of Waters,
Rio del Espiritu Santo)...
& as the prophets foretold
I will make all things new (stutters

Moises, making noises like
Elijah, taking off).
Hart, like emerald elf,
leaps toward her ruby Rubicon –

somewhere beyond Milan, Miranda
(Paris, or Trebizond)...
my aerial's magic wand
fails here, even (lost memoranda).

Only I know that steed King Richard
sought in vain – Pegasus,
rough burr-man mule (Francis) –
drums like a hidden Thunderbird

in his own battered, broken heart
(Earth's fleet beatitude
within his grasp). Rude
hut, strange tent, Somali hurt,

forsaken boat... the Mediterranean
salt will keep each relic
Antikythera mechanic – *as*
my Redeemer liveth (unforeseen).

1.1.16

BIG WIND

Poverty is the best education.
Lady Poverty
& sister Poetry
are twins – identify with a long line

of holy fools, primitive peoples
punished into meekness
by most extreme duress.
Fort et dur (judicial phase).

Abe Lincoln with his Choctaw cheekbones,
Black Elk, Roger Williams,
William Blackstone... hymns
in the wilderness (breeched from stones)

float toward a gray middle ground
of sky. Shy of names –
since the herm what frames
this Percy-dervish meadow-go-round

of constellations... only *Manitou*
will do (for some). Great
Spirit. Big Wind. A late
night pathos, sifting through

cottonwood, magnolia.
Only the geometer
of beatitude & bitter
pain. Familiar Maximus-Bertha

who rises (bulbous) from the plain
senselessness of men
like airy turtle-dove
machine – kind, moderate... humane.

1.2.16

MANGER-HAVEN

Everywhere a vector-vortex,
a 3-dimensional crane-
liftoff. A diagonal plane
of tracer-tracks – trains, trucks,

jet-like chariots surround this
Shriners' hideaway, where
limping children play.
Mute manger-haven, beneath curious

folksy lunar scimitar
insignia. Granddad's
old Buick neighborhood.
Born on Epiphany, you are

a kindly prehistoric whisper-
star, remote but bright.
Hum beneath black-white
acrid mercury bath – Big Dipper

trench-canoe. Grave air-casket
you portage over your head,
smiling beyond dread
fumes of one Martian marble planet...

So every local khipu-knot's
a complex of the six
directions – Shakespeare's
skullcap, Pushkin's troika-stop –

your eschatology through tundra,
mangy Everyman.
Lambent beatitude, then –
shaggy speech, shepherd apocrypha.

1.6.16

FRESH CRUST

The immense raincloud stretched like serpent
or shadow of raven-
wing, on an evening horizon
over the Pacific, just past the unspent

abyss of Golden Gate. Only here
ice scales an ever-brooding
Mississippi – black Earth blood-
stream (like Nile in winter mirror).

My Neva-Neva land folds history
into an origami crane –
an ever-moving terrapin
lapping on a chain (of clay).

A flower clambers from those rings –
a million-pillowed peacock
Rose, whose eyes flock
van der Weyden faces (channelings

of worm-warp smiles). Lyre-kings
hung like Christmas bulbs
from every thorn; their clubs
thronged in night circles, chorusing;

the Word was crumbling, in a whirlpool
(Ocean River, circulating
echoing Hector ring)...
'til Joey the Calabrian (my cool

collaborator) sketched an eagle
plummeting – flipped
up a fresh crust, dipped
in wine & snow – lifted his bugle...

1.7.16

DOVE'S EYE

Arctic air is bearing down now
on this middling Midwestern
flatland plate (limestone).
No sea-breeze moderates the snow

though I remember dockyards of Duluth
in water colors. Seagulls
recollect their coast
with scraping cries. Boaz & Ruth

wend for us all – we ramble through
strange parts, returning home;
Kuala Lumpur's steam-
bath sealed a wedding (one from two).

Love knits together contraries.
This is old wisdom, Sophie;
providential strophe
swung from your native city. Rhody's

ambient orchestra – a certain
mildness in the air,
a temperate clarity...
O ye proud porcelain princes, hearken!

Loveless disdain for one another
serves not to patch up
my cracked American cup.
You bicker with your own twin brother.

Stiff little Nutcracker king, your white
hair flows like rain from grey
dove's eye. Pluperfect Roy...
a rose ellipse (enfolding day & night).

1.8.16

ONE SPRING

The river across the street still flows
under thickening ice, ceaseless.
Its lesser tributaries
(Minnesota, Minnehaha) also

persist – all of them subsiding
into Ocean River
finally (only a quiver
rippling Time). Julius is sliding

a handkerchief across his brow
in 49 B.C.
The die is cast, sez he.
Yokels on Rubicon blow

tubas now – *let War decide.*
World empire in his grip,
peace is ordained. Slip
the noose over each parricide

(Brutus, Absalom); the father's
kingdom will be certified,
et ratified, in blood.
Shadow of a kingfisher

rotating in graffiti'd alcove.
Boethius & father
(Symmachus) share
fort et dur... Ravenna love-

keen (after bronze millennium).
Time's universal –
history's rehearsal
for a mangy star-profundum

*

deeper in the soul o'man
than Solomon arrayed
or Emperor betrayed.
An agate, tossed in Jordan

sand. Halcyon day (of almond
shade, & waterfall).
Life's good, is all –
big benison *de tout l'monde.*

Reaches through the harvest of
your Martian scythe, O
Death, to something more –
the milky Rio of the Blest.

It is *Beyond*. It's over yonder.
Everywoman's Eridanos,
Poe's *Eureka*. Moses
glimpsed it in his heart's far

island (yours, mine) – soul
liberty's Belle Isle –
Eternity (only
a smile from here). Glows, whole.

There were 4 rivers flowing
out of Eden, toward
House of 4 Pines (word
lost on the wind). All knowing

& loving, all doing & being
gathered in a khipu
knot... arc of yew
over limestone grave (one spring).

1.11.16

PRAIRIE SPACE

A beautiful moon swings low over
frigid freeway, tonight.
Distant rays (twice-refracted)
illuminate roadside snow. Up there

floating, one sharp sigh, one smile –
dark rondure of tennis ball
cushions his gradual
descent (unique lunar profile).

Substance of illumination...
State of Union, tonight.
President sheds late
bright emanation (station

on the way). Recognition
of a mission, Everyman –
Goodness is this, right? One.
Gaze upon prairie space (the sun).

Pursuit of happiness. By *we*
the people. Recognition
of a transposition...
humble oxymoron-man (*of thee*

I sing). He play the target-sign,
a threefold ground zero
premier. *Mysterioso.*
Ford Theatre (Dallas denouement).

Roger Williams tracks into the woods
to huts of Miantonomi.
Is finished, sez he –
snowing again (beatitudes).

1.12.16

UPSTART HILLS

Gray coal cars thunder monotonously
across an old iron bridge.
Only a local image
in midwestern bleak. Your poem will be

allegorical, of necessity
since an Earth so various
is only one of a series
on parade (sparkling panoply

du *Cirque Planetaire*). Italian sun
is as a brazen shield
above scarred poppy field;
the moon a candle in Pavian dungeon...

Poema Sacra, Dante's testament
è tutto didascalico –
a climber's manual (to go
from shady gloom to cheerful summit

of Rose Mountain splendor). My sun
rides low in winter sky,
chanting *How Not to Die*
in plain & soulful Minnesotan

(Ojibwa). The dream of history
breaks open at its heart.
All-human upstart
hills (Superior, or Tuscany)

fill nets of silver phosphor –
your soul's a philosopher
in love with twin Mirror
Lakes *(Justitia, Amor)*.

1.13.16

RORSCHACH FIGURE

This gaunt, towering, aged pine,
adorned with a scattering
of obsolete Christmas
lights, draws a straight sober line

lifting its crow's nest to point
of perihelion (invisible sun
behind galactic one).
My ghost-ship creaks with *accent*

grave along her seventh wave
(sky-reckoning) – southern
constellation, borne
on Magellanic surf. An octave

mutely unfolds – an origami
Chinese lantern, spun
outward (on tiny silken
struts) into a diamond *Chi-*

Rho maze – Rorschach figure
of raven, or monarch
brain (Venn-Neva wreck)...
my spider-path, or Chartres lure.

Eurydice of *Dream Song,*
Henry's Sheba down south.
Proceeds by word of mouth –
transfigures saturnine keening

to hopeful whistle. Chickadee,
junco? Woodpecker –
rousing Ravenna *nature*
morte (ligneous crucifix-aubade).

1.15.16

DAWN STREET

In the ash-gray sky, where the ravens drift
in the Bruegel scene, over winter
panorama – harbor
& skating rink, riddle & gift...

In remote perspective, the raven's eye
reaps furtive memory,
most ancient flame. *We*
walked together, you & I

down the dawn street, in spousal light;
only a pigeon-murmur
echoed our passage there.
The hearth's full of embers (life is night).

Old man Boethius steps out
his syllables, each
vowel like a cherished
peach. This radiance will cast

doubt into shade (beneath pine branches
where salted gratitude
savors his fortitude).
Beatrice-Columbia suddenly launches

into sweet aria of praise
when Jonah surfaces
from dove-grey eyes
of everlastingness   Apollinaire's

fumes   filter into laughter
War to End All Wars
a cloverleaf surprise
renders mercy on earth   hereafter

1.17.16

PEASANT DANCE

i.m.MLK

Only an unpretentious oil
beside the door, my mother
painted, 50 years
ago. Backyard. Spring soul

of morning, golden-green – the glow
dappled with jet-black
flock of starlings, yakking &
feeding there (framed by two

young oaks, & the backs of houses).
Bring your gift, starling,
to the altar of everything –
Ocean River, inexhaustible goodness.

O parallactic mercy of
these diamond facets! Water-
falls of liberty – your
moral law, Dove-

cote! Who moves through Memphis stone
like mild summer breeze
or shady swing-trapeze,
to milky matrix of the human

sun. Love's stern ethos is
a camouflage – justice
for joy – ray, source...
O King of Arthur St., she sees

you! One glance of moist radiance
out of the Black Sea book
of *Always*... there, look!
Her garden summons (Peasant Dance).

1.18.16

LILAC BARGE

In the Rock, the library, in Providence.
Snow's hexagon *glissando*
falls on Whitman-Poe
birthday. Athenaeum lens

(blind flash of mercury & lead)
poses twin agate lamps –
of seahorse *hippocamps*
& dread. Envisioning (not-dead).

Dust-labyrinth of pupa-pharaoh.
Curious mummy-volumes
Oedipus exhumes...
– Eureka! I have found you,

Madeleine! In mold of lichen
Venn diagram (Raven) –
Martian crossroad, Jovian
Juliet-canoe... (shade of Ferrara sun).

Saturnine Henry disappears
under the alignment
of these stars' bent
light palladium coheres

& spheres revolve (toward Galilee).
Into Newport *Holy-Land*
sail Jack & Jackie... Helen
Whitman... Eddie Poe. One shy

brown bird, conducting lilac barge
beneath cedar boughs;
bearing between twin prows
her dewy *double-ewed* grail-charge.

1.19.16

SMOKE-SIGNUM

I carry Sophie through the snow
to the summit of Tower Hill.
She says, *It's magical*
(prodigal 2-yr-old). & so

it is. That conical moss-green
Witch's Hat crowns
a Yeatsian limestone
keep (prehistoric submarine

barnacled with biomorphic
hieroglyphs). Isis
the octopus gathers
her segmented sea-worm (limbic

bronze phosphorus monarch child)
in streams of time – before
the 9th planet was born,
or knowledge-tree known (wild

afterthought of smoke-signum).
Chicago *Hiawatha*
arrowed here, truer
than rue – trained consummation,

like soft carnation in Quaker lapel
(hexagonamatrix). Rule,
Scattergood Friends School –
your West Branch harbor (charitable

agape) a hostel in a hostile time.
Justice for orphan, widow,
refugee. Praise be, grey
catenary icon (9-twined lime).

1.20.16

PURE SOUND

i.m. Robert Treuer

Back East, in Rhode Island, the big snow
coming. Thinking of William
Blackstone, hermit-pilgrim – the
one who went to live with Miantonomi

& the other red-men. To the *House*
of 4 Pines – under
cartouche of Little Bear,
North Star. Out of Nazi Austria

sped a peregrine, by grace of God
& pity of strange braves
(Scattergood saviors,
anonymous donors... meek *just good*).

To a tree farm he fostered (in remote
forest). Led into circle
of silent First People,
tending ashes (sitting shiva). Little

prow of acacia, rocking near Itasca-
Nile... your upside-down
fire-drill will drown its
candle in stony Minnehaha.

Sigh, winging out into grey sound
(b-flat at midnight).
The musicologist
from Florence mutters back to ground

just so – back to the pigeon-clay
of primordial, steadfast
Bee (until the last
dragon of Sheol fades away).

1.22.16

REED MAT

Husks of cicadas, limestone shells.
These layers, a palimpsest
of leopard skins (East/
West). Serpentine spells

(*Alph* to *Yezidi*). In graven
hieroglyphs of human
dream – Solomon
& Shulamith (Ferrarese garden

bond). A Mendelssohn mandala-
afterlife, of local
equilibria... after all
the Pharaohs have their sway (*selah*).

Battle of shade & pictograph
resolved by wind. Cool
breeze, troubling pool
of sunken barge (regal riff-raff).

Vernacular archaic culture
architecture – simple
transmission of ample
gratitude for being. Pressure

on the king (of everything).
Grey humming bird
omen signals absurd
sacrifice (pawn for nothing)...

his baby steps (Gypsy to Jew)
toward one wooden
nature morte (amen,
amen). Reed mat, sheik. Me & you.

1.23.16

FARM ROADS

The old poet is a tramp.

Something there is in me that loves
this heavy railroad bridge.
Like an Osiris-ridge
of rust the gyrfalcon oar-hovers

in the antique poem by the worn-out
Beat (Muskeg Al, or Jerry
Don Teo). So very
wistful, warbling his old *trompette*

marine beside the drowsy Miss...
You have to be a hobo
just a little, Jo
to know. How *mutterland* is bliss.

She reaches timely tendrils now
deep through backwaters
of still memory. Neighbors,
children... chicory, mosquitoes... *O.*

Evening stretching infinite
farm roads toward sunset.
& you, caught in a net
of yearning (fluttery disquiet).

She's your Dream, old trampoline.
& I would have you meet
my own familiar fleet
amigo – invisible yet, still gone;

warm shadow, like a humming bird
who beams from evening sky.
Love is perfection (sigh).
A misty rainbow, Hobo said.

1.25.16

TOTEM-GHOST

Winter. An imperturbable water-serpent
flows smoothly south, under
the presiding MN-arch
(Peace Bridge). Cloud-blanket (quiet, lambent

silverthought). Ice-glancing light
of North Star State –
each ray will penetrate
the sixpack hexagons of Snow Rabbit

– that giant Bigfoot totem-ghost
Sophie & Phoebe rolled
to quasi-life (backyard).
Some Hiawatha Teotihuacan (host-

figure, phantom King). Messiah
is a butterfly. *Love,*
Love, and be loved, beloved
Bumblebee – amen, *selah.*

This glossy *lala* glossolalia
is like a peacock's choral
cry, or agate-spiral
Saverin-Canute, out of Iona

(green Columba's jaybird hymn).
At the spare crossrood
of naked servitude –
Boethius, Maximus, beaten

senseless – there Polaris burns,
& melts into the heart
of summer Ocean. Start
your laddie-dance, lass – Roy returns.

1.26.16

MICRO-MOSAIC

This circle of 7 emerald palms
(with 8 red dots across
lifelines) was pressed
by hand – an infant hand, Phoebe's –

under the guiding eye of Grace
(in Providence). Now
I set my cup (micro-
mosaic from Byzantium) in place

atop these marble squares, that trace
brass compass & sundial
of Roger Williams. Trial
by English fire (Coke's carapace)

was his – to bring the Narragansett
word for *liberty*
to London (& to me).
The *sovereignty of good,* in its

vernacular incarnation, is
one global, crystalline,
turtleshell acorn –
Shakespearean lap of happiness

(skullcap, human Golgotha-dome
worn meekly in Ferrara
& Venice – Ravenna,
Providence...) – *What cheer? Welcome,*

warbles Canonicus, chief
Shaker under raven-
falls (Columbian) –
his handshake stronger than belief.

1.27.16

SPECTRA BEE

The spectre of a raven, carved
in ink above the dusty
door, the door to an abyss
beyond the evening river

Nile. Rehearsing my remorse
once more... so toss
Einstein to 529 (Lorenz
aggression-transform) – on course

toward decreation (Eddington eddies
echo in papyrus
reeds). He's *US*
(a relative, at least) – voice-

breeze through checkerboard fabric.
& Raven, O... her shadow
dove into my gray
memorious blender-alembic –

clouds of milk or milk of clouds
from whence the winking
spectra bee. Keening
I owe... I owe... Iona sods

& Iowa rows (dappled Columbia).
A stone in the corner of
RI... reunion-trove
fallen from sky. Cornucopia

plumb with casket (evergreen);
plum turtledove
binding with love
clay child & jealous heaven.

1.29.16

PALM WAVE

This milky February sun
foretells another spring.
Still far-off – winging
eyebrow-arch reflection

of a snow-blue almond bridge.
Yet near... a looming
whisper (out of Red Wing,
maybe) in your ear. Sweet pledge

of union, set sail southward
by wattle-crane basket
to mossy reed thicket
below Delta (*belle Campagnarde*).

Knot-eye of Popeye raptor-
sailor, here trans-
mogrified to mildest
peahen-cockerel (*Eeyore-*

Sophia, high over Frisco Bay).
Equable & everpresent
omni-beneficent
orthogonal well of charity

infusing one & all (mandala-
dome, dominion's
doom). Everyone's
chest *de trésor* – heart's *ah,*

life's *oh*... amended Manitou
of Man. For me & you,
within the vernal blue
of ocean wave (palm-feather true).

2.1.16

BACKWARD THUNDER

The Redeye of these freight cars'
heavy backward thunder
over rubidium crossbars'
X. Where the crooked sumacs are –

their creaky grey akimbo-structures
(rusty *caducei*). *Amorpho-*
phallus Titanium? No,
not quite... but ruddy, like Osiris-

Oedipus (up *3-Way Highway,*
where the pylons meet).
Eddy Parallactic,
relatively paralytic – all that whey

so massive, bending light around
Caesar's own seizures,
jade embrasures
(pyramidical, tyrannical, profound).

The iron Bruegel earth turns so,
in snowy dunes. Until
one feathery perpendicular
percolates up (with bleaker crow).

Light eddied, slow (28, 29...)
where a spring coils
moss-green (*oeuil*
of Bosch, in Kansas City sun);

where Iris plants meek sovereignty
by *Eero-Eeyore Gate* – &
Eurydice, come late
May, rose... (tiny Iona tree).

2.2.16

LOVE-TEMPLE

There's a power vacuum now
below the Black Sea.
Miriam, a refugee
gives birth at stern of carrack (dhou)

& when Rachel picks up Ishmael
off the concrete salt
an angry orphan (Baltic
pattern?) flings his own skull

at sociable Medea (*Simmering*
Mother-of-Pearl Revolver
Hid Woeful Moonstar).
& this is just the *Evening*

Mirror (ravening Wolf-
Mammon). Somewhere near
(gray whisperdame's *here,*
now) Jonah will surf from Gulf –

stubborn mule of humility,
his meek almond eye
only echoes her sigh
(Mary's blues... welling salty

humanity). This continuum
of mother-of-pearl, on
the inner lining (onion-
dome anchoring heavy *ouragan-*

glissando) shapes a simple
turtleshell rainbow –
twilight will bestow
pink robin's-egg Love-temple.

2.3.16

OATMEAL BANTER

Light eddying through layers
of overcast gray sky
whispering, *simplify*.
Willow's underleaf, lyre-players?

Silver. Copper-gray the color
of this beech's mammoth shade,
whose granite roots cascade
light (leaf to leaf, & door

to door). Motionless in time-
space, emitting signs
her gray hide underlines
in graphite (stubborn Balaam's

Hoover-prophecy). The beech,
the book, will not be moved.
Ink trail of raven-dove...
bare gouache, still ground (beseech

thee, spare thy headstrong mule) –
O break the prison mold,
snow-blind brain-cold!
Where father & son meet (fool

with fool) beneath the malachite
green veins, gray matter
of bran (or oatmeal banter).
Strange personal jade wight –

shade-mutter, everlasting
Sheba. Clouds gather
overhead – weather
lit thunder (shackle-blasting).

2.4.16

ISLAND SOUL

I remember that tropic hummingbird
levitating in the garden
in Roger's Providence –
over crimson bee-balm, sailing leeward

toward St. John's (St. Elmo's?) fire.
New World already old
when Williams left the fold
for New-Found Land – an Aztec empire,

blood-soaked under sparkling banners
– *Huitzilopochtli*. Sign
of bestial regression
(eaten by bad table manners).

We seek a sign, & lift it on a pole –
bow down, force others down
before fresh idols of frustration.
Teeth gnash, flesh burns, heads roll...

But it shall not be so with you,
spake Dov the Nazarene.
One sign alone is given –
that lad Jonah, in his whale-canoe.

I recall the scene (*Deserto Rosso*).
Old guy, utterly grey,
cornered by jumbled array
of gray paint cans (cooped-up, *coo-coo*)...

We are all Seekers now, Roger.
Pacific island soul,
deep Ocean swell...
gray-green still humming (shepherd-seer).

2.5.16

LIMESTONE BROW

By the Somme, a century ago
a sum of desolations.
I had a visitation
in a dream last night. Harsh old

Uncle Ezra – driven mad
by madness, muttering
corrections, versing
disenchanted elegiacs (sadness

in my head). After the trenches
he would pit force
'gainst greedy *Usura* –
high-boot it over squamous stenches,

inky pyramids of mental fright.
Let your barefoot Daphne
skip the alfalfa
down the nave then, rancid knight;

your whisper's contrapuntal now
through salty reeds (remorse).
Francesca's creaking hearse
in Rimini. Cracked limestone brow.

Our errand in the labyrinth
is brief, & mostly blind.
The mirror is unkind
to the unkind. A little terebinth

will slake its thirst, where lofty elms
once reigned; our monarch
is lowly – yet in his park
wings fan that once were casket-worms.

2.5.16

PEACOCK TAIL

Dawn light through circumference
of dome conveys some sense
of dreaming weightlessness
as of infinity & omnipresence

so Hagia Sophia & peacock tail
might meet upon a tangent
in Ravenna   Dante's ancient
flame a spark, skimming the axle

of a galaxy, loosed from an arrowhead
flint, striking limestone
footprint (Galilean,
Nazirite). *Behold star in its idea*

redemptio-solidarity
adamant & diamond
centri-petal (almond
mandate) *everybody*

Ordinary & Ionian,
the windswept sea-grass
bareness of the place
tombs of sovereign dominion

lean down to green Columba
(San Franciscan)
his poverty of means
reverberating   simple soul euphoria

& an implicit recognition
of immeasurable flow
bread, wine   now
always   (indelible, human)

2.6.16

CHICORY MENOROTH

There were Goulds for 150 years
plowing granite outcrops
in New Hampshire. Topsfield
nurtured them, with jagged shears,

thick brambles, frozen lakes.
They strove in relative
obscurity – no live
broadcasts, no edited remakes.

Live Free or Die. The grumpy stoic
emits a little light,
no less – the *gift outright*
be given back (one life, unique).

An intuition of *soul liberty*,
that's all – that one might have
life in oneself, to serve
& swerve again (Boethian quiddity);

that conscience might arise like spring
in blustery New England –
a crocus prancing gold
before snow melts; your being

perfect, in a sense (meek master
of your own ramshackle
chicken-yard, O Jacqueline).
You glimpse them off the highway – chicory

menoroth, maybe – glimmering
remote star-woodcuts,
lamps over lonely fields...
just rightness in your bones (beaming).

2.8.16

DEAD RECKONING

In the clear winter light, the bright life
swings through memory
like steady Mississippi
viewed from a bridge. *My wife,*

whispers a tottery unknown Schweik,
hugging his beloved
flak-jacket (bullet-
holes & all) – *Maya Jhenna,* that Mike

mumbles to Neva (ghost of a *muzhik-*
moosh)... my shining
inkling, engravening wing-
back turtledove... (nuncle be sick).

Awhile soul clap in jail, this bird
will penetrate the day –
a wormhole *P*-Jay,
serpentine (heart's own sail-shroud).

Like Raven, still criss-crowing
over Noah's bobble-head –
whose flinty beak's dead
reckoning will note the gorgeous

hillside, blooming afar, over the sea –
so that prophetic castaway
(Hobo-*Jonah*) will play
black Orpheus to *Coulombe*-Bee;

a missive from Petropolis
(long-axled hasp)
plumbs Negrepontis –
limns Clio's last golden gasp.

2.9.16

VERMILION FLEM

Late afternoon. Light sound
of soprano bell, from bass
drone of freight train
over river-bridge. Nothing profound

(just slightly wistful). A poet keeps
time. In the ear's recess,
faint heartbeat-stress
marks passage of the sheep

over the dream-track. Nothing more
nor less. Down N'Orleans way
the Indians are gay
tonight, beaded with coronation *Flor*

del Rio del Espiritu Santo. Amen
& hallelujah, *hey-*
ey-yo. Let us pray
for the grain of wheat, the salty bran

of liberation (touch of soul,
Touchstone). So dance
your way into the trance,
Hal Marie! & remember, all –

tomorrow's Lent (already). The square
of ash upon your brow
a sailor's salty vow
to *steady as she goes* (fair,

kind & true). His hand waves from
the deep – he's called *Acorn*.
He wears an English crown
of oakleaf (he's Vermilion Flem).

2.9.16

FLINTY SEAL

The little height of land, pasture
behind the slough, Heidi,
in Mendelssohn – where we
hunted fireflies together

as on a giant turtle's back
in the dark – like sparks
or bees on a gloomride
puppy stars under the black

sky – sidling, sidereal
in sympathy, friendly
affinity, & simply
love (centripetal

North Star). Vladimir's *Mnemosyne*
within the hazel wood
only pure good –
Time the shady tall ash tree

that leaves its paw-print on your brow
today. A miniature
meteor, or sepulchre
in microcosm, negative snow-

flake, flinty seal of Solomon;
emblematic passion-
flower, heart's icon,
salt for a matrix-flame... O Queen

of the South, nightingale's
bridegroom, at peak of
deep star-well – Love's
rose-nest (crowning pregnant sails).

2.10.16

BRIGHT PENNY

J was for Juniper (*Maia genus,*
Jenna) – an ordinary
quiet little tree –
you find them everywhere in Rus,

U.S. One of the cedar family –
of which great masts are made
in Massa Maritima, she said;
& note the canoe, so beautifully

wrought, that graces this garage
full of rusted implements,
old iron junk (ribs,
tubes, gunnels, *disjecta,* garbage)...

– no, don't kiss me now, it's almost
Valentine's. Here's a letter
in the litter, from your brother
in Minneapolis (him & his boats!) –

expatiating on that Inland Ocean
stretching from Superior's
index, through Mississippi
dells & vales (his new obsession)

leaving these microscopic spirals
...in the pervasive buttery
limestone underbelly
of the land... seashells, fan-whorls;

epitomized in one moist flesh-toned
stony nave & spire
(near 34th & 34).
Meek modern well-proportioned

masterpiece, harmonic matrix
of father & son (elegant
Eero, eerie *Eliel*) – bent
Saarinen ark, soaring to Beatrix

rondure... *O navigators*! Inching
over gravity waves,
black holes, ripe graves
of wombified Vikings... cinching

one planet with your splintery
kaleidoscopes (wind-
buffeted facets of land
& sea) under *Dancing Bear,* Polaris!

I would scratch my cartoon of your fellowship
with the circumference

*

of an almond salience –
one bright Penny's (legal, tender) *skip*.

A dove circles the Bay there, *Columbia* –
where the beats gather
spliced to twine pillar,
shrouds & safety nets of a still *Finlandia* –

wheeling wings, massed between sea
& cedar palisades,
Pacific rock parades
& sigh of spray... enveloping, visionary

finish at the prow of fiery
sunsets! & I recall
the rudder of it all –
kind *capitan* of Little Rhody,

prophet of *soul liberty* –
gold *Independent Man*
atop the mobile span
of Providence – abeam with charity!

Wrapped in cloud, the binding peaks
wink now with *S.O.S.*
Laurentian Divide is
where the waters separate – soul seeks

her Earth, commensurate with hope
– justice of *Manitou*
sluicing like rain (for you
& me) across wide prairie slope

to live-oak bottomland. My faint
hen-scratch... mere filament
to trace the lineament
of *Kalevala*-coracle – St.

Mary's fishing-boat, or Paul's
(vain little man, whose plan
would hook Leviathan) –
one rosy ark, riding the squalls

where refugees huddle for warmth & light.
O womb abrim with life,
grail-casket, *Raven-knife* –
matrix of River's coppery might –

lift up your little pine apex!
Crown my origami fleet
with fir-green fin – beat
time with silver oar (moon reflex).

2.11.16

BOOK

VI

SEA WASH

To turn your glance back, eastward, from
the height of a great orange
pier (*Home on the Range*
in your ear) – immense Pacific foaming

behind you... like a lookout in a crow's-
nest – a single burning glass,
a golden eagle-eyepiece
taking in a continent. Up to Rose

Island Lighthouse (Narragansett Bay) –
to the byzantine capitol dome
in Providence, whose gnomon
is a gold harpooner – looking away

back west, toward you. Photoshot (still).
As when the sun stops briefly
over Jericho, before they
blow the trumpets, & the walls fall;

as if you stood before a Peto
still-life (intricate
& accurate memento
of complete stigmata-scrimshaw hero).

I hear another sea wash, sighing
round salt emerald shores.
Columba's Iona (wars
far off, now) laved with dying kings'

repentance-prayers (touch of blessing
for the wounded flutes
of clay). So lift your lute,
sad Frisco boy. She's leeward (glistening).

2.12.16

ANOTHER CLOUD

Hunchback Richard & the Hunkpapas
were driven off the earth
in hails of lead; their leather
shirts splayed in the newspapers

like ragged flags of slander (flapped
by harrying wind into
nonentity). The men who
cornered them were full of sap –

Miles, Sherman – clinking heroes
for a swell new nation;
never had a notion
of the Lakota they drowned in woe.

The Great Spirit will judge, muttered
Red Cloud. *Old Manitou*
your deeds shall deal to you.
The Rosebud mission doors are shuttered

now. Over Washington monuments
another cloud congeals,
rubidium-fierce. Sky-seals
are torn – rage flows in torrents

through slick marble halls, bears down
skewed scales with partisan
self-servicing, crude
greed, the yap of infinite Mammon –

armored in barking thunder-tread
of heavy weaponry
(gunfire from Albany
to Bernardino – many children dead).

2.16.16

UNBROKEN SMILE

If I murmur a little in your direction,
little almond tree, *lessel*
mandel baum, it's only
because you're a little evergreen

in my heart – still leaving, leaving
from the great ash mast
where you still last, & last...
as if lashed to a breathing & grieving

breeze. Maxims, beatitudes
sing through its rigging
(cicada-susurrus, pinging
from Maximus, Boethius)...

its compass just a simple carpenter's
level's bubble-eye –
a kayak reciprocity-
needle, trained on bent meteor's

immaculate arc (unbroken smile
from sky to Ojibwa midway
way). Immense gravity
waves emanate from a small gray pebble,

tossed off the stern like a Jonah-
pigeon, never to return –
Raven or Betyl-stone
(anchor sunk to seabed zone).

A pyramid of limestone glyphs
guards fair mum-tomb;
your skipper's Sophie-doom
from living lips... (forever flips).

2.17.16

SUNDAY PALM

The muted still-gray river
slides past cottonwoods
& snow, makes hay towards
New Orleans. Fevered *février* –

saison de décision. Party
of the partisans puts up
game faces – trumpets
bray wide, nosing opportunity –

battle flags ahoist, strong words
spray sound (Spartan array).
She moseys on her way,
accompanied by big black birds.

My soul, you tap your Sunday palm.
Must carve down, serpentine,
through plated clay – shed skin
to utmost bone. A Lenten hymn –

let it all go. Beneath gray stone
lies diamond – the fiery
akme of the maker,
kamen of Cape Horn (cross-thorn).

The *Rio* flows toward the Gulf
into the center of the earth.
Where molten rock gives birth
to metamorphs of sheep & wolf –

of black & white, of red & gold.
This alchemy's a *Union*
sparked before the sun –
along still waters (as of old).

2.18.16

SPIDER-THREAD

Late winter gloom. I'm stepping down
an ice-path to the river
like an Incan on his sliver
of Andean terrace (steep, frozen).

Downstream, the dark-eyed Jessie O.
(steamboat captain's daughter,
great-grandmother)
was just a child, coming up from below

St. Louis... *O Jessie Ophelia...*
Cleopatra Desdemona...
Solominka, Marina...
frescoed on a ceiling in *Verona-*

by-Neva, maybe (in a dream).
& I, only mere boy,
half-yearn... imaginary
Longfellow, flaking off the stream...

Your dark water-crossroads, Pawnee-
Hecate. Whirlpool
of Eurydice. School
of Dante's cinder-journey. Three

ways, all phosphoric (thundering
falls). Only to find
that light Diana-mind
Justinian burrowed, for his high welding –

only the lightest spider-thread
from Colchis dawn will do.
For Juliet. You too,
my child, may skip the tightrope-tread.

2.19.16

LITTLE MOTH

Jesus likely would not recognize
what we have made of him –
exemplar (in rite & hymn)
of royal prehistoric Zeus

or Pharaoh-gilded rain. Human
mind climbs out of beast.
Not long ago, the feast
was drunken heads – *the scar remain.*

The ink dries on a twisted pattern.
Tyrant's father-hamlet,
laden sack – fried omelet-
omen (under midnight sun).

A raven zigzags over Noah's
bow (yew, cypress,
acacia). Her nest
will not be found on land, *selah.*

Someone, singing a see-saw
in Galilee. Sea-
shanty (*shanti, shanti*)
maybe. Malcolm? Simone? Naw...

maybe. Light metamorphosis
the order of the day.
Pines, tamarack (way
back beyond Ravenna, Beatrice)...

A little moth molts molten gold
out of black stone,
southwest (of high Zion).
Wings ray to *Nazir* tinder... (fold).

2.19.16

SHADOW-WELL

George Washington was born today;
Sophie Scholl was killed
as well. Her cup was spilled
in order to brim up the bloody

mystery of iniquity that is
our history – an epic-
georgic bio-pic
or tragicomedy (blind *Theseus*

meets *Ariadne* in a maze
of corn – assumes she's
golden *Taurida...* FINIS).
Wings waft into a purple haze.

The moon belongs to everyone.
She set this morning through
a window shade (pale blue
the air, drawn up from Galilean

shadow-well). This labyrinth
contains a *Minotaur*
indeed – his name your
own. The light is very thin

within retaining walls of iron
chicken-wire (chain link);
quincunctial conjunction
for plowman (*Sir Thos. Browne*).

Wisdom B. Justified (in all
her children). *Madre* moon
sheds rain upon human
travail... silvers the plow (*selah*).

2.22.16

MORSE CODE

Once, one limpid winter morning,
at the little white shoebox
with Russian Orthodox
sky-blue-gold Cyrillic writing

trellising the doorway, I noticed
a young man cross himself
climbing its wooden steps
& pass alone into its lamplit

depths. The anthill maze of time
& history is echoed
in the heart's Morse code –
labyrinthine motherlode (of crime

& punishment, betrayal &
remorse); stone battlements
& iron tongues foment
confusion in the stricken mind;

the hungry roar would hush forever
every low flute-sound
of doves (tremulous under-
side of olive leaves, their silver

ripplings). & yet a lightfoot ghost
still paces pine barrens
past tombs of emperors
& saints... his testament recast

the chaos into complex rings
of plenitude, redemption,
commonweal – knotation
of crosstreads (eternal things).

2.23.16

CLAY PERSEPHONE

The fresh air by the Mississippi
that glides to St. Louis
from here – muddy promise
of snowmelt, my clay Persephone.

Among the people that you meet
– around a picnic table
in Duluth, or at that fabled
native board, beside the seat

of Massasoit (near Plymouth Rock) –
one person hovers at
your back, discovers what
you need before you ask (more bock,

mayhap). Like plucky Jeanne d'Arc
– or her twin brother, Tom
o'Hawk – she flies from drum
to flask like Nessie shatters dark

Loch Ness, *grise foudre* scorching east
to west. She's Omnipresence
in *pauvre* disguise – Franciscan
ass with horsepower (a Falcon-Beast).

Stepping forth into canoe
from granite lintel, W.
looks out toward you,
Eurydice de San Francisco –

straight through steely Gateway Arch
midway from sea to sea.
Notes your grave levity
melds plenitude – lark tuning larch.

2.24.16

FINGER-DAB

These sibylline papyrus leaves,
so many shades of raven-
ink, scribe-feathered Ocean
etched with moony mesmer-waves...

The earth's a musty limestone book
Psyche a palimpsest
charting gilt-emerald quest
through eerie *oreille* (slant rook

to woody isle, *Macbête*) – a flickering
archaic *pain-matière*
or wedding ring-structure
spring Geraldine Fitzgerald flung

for blue-eyed boys & one grey heir.
The old man frets in dust
& stone; his ferryman
(*Rouget Blackstone*) fins through the air

from northern Iowa to Eire;
the turtledove they seek
has grown so pigeon-meek
her flutings barely skim the lyre-

string. Once in Calabria
flint-hermit Joachim
pictured a raptor-flame
plummet through time (*vera-*

mente Kiev-pointing). Gentle
Columbia, please ravel up
my rusty finger-dab...
lips' labyrinth, rose-granite mantle.

2.25.16

BOAT-MAID

Primeval spring, at the center of the forest
at the source of headwaters
where mothers find daughters
& fathers, sons... your robin's nest

I sleepwalk toward, beneath half-notes
of chickadee, shrill keening
wail of cardinal, seeking
Persephone (between ice-flotes).

Psyche, Ophelia, Juliet...
your muttered hobo-names
for fishing lures. These games
of avocation... drowsing yet

below Cahokia, the Kore fields
of poppies (Orleansville
or Alexandria)... Île-
de-France... Ariadne's golden wheels...

Old Guillaume with his mummy-crown
smokes goldenrod & wine
beside the snoring Rhine.
Hobo might catch a Jonah-fish, or one

might swallow him (it's all the same)
pining beside the brook
of Lethe... – say there, look
anew, McDuff! Her ancient name

is Cora – she's a round boat-maid
of cedar (juniper);
her berries are pure
blue, honey – she's evergreen (almond).

2.26.16

FRAIL SKY

The sheep in the mosaic, in Ravenna.
Ravens in the scroll,
in the temple (*Emanu-el,*
off Morris Ave). & in Siena,

Lady Pax, lolling like Jenna
on the couch, beside
Justitia. Wide
open, now, your Burchfield *scena* –

wind, grassland, heartache.
What brung them blues, O shy
bird bro? *Frail sky*
disintegrates in Birdy's eye, beak

cradling bright penguin soot of Man.
Handing his crozier
gently to its heir
a sheepish *Father Also-Ran*

smiles, mild as any lambkin
Pontifox. Herder-
gypsies circle ferder
into desert places. *Julius Putin*

frescoes chimp dominion, over
stalag mites hiked to hell –
old human story (well,
there goes the antelope). *Clover*

for meadows, cottonwood for bison...
Amaranth? – or pick
your poison, Hobo Dick.
I'm rippling a *dreamsonge* Union.

2.29.16

PRIMITIVE FRESCO

These cottonwood sentinels beside the river
in the early March sunlight.
May their *sense of being right*
prevail, Persephone return (forever).

My draft of yearning whispers from
bare cave. Slight air
of seashore lingers there,
like early dream of motherland. Home

in a memory of pinewoods, tamarack;
Ravenna in a film
of moss-green idiom –
child-realm of Umbrian yak-yak,

Firenze burble-babble. One gold hinge
arcs sheltering lintel
over intelligible
gate of Jubilee... *& it is so arranged*

we never leave the shining ring.
Like a rock of Magdala
muttering *ephphatha*
our bread & wine are splashed with brine,

salted with everlastingness;
my primitive fresco
roughly points to show
how everything begins to bless –

when *Psyche* lifts from waterfall
& *Raven* (with a flick
of wing) is suddenly quick
Turtledove (threshold within us all).

3.2.16

MINOR TEAR

Bleak winter shades... crows in the trees
beak-gnashing, rasping (*caw-*
caw, hawk-hawk). Low
Earth, rotund *silentium* (dregs, lees).

Stillness of still-life – *Brown Decades*
(hoist Peto). The Just Man
imago is just a man –
barely there, through simple glades

of green. Mirror Lakes liked him,
in Mendelssohn. Only
an infinitely gently-shivery
Rabbi, Hiawatha Honeybear – bro Jim,

our lunky *logos* (penny-loafing).
Who bears it all, past
He- or She-Cat's paste-
up Geryon-masque (a scary nothing).

This maze contains a minor tear.
& through a crevice there
one Ariadne hair
leads you to almond-gold rain-bear.

Earth seethes with ziggurats of fraud
& blind men lash themselves
to violence (*selva*
oscura mitts gorilla code);

but it shall not be so with thee.
Bunny hikes one eye
& looks for wheeling Eli
to come by (benevolent memory).

3.3.16

HIAWATHA DRUM

Old Man Winter with his iron face
is softly melting away.
Soon children will play
in thick mud – clay innocence

& grace rotating, to their source.
The crocuses will climb
into focus, rhyme
purple & gold in petal-vortices;

the tenderness of early things
reminding Thunderbear
that cubs are everywhere
ursine with gratitude, in tumble-rings

of infant glee. Even Ape-Man
has his chance again –
to ravel his last frozen
wrath-dominion in a wreath of cyclamen

& sing the forest into equilibrium
(chaste harmony). Such was
the impulse in the fuse
that lit the fugue – this planetarium

of lambs, this baby shark kingdom;
in prehistoric hamlets
man's relentlessness relents,
somehow. Small Hiawatha drum

or miniature feathered bow
drawn to warm sundial
of Bunny Rabbi smile...
her furry heart (spring-marrow).

3.8.16

TRACERY

They leave a track across time,
the sea-salt souls – faint
& delicate as painted
tracery of April birch-limb

shoots under a pale blue sky;
massive as meteoric
stone flung from the thick
of heaven (dark as a raven eye).

Unreadable *profundum* – yet
a trace of what they loved
remains (as in an alcove
names are tapped in cloudy granite

for a terse echo of foregone delight).
Then centripetal gravity
sheds all formality
& mutters from the depth of night

the soul's original, L-mast
uprightness – earliness;
birchland of quietness,
in boreal Aurora dressed.

Blackstone & Williams, Edward Coke...
such men of merciful Law
& lawful Mercy... & I saw
the matrix of your Liberty – who spoke

with spokes of fire upon her brow.
Psyche, Persephone...
Cana, in Galilee...
primeval Spring, welling forever now.

3.9.16

PLAYGROUND SWING

When Joachim Fiore, hermit-monk
hidden in heel of Italy,
after many a fasting-day
frescoed his Fauve *raptor-hawk*

like a rainbow-feathered calumet
smoking the end of aeons...
When the dust returns
from whence it came (Osiris sunset-

raft, veering to purple bull's-eye)
& bones of bearberry
revert to green hay
& Alma the Corn Maid heaves a sigh

for Land o'Lakes (their vanishing,
twinkling, hexagonal
bye-bye)... then shall we all
rise too, in a Sabbath playground swing

of the Pleiades – & wheel with Mama
Ursa Major, in a New
World Symphony (*Ojibwa*
Lullaby, scribbled on your way

from Minnehaha, Anthony). Because
the whole in the silver bucket
is a river-song (Pawtuxet,
maybe) sweeter than ever was –

is your redemption-hymn, O Solomon.
Sheba the Buffalo Lady
knows it, as does Maggie
Galilee... *The Eagle from the Oven-Sun.*

3.10.16

ONE PINE

I walked down little Dante Street
on Federal Hill (past
the *Venetian Blind King*)
like Eddy Puss, so indiscreet –

playing *Pin the Tail on the Donkey* (me)
or *Cut the Bull, Man* (Tagliabue)
threading a skinny mosey-
prance round metropole, while Ariadne

knotted sunny fleece on Wickenden
(a fateful bumblebee).
A planet's vast & stately
sarabande encompasses all men

& women in the clock-sweep of one
spare hand – like Marsden
Hartley's Dave Jones
locket for H.C. (counting down

to 33 sea-bells) or the swing
of Jasper Johns' yardarm,
marking the twain – all harm
depicted now (a Queequeg thing).

The Son of Man goes as determined
(Berryman teetering on the bridge)
but to him who breaks a pledge
of trust... the way is subterranean

& very long. Multifarious Gaia's
an echo-nautilus – all's
been tolled before. Yet one tall
pine still smiles, Boaz – hers, yours.

3.11.16

APPLE PIE

Hobo drowses in his Einstein field
of asphodel, spooky distances.
Life's tender differences...
only mauve peonies on copper shield.

Irrational yearning for the earth
might be the shortest path
to Providence. Wrath
of History's a concave labyrinth –

your soul must wash a dusty planet
down *Big Muddy*, Hobo.
Rise from your bed of woe;
our Hero beckons from his granite

lintel toward the circling sun.
Path P (transcendental
for each chaste equal
guest of compassing compassion).

The one who went to live with Indians.
Blackstone, Yellow Sweeting
apple-man – his greeting
(like sweet Williams' own) a *Both-Hands*

Welcome, Minnehaha flute –
ray of *soul liberty*,
loop of Easter Rabbi...
Hart, Malcolm, Giulietta's route

bent (parallactic) toward the light.
A catenary smile
or *Life-Saver* will
thread sad grooves into a chariot.

3.14.16

WRY PLANET

The caw of a solitary crow
tracks its own echo straight
through the sonic vanishing point.
Past fanfare of the here & now

through a pinhole in the iris of Osiris
or some other shadow
Everyking from long ago.
Some *Isis Peirce-the-Veil, or Most*

High Elephant from Nile-source
cradling Victoria
for *Homo Sap* (Erecta) –
kindly Melchizedek, primeval Spouse

offering his star-crossed bread & wine
beneath *Polaris* &
the *Twin Cup-Bears*
to lift each soul into his milky Sign.

I hear the rasping of an iron swing.
C-row... *chi-rho... Behold –*
a shepherd in his fold
of 99 lambkins! The last king

looks out from bairn-cupola, a crown
of stars. A gardener
in the graveyard. Mary's
pal, incognito (*Son of Man*).

A retina, streaked with a spectacle
of tears. Psychopomp
beyond Caesar's last trump.
Ocean-continuum... wry planet oracle.

3.15.16

SPRING-STEP

Sunlight glints in flash-of-gold
on blue-gray lashes, curling
sea around each green-
black pupil glancing from cold

Pontus-depths, like lacquered pearl.
Each soul hath such a wild
wee isle – immurèd child
of even-star, whose raven whorl

beams out of *everwhirr* – bright
innocent prinkster, fleet-
footing the complete
spring-step, so shamrock-intricate;

Tara, Soissons, Iona know
how low she twirls, she droops
before her leaping swoops
a coign... *Elijah – let her go*!

Light-nimble Columba... thundery-
coot'red Geraldine... – *fits*
Geraldine, the crown fits
Geraldine! In a wheel of clay

through the eye of time – in a ray
of light, through a feather-
full of waterfalls... *there,*
there! *Look there*! A catenary

clover-span! Four-folded spire,
planted on copper penny-
whistle... one milky-
black Eire-eye rose Paycock-fire!

3.17.16

FLIP SIDE

A silver tattoo at Arlington.
Trumpets (not too far
from Lincoln Memorial).
Apollinaire too (*trompette marine*).

The sacred scar, like a double ewe.
Like lambs to the slaughter
in the last Great War;
vraiment partout (rosemary, rue).

This is our Earth, on copper shield
(*e pluribus unum*). The rain
come spring. Pine scent. Plain
agony (*les jeux sont faits*). Bruise-field.

A raven pivots at the matrix.
Lincoln Center (Ferrara
fall). Fellini mandala
in clown outfit (old Ariosto tricks).

The sovereignty of Providence
is *agape* – beyond
our means, beyond our ken.
The flip side of gilt sentience

is moonlight, filtered through a sunlit
salience. A raven shadow
over Po, it flickers now
like gold in Chartres *coign* – a flit

across a cave crevasse (bat
rite, sinuous scar).
Liberty, in tar
(graffiti). *Morning Star* (Fiat).

3.19.16

BLUE MARBLE

The lattice-work of Ariadne,
barely (in my crepuscular
History Theatre) there.
The river flows on, over yonder –

Eridanos, Mississippi, Po –
moving past this osier
excellence of rare
dear Dr. Wise. Minerva, Virgo?

Beatrice, Julie Littletree...
Maggie... Miriam
of Bethany, or Bethlehem...
limpid over hopscotch Sally

gallivanting crost her vaulting
Paradise of glimmering
frater Pantocrator (wing,
knave, to that sheepfold ceiling).

Meanwhile my double creeps along
like Ezra the Venetian
Blind, touching the stolen
Rimini passage with an aching

brow; beyond his haunts by the canal
& sibylline bone-staves
Franciscans hid in caves,
a living shepherd leaps the wall

(disguised by Ariadne's woof).
These corridors are spongy
depths. So take the plunge –
blue marble veins Vitale's roof.

3.22.16

LAST CALUMET

The Big Sky we all inherited
glows in the subway light.
Glimpsed through the *Reflector-*
Net (right thro' the Western Gate).

Like rays focused on a beam
in Apollinaire's eye,
mass merged in energy
enough to die – you joined the stream

of unknown soldiers (Harry Poilu,
Joe Middleman) fusing
with bronze sea-gong
(tall, serpentine). It boomed for you.

A copper coin, at the bottom of a well
with Choctaw profile, Roman
grin. The cube of Everyman
only squint of salt – a dry seashell.

Roger the Seeker seeks his soul
in that upper air (a wind
so free). Love pinned
him to the still-life door – oak bole

of union, preternatural;
a *chrysos*-oil in old
dry woods (cold
boughs, so late-imperial).

Gold thread, gold hair. Apollinaire
smokes his last *Calumet*.
Salt breeze, dockyard, fishnet.
Doves in grey clouds disappear.

3.23.16

SOLOMON'S SEAL

Morning sunlight on the riverbank.
Old bridge in the background.
Hubbub of human sound
gone quiet here – some time to think.

The ranks of cottonwoods draw shapes
in four dimensions – homesick
willows by Euphrates,
brooding vaults of shady Chartres,

cloisters clad with marigolds
on orange heights (Monte
Cassino) – where they
summon up papyrus scrolls

like hopeful honeybees, reviving
scribble-cribs in royal reels
of pearly Solomon's seal –
fern, aloe, acacia... (ever-living

green confetti, for Easter Rabbi).
I pace these precincts with
a vagrant slouch, as if
I'd missed the point. & then I see

you! – bright invincible
companion – always there
in your cloud-rocking chair
at *End of Time*, & trouble –

familiar storyteller, Indian Guide
whose hearth blazes from Southern
Cross to blue Vermilion – within
Love's angled arc (smile-wide).

3.25.16

LOVE'S KEY

The heavy water of Ezra Pound
subsuming the human tale
to his querulous high-pitch creel,
transmuted suddenly into profound

perilous melody. The charismatic
author, shaken by acidic
lye. Rattled to quick
bones – John Berryman at sick

bay (*delirium tremendum*, guy)
shriven to the marrow.
The prof who would harrow
Hell must round up his own high

insolence. But personality,
like poetry, is excess
on the *History Express* –
a bit gratuitous (to a degree);

won't fold logically into place
aboard the freight car
of any village explainer.
She's obstinate. You're a disgrace.

Whence cometh all authority?
Thrones crumble, powers
tremble – the hour's
getting late. Some mild futurity

yodels an octave through a vise...
the bird's a turtledove.
Love's key to the sky-trove –
exalting the low, humbling the wise.

3.28.16

ROGER WILLIAMS

Eternity, O Eternity! That is our business.

Evocative river, measuring
my time. If I follow
upstream, to the shallow
infant burble of your beginning

– that rush of spring across bright
limestone, agate, flint –
I might catch a glint
of prism-diamond, rainbow sunlight

out of the meteor from whence
we flew. I studied *greatness*
as a bookworm boy; was
wowed by those Prince Valiants

& Teddy Heroes who prevail
(magnanimous & brave)
in moldy Grendel-cave
& gory field (at bookshelf scale);

but not until childhood had passed
did someone jump from stone
canoe, whose doings shone
so implicate with goodness (massed

coordinate with commonweal)
as to rekindle in my mind
each uncreated end
within this flow, earthbound & actual –

as in an icon of the central soul.
Heart-pivot of earth-
planet – integral hearth –
blazing spark in a great oak-bole

*

of clay spheres darting from the fiery
kiln (original
Joie, ineffable).
Star of perfection (seal of history).

Heroes in graven books (sustained
by hungry scrivener-ravens).
Yet the remotest heaven's
slope will be surveyed, garnered, gleaned

by unknown *compadres* (anonymous,
unheralded). Servants
beyond themselves – tense
strings, bowed into major chords.

Two things of opposite nature seem
to depend on one another...
the bond of troth, of lover
& belov'd. Roger's granite door-beam

on the hillside sinks back into dusky
Rhodus billows. Nigh
the steadfast stream, two shy
ephebes lay out a picnic blanky;

an early butterfly, black-gold,
skims toward the shore.
You have hearkened to lore
of skalds who came before – old

poets' conversation, overheard;
now the river moves
in your own heart – Love's
glittering pulse, encouraging word.

3.29.16

FOUR PINES

To imitate Francis, or Guillem d'Orange;
not to turn from the world,
but my own greedy churl
to whom the world panders (strange

profit in dust). In the sweet flame
of yearning day-lilies,
to glimpse a dew-sprung rose
labyrinth... Love's beckoning game.

Transfiguration of a maze of sighs –
of Giuliana's longing,
Henry Cat's sad reckoning...
all those winding trails of Psyche,

Ariadne's ingle eye. The far Gate
shimmers there, in Frisco Bay;
an M, as of a catenary
smile suspended, doubles you (checkmate);

your azure horizon draws its line
between twin vanishing points,
like pillars of four pines
feathered to a target (mine).

The wellspring of the soul is as
a lodestone (from beyond
the Milky Way). Fond
depths of *Holy-Land – Eureka*-adze

or axis of the earth. Bee-mouth,
hinge of honey-door
where uncreated light pours
through... sunbeam, raying north & south.

3.30.16

SPRINGLIGHT

i.m. Jim Harrison

April by the ancient river.
The old bones of the king
remember everything
that he forgot – his yellowed quiver

like a scrollful of desire, old goat,
old Harry son of Harry,
with his dogs, with his '44,
a massif in a cave, disconsolate –

world like a bungled maze, a hive
of killer bees, in a hole
in the ground. *Old King Cole*
with his pipe & his bowl, still alive

somehow. A dust-mote labyrinth
horned by his own shade.
I met a straw-blonde maid
of Provençal, spruce terebinth

from Marseille, or Toulouse – name's
Quitterie – *who kissed*
me sweetly, once
outside St. Martin-in-the-Fields...

*

Turn again, O Man, *from thy insect*
wickedness... a dust-storm
swarms the bristlecone
pine, high in her cold dry cleft,

still evergreen. Through yon spiderweb
of desperate cities
one clear flute-breeze
intones a major melody (*B-*

flat) – frail threads transmogrified
like griffin-chords into
transparent unison – blue
octave through twin pillars (pied,

squared). It was an iteration
out of alienation, empty
heart of vanity –
whose nothingness nested creation.

*

Long ago *el Rio del Espiritu Santo*
rolled, a mighty glacier-
torrent, out of here –
before your *dream-songe* Manitou

brought you to tent among these timbers,
People. April was Earth
before a human birth
lent gentleness & poison (*hers,*

yours, mine). I found a moss-green coin
locked in a cedar fork,
swept past the flooded park
into this punted limb. *Begin the Beguine,*

spun the vapid strings... the *War to End*
All Wars is ended. An old
king crawls from the blistered
bole (emptied orphanman, around

the bend) – shines in the springlight
like a babe newborn.
Roland honks his horn;
Guillaume unwraps his gauze (a *Calumet*).

4.1.16

PSYCHE-GLOW

i.m. MLK

That other Henry, in seclusion
(District of Columbia).
Mourning Eurydice
veiled, so – Isis in stone.

The chaos of the dynamo,
the violence of men
(Mont St.-Michel)... sun
clouded by confusion. Apollo

camouflaged as Hobo now
flickering cigarettes
into the Seine – alights
in Memphis, on a garbage scow.

Columbia, Columbia, murmurs
the mourning dove, *come back*.
Gray sketch in black
& white, along the watchtower.

One ghost dance treads this lambent maze
draws wool into a knot
or chord of charity.
Her milky Manitou is wise.

The profane land, amnesiac
is lifted into tune
by memory of one
who went before – his trouble on his back

your trouble too. A Psyche-glow
to orient the west
toward east, the past
into a future peace – heart's overflow.

4.4.16

MOSAIC SHEPHERD

The knot in the heart is a universal
wedding ring, wherever
you are. Heavier
than iron, *ce diamant mondial*

de l'amande. Bright orange lozenge-
mandorla, shedding leaves
of tears – vicarious
miniature trees (strange

fruit). Like the shady crossroads
with the *Dead End* sign –
a little Chinese lantern
(*glass by LaFarge*). Six nodes

in one honeycomb eye – melodious
riddle of light & shade.
Henry & John, a cannonade
off Sydney Harbor... looming *ficus*

guarding Southern Cross. They sought
a figure for relief –
hoopoe... cloverleaf...
barely-veiled grief. Stray mote

of dark December. Henry looks up
through rose window.
A rim around the *chi-rho,*
hint of shining salt. Red stop

sign on the dynamo, outlined
in cedar-glow (*Mosaic
Shepherd Stands in Lake*).
What the heart seek she shall find.

4.5.16

GRAY PAINT

The vast Flemish panorama
coheres in a raven's eye.
Through haunted oaks, high
wind tosses bugle-calls (*taran*

tara). Bruegel's gray paint congeals
on the perimeter
of the sea... Demeter
wanders like a Walloon reels

caterwauling, *Persephone*!
In Flanders grass, poppy-
purpura (like the sea
around a stubby *Orizaba*) –

only the poem is humble
enough to bear the yoke
of a *poshlost* rude joke.
She won't let you stumble,

Psyche, in your edgy sundance.
That quatrefoil in the blue
mortuary was for you,
poilu (Apollinaire) – *entrance*

to complete volume of sibylline
Mnemosyne. Pine
tree pantomime... a line
of sketchy aquamarine (*shan shui*).

A jasper circumference defines
our Atlantean task,
to reconcile each mask
of pathos (in a matrix of threadlines).

4.8.16

INFANT BROW

At the crossroads, the just man suffers
just for being just –
Job, or Boethius,
or Jesus – carrying a load for others.

Dante whispers in Ravenna dusk
near his exile's end.
Beatrice, penned
in a rose window, sets his task –

to sing the icon that he sees
breathing through granite
as turtledoves through light
gray feathers tune the breeze.

Stillness in time. Iron history
crowns an infant brow...
the *Son of Man,* now
turning evergreen (in Maggie's

almond eye). The desolations
of a nightmare fade
when that rusty parade
sinks into brown decades (stations

on the prairie). Mary Morning Star
signals her six ways
along Path P... *Praise*
Manitou & Manitou-Child, our

big-eared Bunny Rabbi – he
of the octave melody –
which we sang, Adonai,
before dawn, one Epiphany...

4.11.16

TWO CIRCLES

Down by the spring river, tossing sticks
in prehistoric Mizz,
my Jordan – little Isis-
canoes, or Ferrarese six-

wheelers; in my mind's darkroom
recalling you – Love's raven-
haired sybil (guardian
at the Rock's entrance). Your gloom

when my father's birthday wheeled around
each April. The yellow-gold
forsythia enfold
your mother's grave, who died... *O sound*

those flowery depths, Ophelia –
and rise again! He was
a good man – rays
of intellectual *Amor* blessed his day;

he might have walked her from that grave.
A little light only,
through *camera oscura...*
you know. You showed me her cave

in San Francisco's spare kitchen –
where a thin light-blade
infiltrates the Maid
so Piero's hypno-sarabande might spin

anew (red cedar, blue spruce, evergreen).
Rembrandt's *Self-Portrait with*
Two Circles... one light-heavy scythe
defines this wheel's circumference (unseen).

4.12.16

TRANSPARENT SPRING

This wheel's unseen circumference
includes a coffee can
from Hart – a Savarin,
no? – looping a salience

of tulip spires (languid, voluptuous,
orange). *For* Hart, Johns
sounded gray Ocean
& signaled with a palm Love's

one transparent spring (from deep
to deep). A little tree –
lemon? – mustard, maybe;
the orange flourish of a steep

green trumpet, embracing its iron
lattice like a bride
in May... no one can hide
from Love's almond dominion.

This doctrine bides each alteration.
A sigh amid these wheels
rides wingèd heels
from scythe to seedy germination –

Time's origin (space-flowering).
Leaf-whispers from a pair
of olive trees, who share
one catenary pattern... stirring

life-draft, dangled from twin pillars,
lifted toward Pacific
azure – scarred, terrific
sentinels of hope (*hers, yours*).

4.13.16

BREATHING SEA

Old Hobo glances back upstream
as the spring bluets form
an inland sea – a swarm
of peacock eyes (out of a dream-

song dome) across the autumn grass.
Retrospective. Phoebus
in an ochre crevasse,
Magdalenian cave-compass.

Your yearning for Eurydice,
so youthful-hungry, Henry –
out of want, not plenty –
ignorant (in your blind way).

An oscillation of the sun
and moon. The *Q. of Heaven*
looks out from her den,
mild lioness... dusky horizon.

Henry, by his veiled statue,
thinks on Beatrice
(pine-green eyes, sea-
grey). His melancholy's ocean-blue.

Jerusalem, Jerusalem! How
I would have gathered you...
the soul's an orphan zoo
without the smile of Manitou.

A little tree in Galilee
still rustles in the breeze
from a breathing sea. She's
calling you, sailor. *Be free.*

4.14.16

SIMPLE PROW

You see a cat stripe-shadowed
by the slats of a fence.
One of those incidents
from Mendelssohn, out of childhood

infinity... flicker of memory.
Today. Mid-April air
and sunlight. Barely there –
a plainness of weathered cedar, sea-

bells. Sea-salt. Far away
two splendor-pillars
mark the Gate of years
& gravity – *shine, wave goodbye...*

& on the blue horizon line
mother & father join
two hands (bright axle-sign
– a double-axe) under the sun.

Man & Woman, O (*M-W*)...
Come forth, my son,
my daughter, only one –
Time & Space unfold in You.

The mysterious heir of heaven
danced a masque before
Magdalen's cave-door –
mothering the grainy leaven,

heavy loom of Here & Now.
Under faded barn slats,
hidden in straw, the cat's
prowling a kingdom's simple prow.

4.15.16

DELTA QUEEN

The hobo-poem stumbles out of Itasca,
a somno-ambulant mutter
just west of Superior
like a Nile-canoe in Minnehaha

or *Thesée-en-Argo,* lost at sea
in a maze older than time.
A stone-barrow, or lime-
burnt spacetime spruce-vortex (little tree

Apollinaire chased down in Paris
listening to Stravinsky
on the 29th of May).
Distant thunder... blessed senseless

mote. *What acorn happiness*
coils beneath necrolithic
Moscow? What lithe
Pocahontas limns Potomac offices?

Lightning rives gnarled raven limbs.
One glint from gold iris
shakes the paralysis
from icebound Neva aisles – low hymns

drone from limestone fish-caverns;
there is no place on earth
where Psyche's sighing hearth
cannot ray lamplight (ask Jules Verne,

or Edgar Allan – ask St. Joan).
My *Delta Queen* glides on
toward perihelion
engulfing sorrow in her zephyr-zone.

4.18.16

RUSTIC HAY

Like a Prince Hal of the Iron Age,
surrounded by a full staff
of devices (every gaffe
in the book) Henry took a page

from *Stealing Drums in Trinidad*
as they slubbered through the murk
of a flood plain, like turkeys
in a hurricane. It was that bad.

Had to go, blind fool, from Addis Ababa
to Babylon – from Lake Tana
to Concrete Cavern (ah,
Bull-Dance of Hummy Blah-Blah!)

& recapitulate his fancy
infancy – in a shed
built of old dry blood
& scarecrow straw, with Nancy

the Cow & Her Yodeling Shepherds
making rustic hay.
He lived a year & a day
on all fours – eating grass, curds

& whey, locusts, honey, in a swamp
by the Jordan, in Judea...
It's all there, Maria –
in Miriam's mandorla (under the lamp).

Henry wandered thus through drowsy realm
plucking mandolin...
one silver star over dark green pine,
one *cirque* of gold at the Argo helm.

4.19.16

WOOLLY FLOCK

Soon the lilacs will be blooming
in West Branch, Iowa.
Old John Brown's hideaway
among earth Quakers (humming

his grave tune, without the guns).
There Harriet's railroad
tugged through Negus-made
tornado shelters – Grandma's cousins

too. I trace an equilibrium
through reams of loveletters
in turquoise blue (scatters
from Scattergood to end of time).

The clay looms closer on those farms.
Isis herself unveils
just past our Hoovervilles –
beckons with *Everlasting Arms*.

A refuge from the storm, where corn
& flowers grow. *Mild Shaidlock*
led a mighty woolly flock
from Ohio to Muscatine, in 1849

(they write); *his great-granddaughter Mary*
married Jack Ravlin, & thus
they came to Minneapolis...
they rest, remain. Spring memory.

The silence of unvarnished truth
glances from shepherd eyes.
Proud histories of lies
axed by one pine (standing on earth).

4.20.16

KIND FARE

Like a brown wren building a nest
with twine camouflage,
or a Joan in the Stone Age
on her inexplicable quest

to sketch the lineaments of splendor
(milky star-field in a barn
or Jason with a ball of yarn)
– how the sea calls Jonas under!

The booming surf his *Book of J*,
the figure on the prow
with heavy eyes... mild Io?
coaxing him to low brown clay

in gloom, beneath an ancient bridge...
where a rose may lie.
An olive shade skims by
overhead (a palm sweeps its edge).

Between bullhorns, he marks the twain.
Gaunt Maximus, in Colchis,
ancient of days (his
beard like a fleece of milky rain)

burbles an almond-scent breeze
he feels, not sees... melting
aria of everything,
snow-knot of spring (Persephone's).

Like high sea-gates in sunlight, in salt air...
feathers of jasper & bronze
filigree one true coin's
moss-green (Lincoln mite... kind fare).

4.21.16

COCOON-SHADE

We were scrambling through an endless cave,
Mark Trail & I, in the
cartoon – wait – uh...
that was a dream! Mind, now – behave!

There was an independent chap with spear
all gold, atop a globe-
sized turtleshell, adobe –
yodeling (with shimmering lyre)

Good Will I am Good Will...
There was a lowly, sketchy
mule, named *Eeyore,* following
his master, *Donkey Haute,* until

they reached the center of the earth
– a vernal *O,* encompassing
an *M,* a *W* (whelmelding
vertiblur upon a sunlit hearth

all rosorangled in Pacific dawn).
& then I felt wings purring
in my sleep... a chirring
flutter-by of monarch (milky-spun

cocoon-shade of the teeming soil);
a turtledove was crooning
too, for old George – leaning
on his scythe, worn with grave toil.

The axle of the earth, the axle...
muttered he – of rusty
us the icon, see.
Light waves from Chartres pinnacle.

4.22.16

SUNSET GATE

Spring, a project of the Earth.
While she waits for Homo Sapiens
to get over his aggressions –
revert to innocence (a Maypole mirth).

In the beginning... all the *begins*
of the Beguines... the big
innings. Whirligig
of river-prairie syncopations...

I went down into the Bottomland,
down to Monk's Mound.
A Mississippi sound,
a tuning fork of lightning (&

thunder). I looked into my hand
& felt a gentle eye
look back (*speaks Ioway*).
Fishnet... veil of mystery... grand

Isis-Life. Her cryptic tripod
out of Flanders fields
(a Jenna-quivering) yields
Triple-Flem – from Seeker linchpad

over Providence, through keystone
arc, westward... stray
crois (her sunset Gate) –
one orange firetread in the ozone,

warped on muddy waters (surging
to Lousanna). So
the shield of Buffalo-
Mandan feathers her circlet (corralling).

5.10.16

ALMOND ARK

They were farmers & shepherds in West Branch,
cartwrights & blacksmiths, laboring
through pain... the rusty ring
of iron clamps, the thick stench

of horse manure, the pigs & cows...
yet took their time for quiet
in the Meeting House – let
runaways abide, lambs browse.

Their silence lodged in protest against
violence itself –
the insolence of Guelf
& Ghibelline, the gangs, the hunts...

the iron dream of domination
locking the brain-cave
in its frozen grave
(creak-echo of damnation).

There was a spring in Tuscan hills,
coiled like a rusty serpent –
green with moss, bent
into turtleshell... old Williams'

spiral (out of Coke, Blackstone).
Mules' rustic rights
& supernatural delights
limp into leaves of a live-oak woman –

her heavy womb in the cave-shade
like a Negus by the Nile
hidden for a while...
almond ark of spring (oak-apple maid).

5.11.16

SEEDY OWL

Take this canoe : figure in space
afloat upon time.
Like a Venn diagram
of lapping overlappings, Falcon-Ace –

with the footprint of a sacrifice
like seal of royal doom
(where heavy lilacs bloom).
Beneath lilacs, by Lake of the Isles

I turn back down Memory Aisle...
see shades by willow leaves
in Providence. Gold sheaves
of lyres, in single evening file –

there's good gray Edwin, like
a giant beech – there's Voodoo
Queen of Arkansas (*Who-*
Who... her seedy owl's with Mike

now – harps in D.C. laurel branches)...
& Hobo Henry, leaning
back to earth (sing
resurrection, buried man) – launches

out on rolling *River of Dreams*
(with mazy crane dance
in a prairie trance).
E pluribus unum, Roger Williams...

muttering like young apple leaves
from a root in the grave,
out of lips keen to save.
One perfect notion... (so Hart believes).

5.12.16

GRAY THREAD

Out of gray matter of clouds & sea,
matter of Bran or of Bretagne,
slow combers of the brain
surface a fresh conception... see

your own shadow cast by sun
on flesh-tone limestone –
hear the whispering drone
in wave-beats from an unseen iron

spring. Echoing, *the king must die...*
as the palimpsest of legends
from which everything depends
layers the storm with its pearl panoply

in coats of gray... & the first murmur
of the galaxies is almost
silence... & the gray ghost
of Jonah wheels one palm-feather

through the circumference of Time...
& a slight gray thread
drawn from *Ocean* riverbed
dangles in a cat's-cradle (a smiling

rhyme) – emblem of unbreakable
immortal grasp of Love...
as one sea-breached dove
wings its immaculate cable

from far-flung *farfalla* world
to world (your only monarch).
O cedar-scented arc!
Almond *diamonde* – O salty pearl!

5.14.16

SUNSET ROOM

The cutthroat sun over Minneapolis
leaks light into many
dark corners. Rimini
in mind (a limpstone palimpsest

beneath shellfire). *Go & strike*
the tents, men – long way
to Tipperary. Say,
Francesca, if you can – how to make

things new. Peer into womb
of earth-cavern, Ezra –
all the way to Ravenna...
At far end of Pontus rest him tomb

where Theseus stole them golden fleece
Maximus   whose sea-blue
eyes of *geomatrix* (thrum
true)   abstract chamber piece

like waves reiterating   into nautilus
the human sum   reframed
from steel teeth (Somme
bad dream)   the whole shark armistice

To turn   from bull's-eye bulletins
down a narrow corridor
or trench file   war
in the hand, in the mind   sin's

armature   in the marrow   Guillaume
& Jesus   the   steamboat pilot
metymorfs   the whole plot
in a forest   of masts   high sunset room

5.16.16

BIG SHOES

In the deep grain, American
wood flows like river
darkness, Indian-giver
is your claim   start again

with a gamble, shepherd   desert
is your friend   when you
become a   sheep (*who-*
who, keens   Cyclops-owl). My yurt

is yours, pilgrim   enunciates
Canonicus (to the dauntless
youth). His confidence
in the common good   illustrates

the Second Table   of stone
outlines   everyone
understands   Turkmen
& Catholic   Quakers, even –

that the Good   is transparent
& rooted   a charity
branch   shading   the nitty-
gritty (hungry teeth)   your Parent-

Spirit, who is Heir Apparent
&   (apparently)
Ancient of Mondays
also   her name is Clement

or Clementine   she wears big shoes
she drowned   in the river
it was my mistake   her
name   is Jessie (almond   of the Jews)

5.17.16

TEEMING ORBIT

In the old octagonal gazebo
shaded from sunrays
screened from mosquitoes
I think of Marcel Proust, of *Oblomov;*

of the haze of tranquil summers
in an equilibrium
of nature. *Let it come.*
The books fade into memoirs,

epics filigree life's borders
with remote heroics
while the housecat licks
his fur, & children play recorders.

To live life on the edge
of the petunia patch.
To bandage every scratch,
wipe every tear... sea-azure pledge!

Noah's flute-compass – a pilot's
Providence – the homing
pigeon's purple ring
of ocarina *nostos*-pivots...

Deep down in the teeming orbit
of the clay, a blessed
favor lifts each nested
creature into intricate

brush-feathered limestone – emerald
fresco, where white-
haired eagles congregate –
floresce into the parchment (gold).

5.18.16

EARTH-GATE

They're casting another bridge across
the River; saws whine,
a tug toots, the cranes
lift high & gawky, like red-rose

giraffes. *There are orioles in the woods...*
My long-drawn notes
shore up a span that floats
on vague *bleu* Gulf streams – moods

& swings; you have to walk between
the strands of frayed thread
looped onto gravity (dead
reckoning)... *O plum-colored has-been,*

warped by Magdalenian
& riverine diffraction!
Yet one stone section
lifts the key. Giuliana

limns it, with her simple pottery –
the old grey painter
in his deserted corner
emanates intransigent asperity

like mud-splashed cast-off prophecy.
Only the rough rind
of some green kiwi-mind...
her catenary rainbow bend (sea-

sown, high-flown). Yon Earth-Gate
shines at earliest dawn –
solemn mandorla-keystone,
freedom-sign (*gioia* incarnate).

5.19.16

NEVA-LAND

The poem is for lonely you
amidships (*I-&-Thou*
nailed coign to prow) –
& for that grubby neighbor too

next door (George or Georgina
with the garden hoe).
A solitary lamp-glow
lingers in the old cantina –

in William Blackstone's study (*man*
who went to live with...)
– uphill, on the forest path
to *Middy Wewe*'s blithe fountain.

George Washington spins in his grave
to see how we behave
without a mind to save
us from ourselves. Thee must be brave,

& true, & kind, & dedicated
to the perfect good –
that global neighborhood
that shines, wid' green & delicate

kiwi-glow, beneath the rind
of blind & brutal night.
A callow grail-knight
stumbled on it once, near Samarkand –

spry Wolfram rings the tale – &
like an unknown soldier
leapt – O soulman Prospero! –
from here to Skye (in Neva-land).

5.20.16

LOAD-BEARING

Strong wind in Minneapolis
today, & slate-gray
clouds (stone solidarity
on high). *Big Wind,* my father's

nickname (Indian Guides). I picked
West Wind. Some air
in the ceremony there –
pre-Scouts, & pre-Socratic

too. How a breeze shoulders a mountain
into laurel blossoms;
how one lilac sums
a people in a spell (for funeral train).

The *Word-as-Such*... the Word is such
for we who have passed over
Lethe. It is more
than scent of orange – it is a torch

lit by shaping lips, a summons.
One hectoring nation
circles on its chain
thirsting for liberation... the romance

of Spring on earth. It is only a turtledove
salience, a gray-feathered
stone from Petersburg;
just a load-bearing mule, hove-

to before Frisco. & you are called to join
the company of saints –
where Livingstone faints
in swamps of cedar (violet, African).

5.23.16

PEACOCK'S EYE

Path P *stretch in six directions*
out of Cairo, Huck,
sez Jim – *any way you look.*
One of them north-south junctions,

I reckon. There was a labyrinth
of red clay trenches –
dead men in its clenches
like flies hung in a spider's tent

– heavy that clay, so heavy!
Like the bottom of the sea.
How could a little child be
dancing in such dismal gravy?

She's Pueblo, of the clay peoples;
they put away wrath before
the sun go down, f'sure.
Lookee there. & through the peephole

of his fingertips I saw (obscurely
as that garden of Sheba)
a lightning pathway – Sun-Ra
threshing floor – arisen merrily

from ripened Flanders wheat (so
melancholy). Like Van Gogh
seized with a fury-glow
of happiness... Persephone? O

yes! Threading her crane-dance
through a peacock's eye –
purple Hagia Sophia's
woolly poncho-swirl (at cave-entrance).

5.24.16

KIEVAN ARK

This gazebo's tilted octagon
of weathered, worm-eaten
cedar holds off the rain
in Minneapolis, again.

Again, Henry will dream his *songe*
like a train-hopping sponge
& let summer arrange
cloud-peaks of glory (strange

magnet, *fourchette d'orange*). *Concord,*
Columbia – *créatif*
brain-fever of native
mer-wit – good Will's three-cornered

cap of happiness (wasp Osip's
honey-basket on the Hill
of Skull). A game of skill
is Vladimir's, & music too – the ship's

a Kievan ark (turned right-side-up
beneath its choral dome).
Salt-azure breath of wisdom
streams from Maximus (one cup

of simple crumblevine); his prong
is set like Lebanon
cedar beside the chronic
faultline – earthquake birthpang,

epileptic flow. & now one smile
reverses Golgotha
with OK light – it's *manna*-
Madeleine (kneads pain into a grail).

5.25.16

WHISPER-DOOR

Walk back   through a rainy-day memoir
through the watercolor (Grace
Ravlin   *Gloucester, Mass.*)
over a fireplace   wherever you are

down the River Road   by the cottonwoods
through the rose garden   with
a *quipu*-thread   into depths
of summer   Willy's hobo moods

when the eyes relax   deep into green
& a river flows   to the heart-
matrix (*almond, athwart*
twin orange trees)   your ascent   unseen

Father Hennepin   or St. Louis
by the Stone Arch Bridge
on   New World ridge
where *Evening Star*   harps *Liberty*

These harmonic concordances
Apollinaire   *à* New Orleans
Ariadne's contra-dance
in sleepy Paree   sybilline séance

The flute zigzags   *l'après-midi*
sad Adams (Henry) perks
his ear   the password works
once more (*Encore, encore!*)   you see

twin gates rise   virginal   *ange d'or*
with safety net   one golden
thread   *trompette marine*
from Jessie O. to J.   soft whisper-door

5.27.16

BOOK

VII

WHEEL-ROSE

Memorial Day. A good man's ashes
hid in stone by-way,
two steps from coppery
Minnehaha. Her long eyelashes

(Florence) his. Only a mile or so
from viridian jungles
of springtime (Mendelssohn).
His father (Edward) fended the blow

at Saint-Mihiel. & Katherine,
from Reading – with a red
peony, under a shed
in Belgium. *Only 29.*

Red Cross volunteer (unselfish
clear-eyed gaze). Poppies
in a man-made sea
of miseries. *The human wish*

for Providence is octahedral
diamond. My open road
is riven motherlode,
adhesive gossamer. Vein-trail

of cottonwoods, bent by the wind –
a flexible thread of silver-
green, a gusty poplar
grove. Slight syllables will bind

this dream-sail to a *Temeraire*
leaving Galilee harbor
(bound for Superior
beneath the wheel-rose of the Bear).

5.31.16

INGLE EYE

A wild white rose at the side of the house
bloomed just today
like the *city of Dioce*
on green clover stairway   Spouse

Sister   in clusters of stars
Who are you?   Magdala
Stone   mosaic   of gala
winefest   little swirl of squares

corn-maze   around an ingle eye
your single sigh
the keystone   *by-&-by*
(little fiddlehead fern   turning pern-

kernel   the axle of the ax)
as Icarus   burning wax
falls   cataracts
into *Grotto J*   (relax)

on Chartres nave-pavement   discern
the Ariadne pattern
that angry monks   learn
magnanimity   & turn

again   as falcons gyre   into
the sun   (mild   smile
on earth   mile upon mile)
the Son of Man   is fashioned true

whisper those lips   of windblown rue
Jessie Ophelia   your
leaves of grace   empowered
to plow   deep rose   to emerald blue

5.31.16

FROM MEMPHIS

O Lady walking by, in black
jacket & yellow skirt,
you lift me from inert
& vacant thought into a way-back

memory-milieu. The Promised Land
of sunlight at midnight
is nest for monarch flight
& viceroys too (you'll understand

when we get there). The Milkweed King
is Hobo in disguise –
the motherland is prize
for steady Jim (gone huckleberrying

with Oblomov). He walks gently
into rabid disputes,
young Nanabozo – toots
his horn – Rabbi-clown, my

Hiawathee Bigfootprints
of Peace; he's taken down
in order to rebound
into renown, like *Printemps*

Spring-Rain Joan, or *Franny Cricket*
(she of jingling anklets
in the cedar dusk).
There's earthy scent beneath the musket;

there's a penny in the well.
A dinged wingèd profile
traipses from the Nile –
elopes from Memphis (into Israel).

6.1.16

SOFT CATHEDRAL

She came from the rubble-edge of tracks,
my little Jessie, O –
her father gambled so,
her mother sunk low, like a parallax

of sallow sun. Harsh raptor features,
scavenged palimpsest,
thin gewgaws in a needle-nest –
indifferent lights, long-distant stars...

– as if the morning held no lamp
for choppy grizzlies, salt-
&-pepper crowns. *O Walt,*
where be thy warm palm now? Thy camp

amid tin canvases o' cheery braves?
Jonah & Jessie, splintered
by the sea, had wintered
in the bottomland, like jasper leaves;

no voice of kind encouragement,
no ring-dove warbling
could break the iron thing
that iced the whole whale-monument.

Only one bright prong near St. Louis
promised their release –
an upturned kayak, Miss
Virginia (airy gate to happiness).

Slant waves of sorrow wash across
the little pine deck, Jessie
sang, *but comfort thee –*
my soft cathedral floats on moss.

6.2.16

STAR-FIELDS

A monarch sails transparent air
over a sea of grass
toward Mexico cedars.
June hums softly into summer

orchestra – a *Symphony*
of Ocean River (flutes
by Apollinaire). Broom-roots
of harmony brush copper tympani

with nervous splendor. The principle
of the epic poem – Hart
Crane's plangent part
for solo Jonah (sailor's pipe)

merges with cat-gut chords
of choral hymn, Atlantean –
sagas of Everywoman,
Everyman (adze-edge word-hoards).

A stone spun from heaven... King
Tut's meteoric dagger,
sanded to plow much bigger
meadows. Star-fields of the tongue

flicker from familiar cave –
shape speech to love,
vault from worm-grave
to groves of cedar (almond nave

upon a flame-stream, evergreen
to save). Pine-needles
tingle with seedling-
cones; wings fan (bright V-formation).

6.7.16

SCRIMSHAW TRINKET

It's the past that tells us who we are. Without it
we lose our identity. – Stephen Hawking

A raven carried heaven-manna
out of the ark to lonesome
Jonah – him just come
from under the whale-rib (*manna*

overboard) stranded on sand
off Galilee, RI –
& it made him cry.
Those crispy cackles he couldn't

understand – like low gull-talk
sent through a black-
hole paradox;
light straw climbed an orange rock

from the event horizon up to
null infinity –
it was all catenary,
looped in one wave-smile... – who?

Gravity? – or Grace? Eurydice,
maybe. (It was her cave.)
Spoiled meat you crave
is portioned by division – say,

two doves for every plowman's mule.
Queequeg in his casket
(like a scrimshaw trinket)
penned our sempiternal Rule –

each rustic Penny in the well of night
was tender out of love.
Her vernal sparkle-trove
is polyglot – *Euphrasia* (eyebright). *6.8.16*

SPIRIT-WOOD

i.m. Edward Lewis Peckham

Step lightly in my mother's house,
whispered a tiny elf
named ELP – himself
a watercolorist (a yellow lady's

slipper's footprint left the forest
on this day). *Cypripedia*
reginae – Minnehaha's
moccasin – graced this wilderness

as well, making a pair for *Joy*
& *Beauty* (graces
almost three). Time paces
seasoned out of winter, so employ

your dancing shoes, fiery Hiawatha –
roll like Polar Bear
around that pinpoint star,
sing like a loon, like your happy

father (*Thalia*-glad). *Nature*
& *Manitou* join hands;
a *Turtledove* blends
sea-sounds, all about green Eire;

urn burials, gardens of Sirius
swim synchronizing
rhombs on monarch wings
(a rugged Paradise for ladybugs)...

one dance-call through spirit-wood
or jadestone flute
sows dreams of Camelot
(like waves of wheat around a vineyard).

6.9.16

LITTLE BUNDLE

Light cottonwood fluff-motes drift
from high green vaults
along the river, Walt.
Thy hobo-hymn floats like swift

Scythian swallows   over the steppes
Gerrhi   in a land of Gerrhi
gray   *milkers of mares*
Geloni   like Jonah   swallowed up

& cast-off   by the sea again
like an exiled raven
scouring   the salt-sown
slate   for breadcrumbs, broken

limbs, dry vines   any sign
of home, of motherland
Guillaume would understand
Colossus of roses   tall man

grown meek   bemused upon his own
Bermuda   who bears a little
salt-bundle   close to heart
lifted six ways   a hexagon

grown octagonal   a diamond
have salt among yourselves
& plant   peace shelves
atop green Andes   condor-*monde*

Thus crooned the shuffling friar
under orange garage door
over grey sea-floor   as
poplars, nigh Gellone   signed, *Ephphatha*

6.10.16

COMPLACENT WEATHER

A green kid from Appalachia
gone to fight in Fallujah
– someone explain? *Aya,*
Babylon! *O generations*! A

late-night flashback (this time
not a war zone) – the stone
cave, the Mezzo-Eon...
the wooden man (half-lamb,

half-king) splayed on an axle
of Lebanon cedar.
Adam, 2nd mate (bare).
In Aleppo, the shells relax

theological distinctions
(strange how disaster
nets cousins together in
dense swallow-clouds). Sons

remember their angry fathers
in another atmosphere –
benign, complacent weather,
a constant world. Who bothers

to refit owlish waste places?
Earth presses toward
obstructed Adam, stymied
Eve – each watchful heart races

to reach Yezidi Paradise
(jade Peacock Angel,
over the next hill
from Sheol). Sol breaks the ice.

6.11.16

BRIGHT EIDOLON

Like a round dime tossed in a round
lake, hermetic lady
(Mendelssohn, or Galilee)...
the circle of clans closes on a mound

of blue-white clay. With a star
beneath pulsing waves,
to summon all the braves.
Rêve-dream, song-*songe* (*de la mer*).

Smoke rises from Pipestone, where
friars met the chiefs –
an old *Amerique* (Lief's...
Hennepin's, Marquette... *le voyageur*);

Rose de St. Louis, Annie
de Texas... Jessie O.
from N'Orleans – down below
rim-sleep (*full fado,* Ariel).

The fumes are gray & sinuous
veins within rose
windowpane (chartreuse?) –
where a rustic yokel stems the breeze

like mast in steady gale. He's
smiling (thick mute mule,
dumb lamb). You'll
toss him in a hole – he slappim knee.

The frost hurls stern memorials
across blank mirror-ice
(in Mendelssohn). Yet twice
& twice, bright eidelon... (loon calls).

6.13.16

WOOF DAWN

Now vales of *Maia* give away
to peaks of June, plains
emerald after rains;
gold Ghana-threads of yesterday

(encircling *Hermione,*
her *Perdita*) are knotted
in one polyglot,
shade-silvered whisper-crown.

The dream-song of that melancholy
painter in the corner
(Henry Coroner,
or Richard Parking-Lot) might be

a facet of the grey sea's *matière* –
portion of the human
globe (*octagonalmond,*
arched like Nut over the pearl-

sphere of the earth). Hearth-sign
of futurity, through sleep
to an oasis – leaping
Minnehaha (Hobo river-mind).

Someone smiling in an acorn cap
shadows his Georgia garden.
Some apple-orchard man,
repairing limbs... his milky map

renews the face of day. *All things*
woof dawn, old Prospero –
it happened long ago.
Her cartwheel (spun of gold bee-stings).

6.15.16

EVENING ROSE

Day after Father's Day – at cusp
of springing summertime.
Anxious children climb
steep query-spirals – *must the Ship*

break into toothpicks, battered by
cold 40-ft slaps (off
the Tongue)? *Mozartean buff*
Fathers – are they foundering? & why?

Some stately turkeys ornament
our neighborhood. Their very
carriage molts each scary
Bronze Age snood toward merriment,

that used-caruncle dewlap glare
to bustle of 18th-century
quadrille heroine (stray
boa-feather in Ben Franklin's hair).

Down its ravine, the river-myth
is inexhaustible, still
spills, inscrutable (al-
most), its copperhead glide. With

wattle-basket coracle, Huck Frisbee
heels for civilization.
Skinny levitation,
Aesculapland shaman... – *Hey,*

there's Beatrice! Pacing slowly,
lifted above herself,
a white heron (*sylph-*
crane) sure-footed, shadowing me –

long-legged flier in the reeds,
like feathered snow come
from gray clouds.... amalgam
sweetheart-griffin-seraph-steed.

She says: *your frigate's scraping shallows,*
that is all. The ring
of Ocean overhead (sing,
choirs of pilots!) *is harmonious;*

your houseboat made of Lincoln logs
is under beanpole Abe's
Euclidean bien sabe.
His moral compass counters rogue

waves, waves of dead shark-plugs
with a fertile proposition,
proven (fractal fashion)
through o'erlapping plies – Persian rugs,

matryoshka dolls... onion peals
from domes of ever-deeper
& dove-subtle cheer...
'til liberty for all *becomes the seal*

of human Union (universal,
irreversible –
malice invisible,
o'erwhelmed by charity for all).

Doubloons of humanism shine,
winking in mud-banks
near St. Lou. So prinks
the Rio's evening Rose (yours, mine).

6.20.16

MIDNIGHT SUN

i.m. Elena Shvarts

Summertime, in *Oblomov*.
A stately summer read
set in dilapidated
grand estate. Anguish in love,

chaste love blooming too late
for mild aristocrat
sunk deep in all that
lovely lassitude, his summer fate.

Now green shadows shadow green.
An inchworm dangles calmly
from green thread; she
might be Ariadne's cousin, gone

to ground – concrete, though light enough
to float... her emerald measure
camouflaged from Minotaur
into thin air (green limestone bluff).

Pushkin, hid in cedar dacha,
plots another poem
on Elijah; hums
& scratches raven quill. *Da –*

prophet senses feathered friend,
his own spine tingles
under pines... sings –
Shades of Liberty will bend

these iron bars of bone & flesh...
– into something Russian,
titled Midnight Sun.
So (luminous *tenebrae* mesh).

6.21.16

EVENING REQUIEM

The gangly spidery flat-green plant
with the long-speared leaves
my mother (thievishly?)
secreted once, from Zion Mount

in seed-form, back to Minnesota
20 years ago –
lo & behold, just now
began to bloom. Some roseate

variation on chartreuse lances
its mirror symmetry
beside trim cedar trees
into windblown, Ghost Dance expanses.

On a Laplacian continuum
each paper nautilus
folds origami stress
across an evening requiem;

the 44 is full of 22's
until the bison hide
bolsters our flagging pride
& Buffalo Gal pays all our dues.

We flourish like the grasslands,
like the steppes, & fade.
Pacing in subdued parade
horsemen dip their pennants, bands

take up the funeral march, toward
Arlington. We are sown
as wheat for the unknown
dénouement (Jerusalem palm-sword).

6.22.16

GREEN PILLARS

Spell me the *poem including history*
if Providence on earth
blooms, Rhodian... Arthur
ever returning, like waves of the sea –

mesmerized & mesmerizing,
in disguise (as George
the gardener). So merge,
now, emerge, with enterprising

pioneers of happiness, your
boon companions, in
loon-call theremin
borne toward a Lake Superior

of dreams – one cup of fresh water
lifted to the moon
of manna-honey – one
mute field note in the *Chronicle of Mutter-*

Patter. A flimsy paper nautilus
skims her light pinnace
over the sea-surface –
her brood chamber full of caprice,

her *Ocean State* a colony
of Turtledove Cloud-
World. A dream-word
sang out of a rooted cedar tree –

so old, Time had forgotten her;
so strong, her smile
threads from green pillars
outlasting the Wars to End All War.

6.24.16

GREEN SPACES

Bright little icon in the corner
of a peasant hut.
Orange gates flame shut;
a woman hustles away from monster

with serious, calm child (bearing
goldfinch & small orb
in either hand). Absorb
the transposition of the strings

from C major to B-flat minor
played on olive leaves
or almond branches (Eve
or Van at the piano) – far

into green spaces of Mendelssohn.
Errant, vagrant notes are
refugees from time – soar
to primeval cave-womb zone.

Pushkin & Scriabin... scrolled papyrus
harbors the shibboleth
stronger than death,
more jealous than pressed grass

& 4-leaf clovers (planted in
a dictionary). Her hum
from deep Elysium
comes after dragons' angry din;

the very sound lifts pyramids
& ziggurats to dust.
Rose-dust, on lips you must
kiss once... (& delicate eyelids).

6.25.16

FINAL ACT

They've found a fracture in the stone
unnoticed before.
The Holy Sepulchre
is buckling beneath the weight of its own

chapel. & the confessions have
at last made common vow –
the alpha & omega
of restorations. Centuries of

soot from votive candles must
be wiped clean; the vault
shored with titanium bolts
& stabilizing mortar, all the dust

blown free – for a strange energy
is here. *The Holy One*
has set his seal upon
Jerusalem – the seal of a kiss (hey

ey yo). Blind King Oedipus
is *pharmakon* – both
curse & cure; an oath
of the Aranda limns a sacred circus

for the *Origin* beyond hunger
& prey. Man is both Man
& Grub; one handspan
joins them, sacred totem-pair

distinct without division, separation
or confusion. Would
you return to the Wood
where, riven-branching, all began?

*

All the world's a stage. The Totem
glimmers in earth-cavern
like a *mémoire* of perfection;
handprint of omni-profundum,

quiet & invisible as wind.
The hand carves a circle
over gray sea, pearl
of adamantine quiddity – your mind

& heart, your soul, my wounded *Psyche.*
What will they find then,
beneath the slab? One
golden Witchetty Grub? One *Nike,*

linen, soiled by jogging Time?
I think they might unveil
a lost fresco – pale
replica (by Piero) of the same

design that, through the Ice Age,
lifts the crocus. Stubborn,
indomitable baton,
both crozier & calumet – rage

will not overwhelm your calm beauty.
I think of Late Romances
revolving into dances
all around the Globe... O, we

have not yet seen the final act!
Ineffable victory
of meekness... *it shall be,*
because it is, always. O blooming Fact!

6.26.16

SKIN-SWIRL

Wide lonesome chord of milk-train horn
across an Osage plain.
Lilac & star, American
crowd... shy bird calling the not-yet-born.

The microcosm of a Maximus
is like a walnut
brained by teeth. That
worn brown face, in Omaha bus

lounge, spoke quietly. "I am Dakota.
I'm a man." The poem
lifts a sign toward home,
that's all. The sum of Ariadne-

maze, malevolent eye of Minotaur
is in the skin-swirl
of your fingerprint. Roll
back into the vault then, sailor –

shed each blow of monster violence
until you find the mild
eye of the typhoon-child –
immaculate origin of Providence.

I see her hero stepping through the gate
of stone, one hand held out
on a wave of love. Light
scout, scouring the root of hate –

defanging that lamprey of predatory
malice, hostile cruelty –
injustice clamped on history.
With Coke & Blackstone whispers : *Now be free.*

6.28.16

SMALL EMERALD ELEGY

Geoffrey Hill, Yves Bonnefoy, Elie Wiesel

Light at dusk across the grass
salted with white crosses,
poppies... graph of losses
rounding up the Somme. Mass

for the mass of young men gone.
On Cemetery Ridge
the plowmen made a bridge
of bone, unbreakable – and won

the day. *Coraggio,* amigos.
Somnolent River
Time will shiver silver
when *the last full measure* flows

from infant veins, against the grain
of human servitude –
that dominant X (rude
chi-rho, nailed up in the brain).

In the *barranca* (by the monarchs'
den) the battered Consul
penetrated to the well
of Golgotha. His mind sparks

like the last firefly of evening meadows...
a small emerald octagon,
or 4-leaf clover – moon
over Eire, over the raging shadows

of the nations. *Clue vero,* Ariadne-
yarn. A catenary
arc, or smile – an airy
rack of clouds, threading the Neva R.

7.2.16

WILD WEED

The monuments tremble in the mind
like shuddering leaves... the dun-
grey flesh of Russian
olive shoots (wild weed you find

along gray highways). Clouds
resemble ships passing
(or sheep). An everlasting
turtledove of new beginnings crowds

grey folds to elegant mosaic –
peacock splendor, rainbow
tarantella. *Help me now,*
Ancient of Days – the mortal ache

of this wolf spider bite is like a prod
in the bull-dance arena.
I must rotate – ah,
Pocahontas handstand! – God

reward your goldfinch serenade!
Thunder & lightning speed
yon seraphim-steed
across acorn crucible (blade

pillaring smoke & fire upon hill
at Glastonbury, or
Golgotha). Now you are
whittled down to walnut mind-rill...

pirouette... red veins of iron
rivet into diamond.
Bran-*matière*. Pond-
ripple osprey, ranging (*arak*-golden).

7.5.16

PRAIRIE ROUNDELAY

American robin on my fence
I sense you are a friend
& neighbor – here to lend
your orange breast, for salience –

swell-sign of aerial fellowship
in gravid cave-adventure
(blue waves of chicory
pacing old roads, from Boston slip

to San Francisco). How your edgy
yodeling interrogates
our grubby, wormy hates –
sclerotic, squamous tragedy

of shriveled hearts, rancid hypocrisy!
You diagram with song
a madrigal so strong,
so many voices in emergency

merge into blueprint buoyancy –
manifest (garnet clay
prairie roundelay)
a ship-shape evening constancy.

Mute gesture from crow's-nest *G-ray*!
Memory, beyond time
salts a Boethian rhyme-
beat... *in quella Roma onde*

Cristo è Romano. Staunch ruddy
steersman indicates
the palm, the fiery gates,
Pacific O... – *Eternity*! is all his study.

6.7.16

MOSAIC INTERIOR

Hobo sets his sights on Ocean Sky
the cloud-boats drifting
stately, aquamarine
high-masted spinnakers go by

The rusty syntax of the railroad bridge –
necklace for a queen
Romano-Byzantine.
Galla Placidia, maybe... blown to the edge

of warlord chaos, courtier intrigue;
guarding son & heir
with the pale gold hair
(who will not see the Soo Line zigzag

into the forest, north of here).
The mosaic interior
night-blue with stars –
her mausoleum, like an eggshell ear.

Sea-light filters through pinholes
of gold. The grey *matière*
a granite made of air
hides pigeons, ring-dove souls

within its manifold (octahedral
catacomb). Even
Hobo finds his kin again;
the smile of cousin Jeanne will roll

a tensile thread out of the maze
of time & circumstance –
her light ghost dance
where mountains bloom (sheep graze).

7.7.16

RAVEN-SPELT

Cedar shade of Galilee,
Aesculapian shepherd
staff of serpent-
skin, shed (leafing royalty

in vernal memory). Magdala
Stone of good deeds done
O spouse of rustic sun
& witness won... lowly Messiah

come & gone (& come again).
Time flowers on the lips
& salty fate slips
into diamond lantern (homespun

dream of overflowing glee) – a shout
of joy from a windblown seed
of newness sown (whorled
Jubilee) – canoe-galleon, afloat

round Milky Road (unquenchable
Eternity) – that lights
gold *Magna Carta* rights
welded in smiling crucible

of *Manitou*. So on this day
Canonicus & Charles II
framed (raven-spelt) new
Charter, for primordial Way –

experimental Restoration Play
within green cedar
fane – firm oaken chair
of planetary cheer (our Ripening Day).

7.8.16

FISHING BOATS

The old watercolor over the mantle
in my mother's house – the twin
gray fishing boats, the brown
warehouse, the whitewashed walls. Gentle

Gloucester, Massachusetts (Grace
Ravlin *pinxit* – Grandpa's
cousin, from Kaneville, Illinois).
Soft clouds, the upright crosspieces

of lank lanyards (still sea-green
harbor, granite walk).
Thinking of another work –
lone lady at Mount Vernon, culling

flowers for George Washington.
And of another Maximus –
not Gloucester's famous
philosophe, but Maximus, *blue unicorn*

who sketched with Euxine seagull arcs
on stumps (his amputated
medium) one delicate
& sibylline solution. *Sparks*

fly upward from the hearth of Love
– fly outward, penetrate
wolf-packs of *gulag*-state.
This heart simmers like kiln-hot stove

or croon of turtledove, hidden...
violet in tall field grass,
cricket near an underpass.
Willow by slow river (Magdalen).

7.11.16

OLD SALT

Herman riveted to crow's-nest,
Dante wearing out
his shoes... Weldon, forgot
by Golden Gate, & Berryman, a crust

of snow beside the limestone bank.
Moon rose from sea
with magnanimity,
night's passionate gravity... & sank

these antithetical children of the sun
beneath immeasurable Ocean-
wave. Matrix of one
twinkling eye... stuttered translation

from sharks' dogma to *Cutty Sark*
sped rondure-eloquence –
an *Ocean River* sense,
human inheritance (almond birthmark).

The old salt bears his Southern Cross
as shark-tooth earring,
tattooed heart. The singing
shrouds (sea-urge, wave-moss)

remind him of Jonah, lost infant
of the crew – of Jasper,
& Francesca too – Ariel
in Ravenna pines (*al fresco* fundament).

Make all things new. An emerald gong
plumbs planetary tides –
sun-shimmer plies
Gennesaret to Tuscan hills (all-human song).

7.13.16

SILVER THREAD

A raven stitches broken arcs
over Lebanon cedars,
through layers of cinders
on sands of Galilee. These marks

print tracks, embed the shadow
of a shadow (of
a shadow). Whose love
cooled into bottled borders, crow-

foot scars? Etched into sealed eyelids
the guardians of sleep
administer fear, & reap
nightmare (endless cycle in the Cyclades).

I have no wrath, hums the writhing
wheel of flame – *my smile*
will melt stalactite guile
until their funny bones come lurching

from the humus... rows of soldiers
thrown from stone, their hearts
wrung into speaking parts.
Her modulation wove its sutures

out of the basalt lid of night. The ocean
gathers all its woe into
moist glance of pain... you
hear her sigh. Love's Jonah-sign

one silver thread – gray clouds,
gray sea, gray gull, gray
dove... & every way
her wing turns (lifting raven-moods).

7.14.16

GREAT RECKONING

Crusaders racing to the Tomb,
an historical pinpoint
in 1099. Where He went
at 33 (a little room

for some great reckoning). Daggers
in the eye turn every way –
shark swordfish play
for nightmare realms, & beggars

follow San Francisco up a narrow
fuse (to blessedness).
Stigmata (foolish meekness,
humble mulishness). A wheelbarrow

carries mild infant Majesty
into his palmy kingdom,
spiky Jerusalem
(sea-rose of sandy history,

Rome's crabapple). The viney mind
demands firm scaffold,
grid to climb, hold
fast – casket from Samarkand,

mercurial chasm, golden
kaleidoscope... meanwhile
one half-moon wafer-smile
of blinding white sail's sudden

eminence rides on gray wave –
the plummet of an eagle
etches his grave seal,
marking *1132* (full fathom five).

7.15.16

NEW LESSON

Old river the color of rusted iron
you beckon me back before
shell-shocked *histoire*
humaine (long nightmare drill). When

we were as flint people in limestone
hideaways, under
the glare of *Viper-Vulture*
in his ice-eyrie. The repetition

of trauma exudes a pearl-shell
palimpsest (*le Roi*
est mort, vive le Roi) –
one slight Gennesaret wave-swell

is laved to *Pietà* massif, circled by Rome,
lapped by typhoons (of bursting
tears). We are thirsting,
River, for that fluent kingdom

where Ebionite & Nazarene,
snake-handler & Sioux
shaman – every blue
highway mutt, sadsack has-been –

every humiliated woman, each
weakling sissy-boy
undone by bully
chants of dominance – might teach

a new lesson. How once that marble
lifted into cloud...
one dove-grey *noeud*
vitale (breathing *AMOR* into dead fable).

7.19.16

GAZEBO SKEIN

Sultry evening in the Twin Cities.
The earth. My mother's kiln
stoked like Jersey landfill
with Dante's willful souls – at ease

like oil on fire. My moss-green vines
climb the gazebo skein.
Oblomov lived in vain
& died, sweet gentleman. My light declines.

Oblomov dreamt a febrile dream,
icon of idle summer
grace. Her lips murmur
& tickle his ear – *Awake, Sunbeam...*

Dante, shaken, shudders with Love
& epileptic ecstasy;
parallactic *Ocean Sea*
& shadowy Argo up above,

Emperor Henry on chariot-throne
of Rhodian charity.
A band of silver-grey
light-thread knots chords – the drone

of universal B-flat (*Kingdom Come*
with trombones, clarinet
& flute) – *At Last*. FIAT.
Oblomov lifts his balding dome,

his heavy lashes... orange twin
pillars hold one Ariadne-
loop. Pacific naiad?
Juliet? *La Paix*? Her smile shall win.

7.21.16

BLACK DIAMOND

This heart-shaped leaf from cottonwood
dark green & silver-gray
may float down other rivers – say
the Don, by Voronezh... or Eridanos,

through Ravenna (north of Hades)... &
each windblown plum sails
off a shakedy limb, whose spiral
roots corkscrew (like S.S. *Normandie*

propeller) down into a labyrinthine
seine of mounded knots...
a weedy sea-change (plot
of plots). *Black Diamond* is crystalline –

common as salt; an octochoron,
regular, complex;
cubic prismatic Rex
or tesseractic honeycomb (acorn

beanie, maybe). From her, *La Paix*
like some Hermione
dances to life again – see
there! Her coracle – *l'Éternité*!

My raven-tesserae form *nature morte*.
Venn diagram for Orpheus
bent to his Beatrice-dust
in Adriatic backwater – 'til brought

up short, like Slocum, John (Shaker
Indian of Puget Sound)
or like Black Elk, who found
her sun-spun gyroscope (stung-sweet *Makar*).

7.22.16

SOUL SCOUT

i.m. Fr. Jacques Hamel

You breathe a mist over stained glass,
like a cloud over Mirror Lake,
by the trolley road to Blake
(in Mendelssohn). *Rouen, alas.*

In Chartres nave, one dark gray
thread still navigates
J-whorl, on golden agate –
Ariadne's Way (sealed crypt to Day).

Her catenary smile will make
a lazy loop through Space
in Time; her carapace
a turtleshell – sweet curve you take

through clouds like whales, Jonah –
to find an old mercy-go-
round anew. Like Jessie O.
on racy waterwheeler, sunray-

rain-bowed – *Lady Liberty*
an echo of Cahokia,
a salience of *Royal Oak*
(lips' kayak lifting word to be).

Deep breath, *Path P,* Rhodos.
Out of a barbed-wire
cat's-cradle (rust pyre
of Minotaur-empire) you rose –

winded with old George, the breadwinner,
& Maggie, of the *veritas*
caput – where Brandywine flows
into *4 Pine River* (soul scout's honor).

7.26.16

O FLOWER

For a Tear is an Intellectual Thing

This evening light over the sink
& clutter of Mom's pots
dish soap, what-nots
stillness of an eye that doesn't blink

pupil of an unseen commonwealth
Lincoln-logos of a realm
Time cannot overwhelm
where Walter nurses back to health

Hart's broken *farfalla*-tower
& Weldon finds his shoes
again   & Berryman his
balance on that bridge   *O Flower*

Joy   Out of these winter fields
where Bruegel-raven   zig-
zags   over leafless twigs   &
Guillaume's pink turban   slowly   heals

Your graven images of gravity,
Henry   my autumn fall
1132   a burial
at sea   the perspicacity

of buoyant Jonah   one grey gull
white-feathered underneath
lights on a wave   *breathe,*
Dove   lift down from empty skull

my ashen diamond   the snow skims
sparkling   under the sun
& from bright gatherings one
Flamant beams   whose warmth redeems

7.27.16

PINE ARK

Piero the geometer
graphed the perfect dome
(that marvelous human home
& winking sea of gray matter)

beneath the curvature of San Francesco
in Arezzo – a flock of swans
of radiant intelligence
about their Queen, before the portico

(Temple of Solomon). He's hidden
as in a game of hide-&-seek
the wooden matrix (meek
logbox from Tree of Life). When

Helena comes to Jerusalem
she'll draw it out again –
sliver from a lion's
paw, grim rib from Adam's

galley mast. Constantine dreams
his tiny golden honey-cross.
Mary's *Pneuma*-moss
wells in the quiet kitchen... gleams.

Sweet *psyche*-legends circulate
around a forgotten rock
in Magdala. The flock
is scatter-gathered... salty fate

& jittery salts plank-walk the yellow-
black monarchs of love.
Their cedar treasure-trove
is one pine ark (Jonah *chi-rho*).

7.28.16

CLOUD-FEATHERS

The air so brilliant & clear today
beside the Bronze Age river.
The railroad bridge hovers
over its reflection – a light play

of diagonals, like water-spiders
on a pond, or cloud-feathers
above the Jordan, tethered
to a steadfast figure (Jasper's

orant mariner, circumferencing
gray sea with shady palm).
That chanting shepherd, calm
beneath an indigo wheel of blazing

stars... one cheerful face beaming
from the medallion
in Classe (Apollinarian)
under darkened wooden ceiling

of abandoned ship, beached in pine-
swamp, at Ravenna's edge.
Mere icons of a human pledge
so simple, local, omni-Byzantine –

ineffable mosaic sky
where Love bends waves
to lift us from our graves
into a metamorphosis   kind *Aye*

above halo of tears   you streak
with serpentine arches
agios   agios   agios
one river-rainbow   in an eagle's beak

7.29.16

TROMPETTE MARINE

Soft breeze moves the cucumber leaves
climbing the fine mesh.
Each poem starts fresh
upon a labyrinth the wind conceives

the way Dante struggled like a goat
to rise above the black-
white chessboard (epileptic
knight, squirming from Hell's dank moat

toward one firefly-mote of light).
O civil wars of cousin
wolves! Striving in frozen
latitudes of predatory fright-

might, ice-blue treason – all
spite-pirates of the broken
sheep of state – forsaken-
&-forsaking sacrifice! Ravel

me then, Ariadne, in your primordial
& woolen salience
of *J*... into the silence
of a pregnant Jubilee, where Piero's wall

glows in the morning light (& swells
a womb within a cave).
Search the high nave
of the Milky Way – Francesca dwells

up there (with Jenny Littletree) – among
the Shaker Indians, Quakers –
meek *paisans*, peacemakers –
fused by *trompette marine* of song.

8.1.16

IRMA'S FLING

Sly Raven implicates my speech
with folded shade. A bright
dove spangles dew-light
drifting the stream. On the beach

by Mississippi, one yellow-black ensign
of cottonwood, one limestone
arrowhead. An unknown
bird hums wings into a grey spine-

feather matrix – hovers droning
like yellow gyroscope
(totem for sun). *Hope*
is the thing... the Word spins honing

like a drill toward a red diamond,
flaking hieroglyphs
& copper cypress skiffs
for one crossroad encounter (bond

of your voice, speaking soft to me,
from vise of mine). Zone
of Mendelssohn tombstone –
of flint, cracked open for humanity –

to pour through like sprung torrent
& never cease flowing,
as when a raven crowing
from an empty cave (craven, abhorrent)

signals a seed flung by a planet's wing –
smiles through the sea-gate
like Peacock Angel – fate
spannered by a checkmate (*Irma's Fling*).

8.2.16

LITTLE STORIES

Jim Northrup, 1943-2016

The dead cottonwood leans its broken fork
like a Y-brace against
the live cottonwood. Who's
helping whom? The river's work

is steady, seasonal... flows
nearby. Past Fort Snelling
like a hurt knee – swelling
strong west branch waters,

Dakota memory. The boarding school
in Pipestone, pushing English
like a Ghost Dance wish
across calumet plains. Clouds pool

like smoke under their limitless
blue dome. The little stories
join hands – morning glories
vining indigo blooms... a sky-caress

out of heavy red clay. *She will go*
with you to the Happy Land
her canoe made of almond
joy heartbeats, in waves. *I know*

where I'm going... just a change of address.
The flower of a smile
blooms out of dust – the trial
just a test of loving (wilderness).

You'll find the carnation in a sailor's
chest, the rose in a worn
lapel. So being born
will ride the swell, through locks, through doors.

8.8.16

HENRY'S COULOMBE

Muggy August, month of Emperors
& seizures. Hobo Henry
lies in Sharon's Ferry
under the sluggish limestone (worms,

molluscklies, protozoa). He's
coming back to Tuscany,
the Bore (some prophesy).
Huffy, bossy Henry holds the keys,

he thunk. Amid a bole of oaktrees,
under his acorn crown –
like that green Corny Maiden,
one of Igor's fresh catastrophes

(in Paris, 1913). High sign
of times – the *pharmakon,*
the scapegoat, Chosen One –
The barking Kingly Queen

of Carnival, her last crowd scene
(crowing). Guillaume was there,
too – orphic Apollinaire,
sighing for Minka in the black gunshine

of Dallas. *Jenny, we hardly knew ye* –
your sea-cloud camouflage
a fluttery montage
of yellow-black, afloat toward Iona...

America in Henry's *coulombe,* now.
The bird croons at the gates
where Francis celebrates
Pacific pipestone... sea-grey Manitou.

8.9.16

CIRCLET COMB

to Flavia Saraiva

So light she could dance in the palm of your hand
diminutive Flavinha
16 yrs old (4’4”)
spins round a square in Rio-land

revolving figure out of *Faery*   circling
like Geraldine Fitzgerald
with redhead emerald
circlet comb   encompassing

a globe   within her seashell shallop
green mandala made
of hands rosy mermaid
(see Phoebe’s sapient dewdrop

on linen frame   for navigation)
one palm in the hurricane
eye   Persephone
shows leaf again   becomes whole nation

wheeling   in the Great Bear dance
around an oak tree   acorns
reigning like   Golgotha crowns
skullcaps & elf beanies   the romance

of Mnemosyne   *again, again*
the early history
of Buffalo   or Rimini
Ravenn   or Petersburg   Pipestone

or Voronezh   or Minneapolis,
even   along a spiral
fiddlehead   springs tall
her heavy lightness   like   an Okie kiss

8.10.16

SWEET CHARIOT

You rode the midnight Greyhound
through American backwaters.
Past hobo squatters
inside their high lonesome vault (profound

infinite firefly field). No one
forgets their bent magnetic
North, your epileptic
adolescence (endlessness). The sun,

the moon, the Pope, the Emperor...
some bright Hiawatha rider,
beaming father-figure –
Federigo in Jerusalem, hugging an Emir...

History slides by on billboards,
Burma-Shave proverbs.
The Greyhound hums, curves
down Vanishing Road – the Lord's

a baby buffalo. Around the track
the sprinters skim – a blear
of fog machines, the air
nine *tenebrae*. One shady (humpback)

tesseract glides into Galilee –
Gödel infinity
or Miriam smile (she
saw her tall cousin suggest a V);

the mirror of authority
in heaven & on earth
wells supernatural mirth –
sweet chariot of Lady Liberty.

8.11.16

CEDAR HANDS

O calm August river, weaving
under your ceiling of gray
fluff! I'd like to say
you are a figure for Edith, rocking,

singing Sophie to sleep, somewhere
above Ethiopian night.
I'd like to formulate
a lamp in a window, out there

on a foggy lump in Narragansett Bay –
Rose Island Light, maybe –
what stands for certainty
in the midst of rocky sea, the sway

of tide. They're almost finished now
with the bridge repair.
Her double eyebrows bear
their concrete filigree, & show

twin circles in the river's glass.
Their delicate embrace
a fractal carapace
for curving lips of one round lass –

a sea-green pebble, calipered
by radiant massive Einstein
armature. So shine,
my lighthouse pine – like shy brown bird

or Great Blue Heron – one sharp eye
across the moving waters!
Agape holds stars
in loving stillness – rhyming sky

*

with earth. It is an ur-rhyme, personal –
a Neva-petroglyph,
an anchored spider-skiff,
chaste common *akme* (Eeyore-humble);

like moony pleb with sunny Phoebus,
roaming Apollinaire
with domed Apollinaris,
Love is that hearth-melding force

that fuses Unity & Liberty –
soul freedom is the spark
of arcs. I found a monarch,
lonely, in the donkey straw you see

down by the iron river (pausing,
perhaps, between White
House & Soldier's Rest).
We bowed to one another, browsing

sheared grass, cordially.
The song began like this –
a dream made manifest,
Railsplitter... prodigal Boy...

held in grey threads of dog days'
dawnlight. Soft rainbow
pigeon croon – low
throaty turtledove song-maze –

dream-*songe* across the meadowlands
of languages & worlds
farfalla-far – she whirls
& jags... floats into cedar hands.

8.12.16

DAKOTA HEXAGON

This quiet August day toward
the cusp of autumn. Green
vine-light in the cavern
where Henry hides his raven-word.

That empty chair in Dante's sky-
deep rose, for all the hoped-
for prophets, emperors...
& here's Sophia's little throne (my

dancing-master's rosy resting-
spot). Let her skip
fearless across the ship
of state, her toy basilica, questing;

the *Greyhound* of the Lord, her
vengeance, comes to this –
gray clouds of Providence
replete with rain; a pregnant mother

radiant with clearing day; the shades
of persecution blown away
by ocarinas (clay-
shell turtledoves, dolphin parades).

Ineffable golden Hephaestus-net...
veil of corn fleece over
a West Branch face. Her
sister in D.C. (Adams duet) –

icon of Miriam & Magdalen,
Dakota hexagon
implicit in the sun
of Washington... cartwheels, Columbian.

8.13.16

DOUBLE-DECKER

Hobo lounged by the great gray Ocean
River, his old hide detached
a little from his mind,
like Don in Key West, his one-

time winter host (at the Q Motel).
Distanced a little from the
whitecaps, red & blue,
that molder to a stucco frieze of Hell

sometimes. He remembers wild violets
that peek beneath gray toes
of an elder copper beech, whose
crown shades Providence; those roots

drill deeper than the black & white
of shaky party platforms.
Down beneath worms
mining resentment & indifference, the bite

of greedy centipedes, the slugs
cold as a winter street
in Minneapolis, whose neat
chewing fattens themselves alone (bugs

do not think about their neighbors).
Whose murmurous gray arms
have framed the milkweed farms
of metaphysical *Hope*, that anchors

Roger Williams' canoe –
Love's almond chariot
that smiling *Faith* built
out of flocks of *can-do*

monarch wings, green palms
circumferencing the gray
scallops of yesterday –
twin limestone radials (emblems

of spousal harmony, *e pluribus*
unum). Whose tap sinks toward
the center of the gourd,
the hearth Love stokes, wells tears...

& where a voice from her grey mirror
sang in Hobo's ear –
Behold the Platonic Year
revolve at last, aboard my double-decker

Greyhound! *When the game of suits*
& spades & royal clubs
gives way to hearts purple
& ruddy diamonds – twin 52s

orbit an orange origami octagon,
one Chinese lantern, standing
in the night garden – bring
Hobo to the table, then! It's done!

He pondered pumpkin murmurings,
& mooned there, by the muddy
banks. *The breeze of poetry...*
only a feeling (sighed). Our burdenings

borne by that humble muse, whose trust
in some deep loving cloud
grey Manitou's abode
will wave back (Noah's buoyant crust).

8.15.16

DANTE SCHOOL

Long ago in Florence, Alighieri
smashed the limestone font
at the Baptistery – *Don't*
Panic! – to save a little boy

from drowning. His prophetic sign,
a riposte for his own exile –
sluiced out with bile
& blood of lawlessness (Italian

style). The sea rides high, the rain
seems endless. Human
callousness a given,
leaden sinker-weights anchored in pain

call for a coracle, a basket-woven
safety net (to keep
the child alive, upon
the deep). Cross-stitch the waves then,

Raven – paint Noah's yawl afloat
until we memorize the name
that hawsers through this game
of crosshairs (golden, black & white).

Only a shadow over the sea;
an eyelash, lancing
a tiny tear. So bring
your harp now, Queequeg – free

that pearl-feathered quasi-gull
whose omnipresence bobs
the wavy globe. *Corncobs*
& acorns in Polenta (Dante school).

8.16.16

PINK TUGBOAT

I retrace my steps again
along the River Road
past Granddad's solid old
brick fortress. A trumpet vine

shines orange & green, climbing
a mud-brown corner into
August light. I'll go
down to that riverbank now, rhyming

with Nile & Jordan, Voronezh, Po –
a stream that crosses borders,
winding *atlatl* corridors
so sinuous & serpentine, into

the gray *matière,* the mutter-mouth...
sea-grotto of an Ocean
State (salt origin
of shanty-song). From north to south

diagonal, my yellow gyroscope
leans, vaulting on thread
from Gate of the Dead
(whose soft, dense orange-&-azure rope-

ladder lifts up the gravity of stolid
steel & staggered stone)
to Magdalenian
interior... & cartwheels there – Bride

of convex grassland cave-complex –
Cahokia coyote-
gal, whose Galilee
glee-zone (primordial) sketches a hex-

*

agon – galactic rumble-stir
of light-warp milky skein
or reign of windy Wayne,
pouring a *Who-He*? mirror-

ray into the rainbow trine
of spray-tossed clement
Clementine. Cement
shoes will not keep her in the brine

of Poseidon forever – see her shadow
stride the surface now!
With pink tugboat in tow
paintered to Ariadne's golden bow

– refracted ball of lambswool, bent
through Roger Williams' granite
lintel – Dante's bright
brooder-line. *The Great Commandment*

coming down from Manitou
like light... it is
not liable to conquest –
conscience is free, a gift to you

who seek for Me. A wheeling sword
glinted above a garden;
a ring of apple trees, hidden
in shade of Sant'Apollinaire. Word

melody   green hummingbird vine
Guillaume's *trompette marine*
a secret acorn   Queen
of *Royal Oak*   (she is a 5   & 29)

8.17.16

ROOSTERS CROW

for the rescuers

A gray light shines through the normal world
a silver-scale dawnlight
like the sea-sound in the right
chord on an oud, like a sail unfurled

on a cedar mast, standing simply free
on a fishing boat, out of Skala
Sikaminias, on Lesbos. *Ah,*
sighs the wind, for the drowned refugee –

Oh, keens the seaman, for the ghost
of his son (a scarecrow
helped to shore). Hard row
now, for Samaritans – for the host

village, gasping by the sea, in the normal
world, in the feathered light
of the mourning dove, so quiet
here (in the soughing wind, in the tall

cedars, in the shy bird's nest, in the forest
dusk, in the soft
dawnlight, in the gray gull's loft,
in the normal world). *Plain salt is best.*

On a concrete floor, someone traced a star
like an octagon, in a Sapphic
ode – under harsh traffic,
under raving codes, like a graven bar

on a looping ply. In a rosy key
sailors skim toward home –
from a morning comb,
roosters crow for Lesbos (merrily).

8.18.16

SILVER CHEST

Uncle George the plowman zigzags calmly
weaving his furrows back
& forth (west of Fond du Lac).
Laboring almost at rest, along his way.

The black soil teems with memories.
Childhood in Mendelssohn,
a helium balloon –
only now the fatal pine shades Miriam's

plein air Jubilee (specific gravity
of coffin-keel). Time,
History here touch the rim
of a labyrinth (*Fro-Back,* so corny)

whose perimeter outlines her face –
smiling, dreaming, lost
in the supple meadow-grass
of Eros flowering to Agape (*O Grace*).

Spruce Mountain rises straight ahead,
pilgrim – just south of Bonnie
Craigielee. Matilda will be
waltzing there, in a tamarack shade

not far from the sea; she will take your hand
where kids' bird-voices
boomerang – where earth rejoices
in equilibrium, & equity. One command

radiates Franciscan swag of turtledove;
one cloud sheds orange arcs
over antipodean parks
of aboriginal penitence (blue *Jonah*-love).

8.22.16

LAST WORD

Scavenging Raven found a crust
of broken mirror for
his nest above the river,
in a craggy oak (*Blackstone,* dust-

laden, winding her copper yarn
just east of Providence).
Po (or Eridanus)
glinted in that shard; a purple crayon

traced a spiral crane-dance there,
pinned to a dove-grey water-
wheel (by hand). The daughter
of Caesar trolled a welded cluster

of rust-rose keys just below the surface –
keys to the worm-riddled door
of haunted Sant' Apollinaire
in Classe (where Pharos ghost-sails

teem for Stilicho, Galla Placidia).
At his perch, Cautantowwit
reads smokefires lit
from Paris – *On 29th of May*

Corn Maiden will pirouette
one Final Show (a Waltz
to End All Wars). *Salt*
is good, croaks the haunted vet –

share salt amongst yourselves, &
be at peace. The night bird
oars southwest – his last word
whistled into silence (prairie-land).

8.23.16

ANCIENT KEY

No estoy yo aqui que soy tu madre?

The spiral molluscs from Precambrian seabed
in the limestone facing by the door
remind me of you; the bent lyre
of the cottonwood by the riverbank led

me back to you too – bent over your clay
wheel, shaping the river-mud
into a smiling *imago*. We tread
your maze toward home, thread-spun Ariadne.

That Mexican *Last Supper* diorama –
chipped clay bread-&-wine feast
you repaired... bones of a beast
lifted from bloodlines, toward a panorama.

Light from a distant prison window
gleams in Colchis. Maximus
knots three bright strands
beneath a keystone arch – mingled so,

they mark a brow with perfect diamond,
one spark of dancing flame.
Perfection is the frame
of right accomplishment – the ripe almond

of *what thou lovest well*. Well-founded
Gateway Arch, the light flows
east to west – what *Rhodos* grows
for liberty, for justice (lightning-grounded,

here & now). Crossed in St. Louis
by *Rio del Espiritu* – & there
one eerie soaring flare
of Raven passing through (southwest)

*

inks the last answering *quipu*
to that sweet hypothesis
of sea-blue Maximus –
the *imago*, a kind of kindly Manitou-

insignia. Seal of copper Penny
gleaming from the bottomland;
Columbian wish-well (one hand-
eye palms its moss-green rim... see?).

Southwest, southwest... Cautantowwit,
drawn like a Malcolm, like
a black-orange monarch
through the double dove-doors of that

moonlit mirror, into Mexico –
to touch the orange checkmate
of an azure Golden Gate.
Stubborn, impoverished, soft Frisco

mule! Lifting the ancient key
of human harmony
again, for you, for me –
netting the breathing sail of safety

there, at last – for Juliet,
for John, for Weldon,
Malcolm, Hart... for everyone
yearning, unreconciled, disconsolate;

& across vast timespace hollows
her winged hands & face
stir courage to embrace –
Grace penetrates the Gates (& Rose).
8.24.16

MORNING CAVE

Late August. Royal touch of autumn.
Comfortable king
of tenderness, bring
me down to your brown river once again.

The cottonwoods are silver-green
but turning gold. A monarch
speeds black-orange – sparks
up the path, to vanishment (unseen

morpho-sprint). My chunk of lumber
floats off too. Fine meteor
pumice, sanded to pearl –
gray weathered pebble, unknown soldier...

The State Fair's starting up today.
Princess K of the Milky
Way will crownèd be.
Black milk of bitter history

we sipped... fed roots of almond tree.
Cryptic redemption
on knife's edge... Raven
remembers (Hazel, breathing free).

The *King of Milk* is by the riverside.
He washes memories
like Papa's hand – a breeze
murmuring, *Everything's OK*. I sighed.

A child is comforted. The Earth
will be. Like Magdalen
or Beatrice – when the sun
colors a morning cave (in Nazareth).

8.25.16

ABOUT THE AUTHOR

Henry Gould's poems, essays and reviews have appeared in various journals. He maintains a poetry website called *HG Poetics* (hgpoetics.blogspot.com). His books include *Stone* (Copper Beech Press, 1979) and *Stubborn Grew* (Spuyten Duyvil, 2000); he also co-edited an anthology in honor of poet and scholar Edwin Honig, titled *A Glass of Green Tea – With Honig* (1994, distr. by Fordham U.P.), and edited a volume of Honig's collected poems, *Time & Again, Poems 1940-1997* (XLibris). After living for many years in Providence, RI, he recently returned to his hometown, Minneapolis.